LIFEWORDS

by REV. MARK ATHERTON

Lifewords

Written by Mark Atherton

Published 2019.

ISBN: 9781674072531

Acknowledgements

I could not have written this book without these people: Steve Wilson, Karen Cummings, Cheryl Sabo, Josh Cougle and Adam Ladd. These folks helped me immensely with editing, formatting and cover design. Thank you to the board at Xenia Church of the Nazarene. They granted me a 12-week sabbatical during which I did much of this work. I would not have been able to finish this project without that concentrated time away.

Finally, thank you to my wife, Sue. She held down the fort at home while I was away on the sabbatical. Also, she did the final proof. So, if there are any mistakes, blame her!!

Happy New Year! Let's start the new year off with this truth: Because the church is made up of flawed human beings, it is now and will always be a flawed institution. Why does that bother people? We keep all kinds of imperfect people, things, and organizations in our lives, so why does the church have to be perfect? It will never be because it's made up of people like you and me. We're kind of like the Apostle Paul when he says, "The things I want to do I don't and the things I don't want to do I do." That's our lifeword today from Romans 7:19.

If you are looking for perfect institutions, you would not have joined the Rotary, the YMCA, the PTA, or the neighborhood MOMS association. As we start the new year, choose to be a part of a church. We need more imperfect people to help our imperfect institution.

While each person must receive new life in Christ individually, it's been known for years that the best environment for this new life is in the imperfect place called the church. The best place for the development of Christian maturity is among other people. It is in the church that the Christian can best use the gifts and talents God has given him. The solitary Christian may enjoy not dealing with the imperfections of others, but the one who walks alone is not fully Christian. Hebrews 10:25 reminds us to "not neglect the gathering together." It's in that gathering, as we deal with the imperfections of others, that we grow and mature and become fully Christian. As we enter the new year, resolve to become involved, or more involved with other Christians through the church of your choice.

The Bible says God has given a gift to the church: pastors and teachers for the building up of the body of Christ (Ephesians 4:11-12). Now, these pastors and teachers aren't perfect. I'm one of them, and I know lots of them. Imperfect churches are led by imperfect pastors. Even so, why don't you avail yourself of God's gift to you? This New Year's Sunday, attend the church of your choice.

On this 2nd day of the new year, may I pray for us? Father, we confess we cannot deal with what's ahead in the new year on our own. Only You know what this year has in store for us. Help us to remember to trust You no matter what lies ahead.

May we remember your unchanging love for all of us. Help us to rest in that love even when we don't feel loveable. Because of Your love, may we love others. Keep us from thinking this world centers around our issues.

Father, we pray for our nation and its leaders. May they have the wisdom to know that "Blessed is the nation whose God is the Lord." We pray for Your protection on all those who serve in the military. Be with their families as well.

We thank You for Your goodness to us. You are a good God, and we are a blessed people. May we never take that for granted. Help us to live close to You and sense Your nearness in everything we say and do. May our ears be inclined to Your leading.

Forgive us when we fall short of Your design for us. Make us aware of sin and allow us to be sensitive to it. May we confess and repent quickly of all that displeases You.

Thank you for salvation. Thank you that you are committed to our well-being. Renew our commitment to You daily. We pray this in the only name under Heaven by which we can be saved, the name of the Lord Jesus Christ... Amen.

Every January, millions of people begin their year resolving to lose weight, exercise more, eat healthier, and manage their finances better than last year. What have your resolved for the new year?

I don't know about you, but my tongue needs work. Sometimes, it's too harsh or too short. Often, it's not gracious enough. I really need my tongue to be tamed, but that's one New Year's resolution that can't be made. The Bible says in James 3:8 that "no man can tame the tongue."

James 3:7 points to an amazing human achievement: the taming of all kinds of creatures. But we can't tame the tongue. More specifically, we can't tame our own tongue. It's not an ability we have the power to do. Our tongues control us just as a tiny bit guides a horse or a rudder steers a huge ship.

James paints a grim picture of our tongues. He describes them in a way that leaves no room for comforting ourselves. He even goes on to say that when we use our words for good, we may use them for harm in the next moment. James, writing under the inspiration of the Holy Spirit, says our tongues are uncontrollable, powerful, and hurtful. Wow! James says earlier in his book, "Those who consider themselves religious and yet do not keep a tight rein on their tongues deceive themselves, and their religion is worthless" (James 1:26).

All this negativity screams for some good news. James gives it in 4:7: "Submit to God. Resist the devil and he will flee from you." This is our lifeword for today. The answer is full submission to God combined with our intent and will. One requires the other. We cannot submit and still indulge the temptation. Also, we cannot resist the Devil without first submitting to God. We need His power to resist.

As I write this, Kanye West, a celebrity, who was well-known for his sinful lifestyle, is testifying to new life in Christ. Some doubt his conversion while others think it is real. His life does seem to be changed, and until we see something different out of him, we must believe him. Time will tell the validity of his claims.

We sometimes hear politicians, usually around election time, speak of their Christian faith. When they address Christians, they speak of prayer and their great faith in God. After the election is over, we don't see much fruit of their election season conversion.

I've known people who say they are Christians, but after some months, they return to their old ways again. I've heard statements like, "I tried faith in Christ, but it didn't work for me." I think the reality is that they never were saved in the first place.

In my years of ministry, I've seen many who turn to God when they hit hard times. But when things get better, you see them going back to their old ways. Though only God knows, I don't think many of these people were Christians in the first place.

At the beginning of the new year, many people turn over a new leaf. But when Jesus Christ comes into our lives, there is real change. Turning over a new leaf may change us on the outside, but only salvation makes us a "new creation in Christ" (2 Corinthians 5:17). Our problem is deeper and cannot be solved by turning over new leaves. Jesus must change us from the inside out.

Our lifeword today is from Matthew 23:26. Jesus told the Pharisees to "First clean the inside of the cup and dish, and then the outside also will be clean." My sin problem needs more than a new leaf. I need Jesus to do something for me that I can't do for myself.

I've been a Christian now for over 20 years. The older I've become in the faith, the fewer convictions I have about certain elements of the Christian life. I hope that doesn't mean I'm compromising. I trust it means I'm no longer a baby Christian. I think I've realized that a lot of the things I once thought were important, aren't that big of a deal. As a young Christian, I used to take a stand on lots of issues. Now, I don't think those areas are as vital to my Christian walk as I used to. When I was younger in the faith, I was quick to tell you where I stood on this or that issue. Now, I'm much slower to open my mouth and enter the realm of what the Bible calls "disputable matters." I hope this means I've matured as a Christian. Paul says in Romans 14:1 to "accept those whose faith is weak, without passing judgement on disputable matters." Those are our lifewords for today.

Concerning disputable matters, things that aren't black and white in Scripture, the Bible says I should accept people who disagree with me. As my dad used to say, let's agree to disagree. What are "disputable matters?" They are usually issues of doctrine that make my denomination different from yours. Now there are many doctrinal beliefs that are vital to our understanding of Christianity. Core beliefs would not come under the heading of "disputable matters." However, there are some things the Bible is not clear about that are up to an individual's or a denomination's interpretation.

A few examples are: the different teachings on end-times, Calvinism or Arminianism, frequency of Communion, modes of Baptism, issues of church polity... just to name a few. These are secondary issues, and yet they cause conflict in the Church.

So, what do we do about disputable matters? The Bible says not to argue about them. Agree to disagree. Deal with differences with grace and love. As we accept others, we come to a fuller understanding of the faith.

We're looking this week at Paul's admonition to us in Romans 14:1 to "accept those whose faith is weak, without passing judgement on disputable matters." Those are our lifewords for today. The words "disputable matters" are not speaking of the areas where the Bible says "thus saith the Lord." It's talking about the many gray areas of Scripture where God seems to allow me to make up my own mind. And invariably, when I make up my own mind, someone will disagree with me. I must accept that all people don't think like me.

People are different, and that makes life difficult. We were raised differently with different morals and values. We were raised in different places with different cultures. We have different gifts, different likes and dislikes. We're all at different places in our spiritual journeys.

Despite our differences, we need to understand that we are all brothers and sisters in Christ. Instead of magnifying these differences, we should appreciate them and the roles they play in the Body of Christ. Let's focus on areas of agreement and make a big deal out of those.

Paul pleads with Euodia and Syntyche to be united with each other in the Lord (Philippians 4:2). The key phrase is "agree in the Lord." We can speculate that the differences were on disputable matters because Paul says "agree in the Lord." Agree on what we have in common—the most important thing—our mutual faith in Christ. Whatever the differences were, Paul says to put them aside for the cause of Christ. Paul calls on the church to help these women work out their differences (Philippians 4:3).

Romans 15:7 tells me that I should accept you because God has accepted me. If God has accepted you, I should accept you as well. Let's extend the grace of acceptance to others, just like God extends to us.

Even though we all are different and those differences will cause conflict and misunderstanding, God's Word is plain: accept one another. Many times, people don't make that easy. If you are like me, we sometimes don't feel like accepting them. We would much rather give them a piece of our mind. The command "accept one another" is not easy and does not come naturally. If it did, Paul would have had no reason to remind us of the necessity of it.

If Paul had left it with "accept one another," we might sidestep that command by rationalizing that God meant to accept acceptable people. But the totality of Romans 15:7 is this: "accept one another, then, just as Christ accepted you, in order to bring praise to God." Those are our lifewords for today. That "just as Christ accepted you" part is the rub, isn't it? I don't know about you, but I wasn't too acceptable when Christ accepted me. In fact, I identify with John Newton when he calls himself a "wretch" in the hymn "Amazing Grace."

The Bible has many examples of people not accepting each other. Jews and Gentiles did not get along, even after salvation. The Jewish Christians thought the Gentiles should be more Jewish, and the Gentiles were convinced the Jews should be more like them. But Paul addressed this matter plainly. In Ephesians 2:14-16, he says, "in Christ," these two groups are one. At the cross, Christ put to death their hostility toward each other.

If I lived back then, I would be quick to say, "Somebody straighten these legalistic Jews out!" But the truth is, Jesus didn't require me to get straightened out before I was accepted. Biblically, straightening people out is not my job; accepting them is. Now, God may use me to speak to these people in an effort to bring them more in line to the truth of God's Word. But that will always come *after* I accept them. Only after people have felt the grace of acceptance do they let their guard down enough to accept direction from someone else.

"Accept those whose faith is weak, without passing judgment on disputable matters"(Romans 14:1). Those are our lifewords for today. This week, we're trying to get a handle on this verse. As we read this closely, it instructs us not simply to accept others, but to accept those who are weak in the faith. What does that mean? Are some Christians strong and some weak? What does it mean to have a weak faith?

As always, context is crucial, and the surrounding verses are speaking of eating certain foods. This seems odd to us, but it would not have been to first-century readers. If someone with a weak faith sees another believer eating meat that has been sacrificed to idols, the weaker brother may be horrified. Much of the available meat in that day was sold to the public after the animal had been sacrificed to one of the pagan gods. Some "weaker" believers would not eat this because it was tainted because of the pagan worship. Some of the "stronger" believers knew that pagan worship was false, and they had no problem taking that steak home and cooking it for the family. They knew their faith was firmly in Christ, not in whether they ate food sacrificed to idols or not.

To be weak in the faith means not having confidence that Christ's death was sufficient for the payment of sins. It's mixing other do's and don'ts in with the cross. The weaker believer may know that Christ died but is not strong enough to stand on that and that alone. The weaker believer cannot sing the old hymn "Jesus Paid It All."

How about you? Do you have a weak faith? Is your faith diluted with cultural do's and don'ts? Don't get me wrong, some of those cultural things may be wise. But remember, they don't have the power to save. Christ and Christ alone is sufficient for that. Confidence in anything I can do is confidence in the flesh (Philippians 3:3). The strong believer is leaning on Jesus, putting their full weight on what Christ accomplished on the cross.

Let's continue where we left off yesterday. Our lifewords today are from 1 Corinthians 8:9: "Be careful, however, that the exercise of your freedom does not become a stumbling block to the weak." Paul goes on to say in verse 13 that if eating meat causes another believer to sin, "I'll never eat meat again."

Paul does not argue that eating meat sacrificed to idols is sinful in and of itself. Instead, he is concerned about the impact it can have on others. Paul says in 1 Corinthians 8:10-11 that if "my freedom causes the weaker believer to violate his conscience and eat something he thinks he shouldn't, I have sinned against my brother and against Christ." In verse 12, Paul says we must always consider the effect our actions have upon other people.

We understand submitting to the weak. We do it often, without reservation, in other areas of our lives. A crying baby controls your day. The sick child controls a lot of your time. A broken ankle determines your mobility. In the same way, Paul calls us to place the spiritual needs of weaker believers ahead of our desires to exercise our freedom in Christ.

Some may say we have the "right" to exercise our freedom. Here, as always, Jesus is our example. Jesus gave up all of His rights for us. As the Alpha and Omega, He had the right to stay in Heaven, seated at the right hand of the Father. As the Son of God, He had the right to be worshiped. But He humbled Himself to come to this earth as a mortal man, not for His sake, but ours.

No wonder the New Testament places such an emphasis on others. Love one another, forgive one another, submit to one another, be devoted to one another, instruct one another, greet one another... I could go on and on. Paul tells us to be careful what we do—even limit our freedom—because our actions have an effect on others, especially the weaker ones among us.

You've heard the slogan, "What happens in Vegas stays in Vegas." This means what happens in Las Vegas has no bearing on the rest of my life. I wonder if some Christians are living their faith this way. When we compartmentalize our faith, the slogan becomes, "What happens at church stays at church." This could mean what happens at the church has no bearing on the rest of my life. I think we all know the Bible has no understanding of that kind of a Christian. In fact, John Wesley, founder of the Methodist Church, would call this person an "almost Christian."

I had a friend tell me once that he separates his religion from his business. I was a high school and college basketball coach for many years. A friend of mine who coached at a neighboring school told me when he gets on the court, he loses his religion. Those two guys didn't understand the wisdom that comes from our lifeword today: "Acknowledge God in all your ways" (Proverbs 3:6).

To these friends of mine, it seemed perfectly acceptable to compartmentalize faith from the other areas of life. Many have a box named Faith that doesn't interfere with any of the other boxes named Work, Finances, Family, Recreation, and so forth. The Bible speaks against that in many places. Romans 12:1 in The Message translation says, "So here's what I want you to do, God helping you: Take your everyday, ordinary life—your sleeping, eating, going-to-work, and walking-around life—and place it before God as an offering." Those are our lifewords for today.

The Bible says, "Trust in the Lord with all your heart and lean not on your own understanding; in all your ways acknowledge Him and He will direct your paths" (Proverbs 3:5-6). Did you see the emphasis on the word *all*? The verse says to trust with *all* your heart and acknowledge Him in *all* your ways. Compartmentalizing my faith would be in direct contrast to *all*. Let's not be almost Christians, but be as Wesley would call (all) together Christians.

Let's take a deeper look at yesterday's passage from Proverbs 3:5-6. "Trust in the Lord with all your heart and lean not on your own understanding; in all your ways acknowledge Him, and He will direct your paths." I find it interesting what the Bible *doesn't* say here. It doesn't say to trust and everything in our lives will be great. It doesn't say to trust and everything will work out the way we want. It doesn't say to trust and everyone will live happily ever after. The Bible simply says to trust and God will direct our paths. Nowhere in God's Word are we promised an easy passage through life. The promise here is that God will be with you to direct your path even though that path may be difficult.

The apostle Paul writes, "...but we also glory in our sufferings, because we know that suffering produces perseverance; perseverance, character; and character, hope" (Romans 5:3-4). Those are our lifewords for today. This teaches us that Christians go through tough times, and God desires that those times produce qualities in our lives that lead to maturity.

We accept this truth in other areas. In athletics, we call it "no pain, no gain." Only when I go through the difficulty of exercising my body will my body come back stronger and able to deal with increased amounts of exercise. As a parent, we don't save our children from going through difficulty because we know it's that same difficulty that helped us grow up and mature.

Jesus says it plainly in John 16:33; "...in this life you will have trouble." Only in Heaven can we have days with no pain, laughter but no sorrow, and sun without rain. Nowhere is a comfortable existence promised on in this lifetime. What is promised is that through the hard things of life you will become the person God wants you to be. As we trust and lean on Him, He will direct our path. But that direction is not always to an easy place.

You can set up a lot of things in your backyard: picnic tables, swing sets, volleyball nets, a barbeque grill. There's a story in Judges 17 about a man named Micah who set up his own church in his backyard! He even hired his son as priest! Judges 17 says, "Now this man Micah had a shrine, and he made an ephod and some household gods and installed one of his sons as his priest." Those are our lifewords for today. Before we laugh, let's make sure we're not doing this ourselves. Oh, I know we don't build a church in our backyard, but we may set up our own little religion, a religion of our own making, One that suits our preferences and desires. But God will have none of that. When it comes to faith, God has revealed truth to us in His Word. Whether we like it or not isn't really the issue. The question is whether we will submit to it or invent our own backyard religion—just like Micah did.

As the story unfolds, we see that neither Micah nor his mother take sin seriously. Micah stole money from his mother, and she evidently doesn't think it's a big deal. In fact, her response to his theft is, "The Lord bless you, my son" (Judges 17:2). A faith that winks at sin is not biblical and certainly is backyard religion. Sin costs Jesus His life. It's the only thing that separates us from God. Romans 6:23 tells us the wages of sin is death. God takes sin so seriously that He sent His only Son to die for my sin and yours. To wink at sin, to minimize it, is to discount the sacrifice that Jesus made on the cross. The flippant attitude that both Micah and his mother display toward sin is irreverent and unbiblical.

If people won't take sin seriously, they may have a religion of their own choosing, meeting their preferences and avoiding anything they dislike. They may have backyard religion. Avoid it at all costs, and be sure you have the real thing... a biblical faith that takes sin seriously. After all, it cost Jesus His life.

Yesterday, we learned of a man name Micah who set up his own church in his backyard. As the story continues, we see Micah has a desire to get the right priest for his backyard church. He had installed his son as the priest. All of a sudden, however, the grass looked greener on the other side. A Levite from Bethlehem wandered by one day, and Micah saw the opportunity to upgrade his backyard religion. A Levite! These guys were assistants to the priests in Jerusalem. Micah must have thought he had the next best thing to a real priest. The Bible says that Micah and the priest negotiate a salary package. Before you know it, Micah fires his son and installs this Levite in his place. Judges 17:13 records Micah's words as, "Now I know that the Lord will be good to me, since this Levite has become my priest."

In Micah's backyard religion, if he gets the right priest, God will bless him. He's concerned with getting all the trappings of his backyard church right, but he leaves out the most important thing...getting his own heart right. Getting his heart right goes back to stealing his mother's money. We still see no repentance for that.

Backyard religion will always look nice. It will say and do the right things—at least on the outside—but it leaves the heart unchanged. Jesus says to clean the inside of the cup and then the outside will be clean as well (Matthew 23:26). Those are our lifewords for today. When the New Testament looks back on an Old Testament character's life, these words are used: He (King David) was a man after God's own heart (Acts 13:22).

God is desirous of our heart because He knows when He has that, our walk and talk will follow. Backyard religion will sing nice songs, read nice verses, build nice buildings, have nice preachers who say nice things. But they will miss the most crucial thing... a heart after God.

As we continue to look at Micah and his backyard church, we see a man who was certainly zealous. Micah built a shrine and fashioned an ephod to use in worship. An ephod was nothing more than a garment to be worn during priestly activities. He carved out some idols and even hired his own personal priest. He was especially excited about the priest as he said, "Now I know that the LORD will be good to me, since this Levite has become my priest" (Judges 17:13). However, Micah sought to worship God the way he wanted, not the way God had commanded.

Worship is NOT a personal thing that can be expressed however you choose. Jesus said there is a kind of worship that God desires. If that is true, there must also be a kind of worship He does not desire. Our lifewords today are from John 4:23- 24. There, the Bible says that true worshipers will worship the Father in spirit and truth. It even says the Father is seeking such people to worship Him. The passage says if we are to worship God, we must do it in spirit and truth. So, it's imperative that we worship God this way. That begs the question: What does true worship mean?

True worship is to worship God in Christ. To worship in truth is not merely to worship in sincerity, but to worship God through Jesus. He is the "Truth" (John 14:6). True worship is for all people… Jew or Samaritan, male or female (John 4). True worship is not limited to a place. True worship invites whosoever to worship God wherever they are. God's presence is in the finest cathedral in Rome or the humblest home in Papua New Guinea.

Worshipping in spirit without truth is nothing more than emotionalism. Worshipping in truth without spirit is dead orthodoxy. May we not make Micah's mistake. May we worship in knowledge, which is informed by God's Word and points us to the truth that is found in Christ Jesus.

Eventually, each one of us will have our faith tested by hard times. Things will not go as we think they should, and our Christian experience may seem less than what was preached or taught to us. We become disappointed, confused, and even mad. What do we do then?

In Judges 18, Micah loses his priest and his church with all his religious symbols. He's crushed and says in Judges 18:24, "You took the gods I made, and my priest...What else do I have?" Micah feels he has nothing left now that his backyard church has been destroyed. If your faith is on the inside, it doesn't matter if your church house burns to the ground, if your pastor leaves, or even if your church closes. Your faith will stand in hard times because it's in you. It's in your heart.

Whatever can be taken from us is of man. Eternal things are not of this world and are not dependent on the happenings of the world. Storms may come, mountains may impede your progress, rivers will flood, maybe your church will burn down, and your pastor will leave. All of those hard times don't affect what John Wesley, founder of the Methodist Church called "heart religion." Wesley (and the Bible) stressed the need for spiritual reality. For Wesley, "heart religion" stood against a mere formalized or intellectualized religion.

Wesley was not against outward decorum and a beautiful liturgy. But He never put weight on them and even said they are expendable. "Let no man dream that they have any intrinsic worth; or that religion cannot subsist without them." Wesley was not saying to throw all liturgy aside, but experience had taught him that they could not be substituted for the real thing. In Wesley's mind, the real thing was the reality of heart religion.

What did Micah have left after he lost his church, all of its trappings, and his priest? He still had God, His presence, and His power. That's enough to get us through the hardest times.

Yesterday, we looked at a difficult time in Micah's life. He lost his church with all of its trappings, and even his priest got a better offer from another church. Micah lamented the situation he was in by saying, "...what else do I have left?" (Judges 18:24). Micah and his backyard religion didn't stand up in tough times. A faith based on mere formality never will.

Micah appears to be religious in name only. His faith seemed to be based in outward things only and not in his inward feelings. He certainly made a profession of faith, but in reality, did not possess it. For today's Christians who profess but don't practice, their Christianity may hold up on Sunday but won't on all the difficult Mondays of life.

Jesus spoke of this often. To the Jews of His day, Jesus had hard words: "These people honor me with their lips, but their hearts are far from me. They worship me in vain" (Matthew 15:8-9). Those are our lifewords for today. He constantly criticizes the formality of the scribes and Pharisees. Over and over, He says to them, "Woe to you, scribes and Pharisees, hypocrites!"(Matthew 23).

Paul tells the church that met at Rome that a man is not a Jew who is one outwardly only. He says the important Jewish ritual of circumcision avails nothing if it's merely physical. "No, a person is a Jew who is one inwardly; and circumcision is circumcision of the heart..." (Romans 2:28).

Micah's faith was not in the living God. His faith was in "faith" with all of the outward displays of devotion. But Micah's faith is not the issue today.... it's my faith and yours. Will it stand up to the difficulties of life? It will if it's the "heart religion" we spoke of yesterday. That's a religion based on Christ's work on the cross. This kind of faith is so real that it permeates to the very core of your being. It cannot be taken from you even in life's most difficult times.

We've been looking this week at a story in Judges 17-18. It's a story of a man who had backyard religion. One of the key verses in this account is Judges 17:6. It says "In those days Israel had no king; everyone did as they saw fit." Some translations will say, "everyone did what was right in their own eyes." Others will say, "everyone did what they thought was right."

That didn't work well in the Book of Judges, and it doesn't work well today. All of this sounds very up to date, doesn't it? It's the philosophy of the age. Do what you want. Do what you think is right. If it's right for you, who am I to judge? This is called Individualism. That's buying into the lie that we're the gold standard for our lives. In our Western world, individuality and my choice are vital to our modern lives.

If everyone is doing what they see fit, that pretty much leaves God and His Word out of the equation. In the blink of an eye, in just a few decades, we've removed God from important areas of our lives... from our schools to our government to the media. The worship of God is okay if it's limited to Sunday mornings and doesn't interfere with what others deem important.

When everyone does what is right in their own eyes, we're told that there are no absolutes — what's true for you may not be true for me. Of course, when you make the statement, "There are no absolutes," that is an absolute statement in itself. When people assert that no absolutes exist, they really claim that God doesn't exist because God is the ultimate absolute. That's the end result of individualism. When everyone does what's right in their own eyes, the individual is king; the individual is absolute.

Without a commitment to truth and the authority of God, the consequences to our society and for us as individuals are staggering. It all starts innocently enough, with everyone doing what is right in their own eyes.

Throughout this week's discussion of Micah and his backyard church, I've used the word "religion." Some of you were taught that this is a bad word and opposite of Christianity. Some of us grew up with phrases like, "Religion says do, Jesus says done." Maybe some of you remember this one: "Religion says slave, Jesus says son." Most of you have heard that Christianity is a relationship, not a religion. Many of us have heard someone piously say, "I'm not religious, I'm spiritual."

There is no question that using the word religion or religious can have a connotation of a legalistic and rule-following type of Christianity. Unfortunately, it is common in our country for religion to be nothing more than ceremony and tradition that is void of reality. This kind of empty religion is why the word religion has such negative implications to some.

Into this discussion, we must bring God's Word. The Bible has nothing negative to say about the word religion. In fact, it's just the opposite. Biblically, religion can be a very good thing if it spawns action in our lives. "If anyone thinks he is religious and does not bridle his tongue but deceives his heart, this person's religion is worthless" (James 1:26). That's our lifeword for today. The Greek word here, translated religion, simply means worship. So, James is saying that worship of God that does not translate into daily activity in our lives is worthless.

James continues in verse 27: "Religion that is pure and undefiled before God the Father is this: to visit orphans and widows in their affliction, and to keep oneself unstained from the world." God has plainly revealed in His Word what is of value to Him. Without a doubt, God has a heart for orphans and widows and those who cannot care for themselves. No one can read God's Word and doubt that. So, religion that honors God is practiced in accordance to His Word, in this case, giving yourself to those who need you. That's good religion. Let's not run from the word. Let's practice it.

Singer and songwriter Bob Dylan wrote, "You may be a state trooper, you might be a young Turk. You may be the head of some big TV network." Dylan was trying to convince us that everyone must choose to serve somebody. The most important decisions we have to make are spiritual. Dylan wrote, "It may be the devil or it may be the Lord, but you're gonna have to serve somebody."

The decision to serve God may not be an easy one. Sometimes, it comes with hard consequences, such as choosing to obey God or man. We can all remember at least one time in our lives when we chose poorly because of peer pressure. Maybe that's why the Bible talks again and again about the importance of choices. Our lifewords today are from Joshua 24:15. The Bible says, "Choose for yourself this day whom you will serve."

Every day, we make hundreds—maybe even thousands—of choices. Some are simple, and others mean a great deal. Our lives are not a roll of the dice or something that happens randomly. The power of choice is basic to being human. This freedom sets us apart from the rest of God's creation. It's part and parcel to being created in the image of God.

God could have made us so that we would robotically do His will. That would not have served His purpose though. He wanted people who would love Him and love others. Love cannot be forced or compelled. It can only be freely given.

God will not compel you to do His will. He will always guide you in the right direction, but He won't make that final choice. That one is up to you. Bob Dylan was right, "you gotta serve somebody."

"I've had choices since the day I was born, there were voices, that told me right from wrong. Now if I had listened, I wouldn't be here today. Living and dying with the choices I've made." Those words aren't Scripture. They are from a country song by George Jones. While the words don't have a chapter and verse I can attach to them, they sure are biblical. God's Word teaches us that our lives are nothing more than the sum total of the choices we make.

Every day, we make choices that affect our future. Do I go to bed early or do I stay up late? Do I choose a candy bar or an apple? Do I spend money or do I save? All of these choices are small in and of themselves, but viewed in the totality of life, George Jones was right; we're living and dying with the choices we make. Our lifewords today find Moses encouraging the people of Israel to make good choices. "See, I set before you today life and prosperity, death and destruction (Deuteronomy 30:15). He desires that Israel choose well because He knows that their lives are nothing more than the sum total of all the choices they make.

Sometime today, you will have a choice to respond to God or to ignore Him. How you respond will determine the type of tomorrow you will have. Joshua 24:15 offers a clear-cut choice. "...choose today whom you will serve." In one of the most dramatic stories in all of God's Word, Elijah challenged the prophets of Baal saying, "How long will you falter between two opinions? If the Lord is God, follow him; but if Baal, follow him" (1 Kings 18:21).

Your choices matter. I'm an old math teacher, so this equation makes sense to me: Choice + choice + choice + choice = your life. That mathematical equation makes a good country song, and it makes good theology as well.

One of the most important choices God has given us is how we will raise our children. Today's lifeword is from Joshua 24:15: "...choose for yourselves this day whom you will serve, whether the gods your ancestors served beyond the Euphrates, or the gods of the Amorites, in whose land you are living. But as for me and my household, we will serve the Lord."

Joshua says, "As for me and my house, we will serve the Lord." Our Scripture portrays a united home. "As for me _and_ my house, we will serve the Lord." Raising Christian kids is a hard task, but in a home where Mom and Dad are united in their faith, it's a little easier.

This verse applies here: "Do not be yoked together with unbelievers. For what do righteousness and wickedness have in common? Or what fellowship can light have with darkness?" (2 Corinthians 6:14). A yoke is a wooden beam used between a pair of oxen that allows them to work together as a team to pull a load. An "unequally yoked" team has one stronger ox and one weaker. Instead of working together, they are at odds with one another. In this verse, Paul discourages an unequal partnership with unbelievers because believers and unbelievers are opposites, just as light and darkness are opposites.

Of course, the closest partnership one can have with another is found in marriage. This relationship is so close in God's eyes that He refers to a married couple as "one flesh" (Genesis 2:24). Uniting a believer with an unbeliever makes for a very difficult marriage relationship.

Hear this today from the heart of a pastor. Don't get married to someone you are not compatible with spiritually. Single men, wait until that special woman comes along who loves God as much as you do. Single ladies, don't get impatient. The right guy is out there. Don't compromise. Wait until you both are united spiritually.

Tommy Lasorda, former manager of the Los Angeles Dodgers said, "The difference between the impossible and the possible lies in a man's determination." Joshua, of Old Testament days, and Lasorda lived in different times, but both knew the importance of determination. Our lifewords today are from Joshua 24:15: "As for me and my house we will serve the Lord."

I hear determination in those words of Joshua. It certainly isn't easy for us to raise Christian kids. Our kids see, hear, and experience things daily that are opposed to the things of Christ. It's easy to throw our hands up and go with the crowd because everyone else is. It's at those times we must be determined. Another word for determination is grit—a relentless determination to pursue a desired goal.

The Bible is full of examples of grit. Noah built an ark that took decades as he waited and believed in God's promise. Joseph, when he was stuck in a prison, waited and held on to the belief in God's promise. Moses led a bunch of grumblers as they walked in circles for 40 years as he waited and believed in God's promise.

When times got tough, my dad would tell me to grit my teeth and get through it. Biblical grit is different than that. It has, at its core, a faith that rests on the promises of God.

As a parent, I must be determined to raise godly kids. I must have the resolve to paddle upstream when the world seems to be going the other way. I must have the grit that believes God's greatest desire for my life is for me to pass on my faith to my children.

This determination is a gift of God's grace, empowered by His Holy Spirit, and is there for the asking. You'll find God's grace sufficient if you are gritty enough to say, "As for me and my house we will serve the Lord."

President Harry Truman was fond of saying, "The buck stops here." Joshua, an ancient leader of the people of Israel, would agree, at least when it comes to child rearing. There was a day over 3,000 years ago when he stood and challenged the people he led by saying, "As for me and my house, we will serve the Lord." Those words from Joshua 24:15 are our lifewords for today.

The families who are successful in raising Christian children take responsibility for their kid's spiritual condition. You can hear that in Joshua's words, can't you? "As for me and my house, we will serve the Lord." It's almost as if Joshua is saying, "You all can choose whatever you want, but here's my choice. Even if the rest of you choose to forsake the Lord, here's my choice."

There are many ways moms and dads can seek assistance. There are a multitude of resources to help the Christian parent. Christian parents have never had more help than they do today. I'm thankful for all of those. But, in the end, the responsibility is ours. No children's pastor, Sunday school teacher, or youth pastor has more influence than we do as moms and dads. Parents, please don't underestimate the power you have.

It is God's design for parents to leverage that power. In Deuteronomy 6, Moses told the nation of Israel the value of parental discipleship. "These commandments that I give you today are to be on your hearts. Impress them on your children. Talk about them when you sit at home and when you walk along the road, when you lie down and when you get up" (Deuteronomy 6:6–7). Moses called upon mothers and fathers to make the home the primary place of discipleship. God placed firmly on the backs of moms and dads the responsibility of teaching children His ways.

Moms and dads, don't pass the buck. Take the responsibility and the power that comes along with it and say as Joshua did, "As for me and my house, we will serve the Lord."

As a pastor, I wish all the parents in my church fully understood the power they have as parents. This power is taught in many places in the Bible but nowhere more plainly than in Proverbs 22:6, which are our lifewords for today. It says, "Train up a child in the way he should go, and when he is old he will not depart from it." This verse is not a promise, but it does speak of the power a parent has when they intentionally direct a son or daughter. The parent's power is so strong that the child will not be able to get away from it, even when they are older. In fact, as we model a Christ-like life for our children, as they get older, the more powerful a parent's influence will become.

I've often heard people say, "Do as I say, not as I do." Of course, that acknowledges the truth that it's tough to live up to what you teach your children. But no matter what mistakes have been made in the past, if a parent will admit them, seek forgiveness, and make amends, they can set a tremendous example for their children.

While it's crucial to start this modeling early when the kids are young, it's foolish to believe that as our children get older, we lose the power to influence them. I could argue that modeling faith is more important as the children hit their teen years and beyond. As they learn more about the faith, they know you are living out a true faith instead of putting on a show for them. Younger kids have more difficulty distinguishing between the two.

I'm continually amazed at the power of parents, and I'm convinced most parents do not understand the level of influence they have. If they did, they would leverage it far more often.

Our lifeword today is from James 1:26: "Those who consider themselves religious and yet do not keep a tight rein on their tongues deceive themselves, and their religion is worthless." As we attempt to set godly examples for our children, our tongue plays a major role in that. In fact, this verse says our kids will view our religion as worthless if we make poor choices with our words. As we live out our Christian lives in front of our kids, and as we intentionally disciple them, attention must be paid to our speech.

One of the best choices we will make with our tongue is not to use it. "When words are many, sin is not absent, but he who holds his tongue is wise" (Proverbs 10:19). "Do you see someone who speaks in haste? There is more hope for a fool than for them" (Proverbs 29:20). We could go on and on with biblical admonitions to not speak, but this last verse is my favorite: "Even fools are thought wise if they keep silent, and discerning if they hold their tongues" (Proverbs 17:28). My dad drilled that verse into my head this way: better to keep your mouth shut and be thought a fool than to open it and remove all doubt!

Talk, talk, talk, talk, and more talk is the mark of a fool. We know that biblically and experientially. Teach this to your children, and may they learn it from your example. Moms and dads, practice and teach James 1:19: "Everyone should be quick to listen and slow to speak."

This is a self-control issue, but it is also a heart issue. Jesus said in Luke 6:45, "...out of the overflow of the heart, the mouth speaks." What comes out of our mouths is an indication of what's in our hearts. We all need God's Holy Spirit to do deep work in our hearts. Ask Him for that work today.

When I was younger, I was a big Eagles fan. I bought all their albums and 8-tracks. Wow, I'm dating myself, aren't I? One of my favorite songs went like this, "Get over it, get over it. All this whinin' and cryin' and pitchin' a fit, Get over it, get over it." That may sound harsh, but getting over the past is a huge issue. Many people are dragged down because they can't let something go. It may not be easy, but we must do everything we can to get over it.

Our lifewords today come from 1 Samuel 16:1. God says to His prophet Samuel, "How long will you mourn for Saul?" Saul was the first king of Israel and because of his poor choices, God had rejected him. Samuel was mourning over that, and God came to him and asked, "How long?" How long will you be stuck in the past? How long will you be looking backward when it's time to look forward? How long will you be stuck here when I need you someplace else?

If Samuel had continued to mourn, he would have missed the new thing God had planned. He would have missed King David and the critical role Samuel would play in his life.

Any day is a great day to leave the past and walk into God's future. That may mean getting over a hurt. It may mean forgiving someone. That may mean going to the person who hurt you and having a difficult conversation. You may need to ask someone to forgive you for a past offense. None of those things are easy, but they may be required if you're going to get over it.

January 27th

Today's lifeword is from Proverbs 17:9: "Love prospers when a fault is forgiven, but dwelling on it separates close friends." Are you dwelling on something you need to let go? Oh, I know what they did was wrong; there's no disputing that. But how is dwelling on it helping you? They should not have said it; there's no doubt about that. But is dwelling on it helping you get past it? Hey, I get it; they were wrong. I'm not saying they were right. But how can you change the situation by dwelling on it?

You can always count on other people irritating and offending you. That's a given. But what you do with that is the key. By not dwelling on these almost-daily irritations, you make it easier on yourself and the people around you.

Be the type of person who doesn't get their feathers ruffled easily. A Christian shouldn't dwell on minor irritations that commonly occur. Here's one of the reasons why: a Christian knows they been forgiven much, so it is easier for them to forgive others. (Colossians 3:13)

Our lifeword says, "Love prospers when a fault is forgiven." Forgiveness is one way we show love to others. If I dwell on it, I'm tempted to gossip and whisper about the person who wronged me. Not letting it go may convince me to repeat rumors that may harm a person's reputation. Dwelling on a wrong makes me a miserable person. Why would I do it? Why would I not let it go?

God's Word encourages us to do just that. Are you dwelling on something that happened last year, 5 years ago, or maybe even earlier? Don't allow what's in the past to turn you into a bitter person who won't get over it.

Our lifeword again is from Proverbs 17:9: "Love prospers when a fault is forgiven, but dwelling on it separates close friends." We're encouraged here to let things go because holding on may break friendships. Obviously, the writer is speaking of the friendship of the one who offended you, but also the friendship of others as well. When I'm bitter, unforgiving, and continually dwell on something that happened in the past, it doesn't make me a person that others want to be around. When I get over it, not only is my relationship with the offender mended, it also improves my friendships with others. No one enjoys being around a bitter person who is clinging to past hurts.

Another translation of Proverbs 17:9 says, "He who conceals a transgression seeks love, but he who repeats a matter separates intimate friends." To conceal means, in the Hebrew language, to cover up. Does God want me to participate in a cover-up? Why should someone conceal a transgression? That sounds like stuffing it under the rug and not dealing with it honestly. That doesn't sound Christian, but let's look deeper.

Love demands that we choose to forgive and set such things aside. Rather than bring up the transgression again, we choose to drop it. That's a huge part of forgiveness: never bringing it up again. If the issue is big enough, there may be a need for reconciliation. An honest, heart-to-heart discussion may be appropriate. This isn't a cover-up. Instead, it's a path for getting over it.

As Christians, we are to seek the way of love. One way to do that is by forgiving the fault and covering the transgression. Choose to forgive today and drop the fact that they've blown it. That will help everyone *get over it*.

The last few days, we've been talking about getting over past hurts. We've been encouraged through God's Word not to dwell on the past. God comes to Samuel and says, "How long will you mourn for Saul?" (1 Samuel 16:1). We've seen that covering a sin not only means to forgive; it also means to not bring the issue up again; to not repeat the matter. Peter elaborates on this in the New Testament. "Most important of all, continue to show deep love for each other, for love covers a multitude of sins" (1 Peter 4:8). That's our lifeword for today.

We've all had friends that hurt us. Something in us wants to share that with others. That's probably our flesh, our sinful nature. But God speaks to us through His Spirit and says to keep our mouth shut. "Love covers a multitude of sins." Love means not bringing it up again.

Solomon tells us in Proverbs 17:9 that it's the one who "repeats a matter" who separates intimate friends. The word "repeats" is the opposite of covering up or concealing. It means that the issue has been brought out in the open. It is talked about here and talked about there. That's not forgiveness. A godly cover-up happens when the issue is resolved, forgiveness is asked for and accepted, and the situation is never mentioned again. To uncover someone's sin by repeating it to others is not love. It ruins friendships.

Repeating the matter refers to sharing it with others, but it also relates to reminding the one at fault of their error again and again. This is not love, and it will separate good friends. The true friend forgives and moves on, choosing to remember it no longer. A true friend is kind of like our God, who "remembers our sins no more" (Isaiah 43:25).

As we've been discussing past hurts, it occurred to me that many of you have been hurt by church. Someone in that church, maybe even a pastor, has said or done something you just can't get over. You're hurt, even bitter, and may have stopped attending. You're having a hard time letting go. Getting over it seems impossible. Dwelling on it is a daily occurrence.

As a pastor for over 20 years, I know hurt people don't want to be hurt again. They may even question whether church is for them. Church is not and never has been a perfect place. The Bible is full of accounts of church squabbles and problems. Even in New Testament times, it was not a perfect place. 1st Corinthians was written to a church full of problems. The Book of the Revelation (chapters 2–3) speaks of a church that was so messed up, Jesus wanted to vomit it from His mouth (Revelation 3:16).

If you've been hurt by church, may I encourage you to love. That may sound simplistic, but it's the biblical response. That response is in 1st Corinthians, where Paul is addressing a very messed up church. It's to that church that he writes the "love chapter." A part of it will be our lifewords for today: "Love is patient, love is kind. It does not envy, it does not boast, it is not proud. It does not dishonor others, it is not self-seeking, it is not easily angered, it keeps no record of wrongs. Love does not delight in evil but rejoices with the truth. It always protects, always trusts, always hopes, always perseveres" (1 Corinthians 13:4-7).

Getting over past hurts, letting them go, not dwelling on them, forgiving faults, and not repeating them—all are examples of love. After all, the Apostle Paul defines love as keeping no record of wrongs (1 Corinthians 13:5).

Many times in life, we have to give something up to gain something else. If I want to lose weight, I must give up my desire for late-night honey roasted peanuts. If I want to be an effective leader for our church, I must give up my desire to please everyone. If I want to be a good father and husband, I may have to give up some hobbies that take me away from my family. The same is true of our spiritual lives.

Our lifeword for today is from Philippians 3:7, where Paul writes, "...but what things were gain these I have counted loss for Christ." Paul lists his religious resume, things he once counted on for right standing with God. Do you have such a resume? Baptized? Confirmed? Church member? Tither? Good person? Resumes aren't bad unless they keep you from accepting the grace of God. If I count on my resume, if I trust in it, put hope in it, then I'm not counting on, trusting in, and putting hope in Christ. Paul says whatever things were on his resume, he counts them loss.

He goes on to say, "I count all things as loss and consider them rubbish, that I may gain Christ" (Philippians 3:8). What things did Paul consider rubbish? It was his religious resume. The Bible says those things are rubbish if we're depending on them for salvation. The word rubbish in the original language of the Bible means human excrement. That's what Paul thinks of the things we count on instead of counting on Christ. Resume = rubbish.

Religious resumes aren't bad unless you're counting on them for right standing before God. If that's the case, you need to lose it. Count it as rubbish and give it up so that you may gain Christ.

Our lifeword for today is from Philippians 3:9. Paul says, I don't want to have a "righteousness of my own" but that which is through faith in Christ. Yesterday, we spoke of Paul's religious resume. For years, Paul had a righteousness of his own based on his own efforts. That's what he counted on for right standing in front of God. You know what the Old Testament says about that, don't you? Isaiah 64:6 says our own righteousness is "filthy rags." Now, "filthy rags" is not a literal translation. The translators cleaned it up a bit. Literally, it's menstrual rags, the rags of a woman's monthly uncleanness. Wow, Paul is pretty graphic when he encourages people to trust in Christ. In yesterday's devotion, Paul used a word that means human excrement and today, he uses menstrual rags! Paul makes it very clear what he thinks of our own attempt to be righteous in God's eyes.

When we try to earn God's approval or somehow try to add to Jesus' work on the cross, God is not impressed. The price He paid for your salvation was so large, to add anything to it is insulting to God.

Now, don't get confused. This passage is not condemning all our acts of goodness as nothing more than "filthy rags." God is pleased with good works from us. He commands them. We were saved for them (Ephesians 2:10). But if these works are used to somehow curry favor with God and add to the work of the cross, God sees those efforts as filthy rags.

The question for you and me is this: Do we have a righteousness from God (Romans 3:21), or do we have the filthy rags of our own righteousness? Is your faith in Christ and Christ alone?

February 2nd

At my age in life, I've noticed forgetting is becoming more common for me. That's usually thought of as a bad thing, but in Philippians 3:13, the Bible says it can be helpful spiritually. Paul says, "Forgetting what is behind...I press on toward the goal." Those are our lifewords for today.

Paul may want to forget his spiritual accomplishments. After all, he refers to himself as a Hebrew of Hebrews and faultless when it came to keeping the law (Philippians 3:5-6). Remembering our spiritual successes can keep us from pressing on to the higher ground of Christian maturity. By the grace of God, He's allowed us to grow as Christians. We don't think the same as we used to, and we don't do the same things we once did. Thank Him for that, but don't rest on your laurels. While we must be eternally grateful for what God has brought us out of and into, we're not satisfied with that. We want to tread into deeper waters of His grace. The old hymn says, "Still praying as I'm onward bound, Lord, plant my feet on higher ground."

Paul may have had a hard time putting his spiritual failures behind him. Remember, Paul was Saul who persecuted the Church violently. He gave approval for the stoning of Stephen, and guilt and shame may have plagued him. But Paul was reminding us, and maybe himself, to forget the past. In the past, he counted on his own efforts for right standing with God. Possibly Paul was aggravated with himself on how blind he could have been to the truth of Scripture that says there is "none who are righteous" (Romans 3:10).

I thank God for all that He's done for me. He's brought me a "mighty long way" as the old gospel song says. But if I look back to good times or bad, I will slow my progress of pressing on to spiritual maturity. So, I don't want to dwell on the past. I want to forget it and move on to the new things God has for me.

I've pastored Xenia Nazarene Church for many years now, and I find that I repeat myself quite often. As I look over past sermons and Bible studies, I notice that I go over the same things regularly. Is that a sign of old age, or is it a spiritual necessity? The apostle Paul writes, "It is no trouble for me to write the same things to you again, and it is a safeguard for you" (Philippians 3:1). Those are our lifewords for today.

As he writes one of the most crucial chapters in all of God's Word, Paul says that he is repeating himself. In the AV translation (Atherton Version), he writes, "I know I have told you this before, but I need to say it again. Watch out for those who lessen the grace of God by making you think you have to add something to the cross of Christ." Paul must have thought we all need reminders of the most important things.

We learn by repetition, and Paul must have known there were some who had not learned the spiritual lesson of salvation through Christ and Christ alone. False teachers were promoting things like circumcision as a way to make sure you were saved. Paul doesn't play nice here. He calls these teachers "dogs and evildoers" (Philippians 3:2). Dogs weren't household pets in biblical times; they were wild and filthy. First-century Jews often used this adjective to describe people who they thought were unclean—mainly Gentiles.

As humans, it's hard to accept God's free gift. It goes against what we've learned about earning our way. Some want to do something to seal the deal. But Paul's response was harsh: You're a dog! That's what Paul thought of those who found Christ's work on the cross insufficient. And if there is one New Testament truth repeated over and over, it's that salvation is by grace. Because we're slow learners, let's repeat that again and again.

Having confidence is vital to success in many areas. As I write this, I'm teaching my son to drive. I'm reminded each time we go out that confidence is important. As a young driver, he's tense and worried that he will make a mistake. He has to put more time behind the wheel to acquire the confidence to relax. While confidence is a good thing in driving, Paul warns us against confidence in the spiritual realm. In Philippians 3:3, Paul defines a Christian as one "who puts no confidence in the flesh." Those are our lifewords for today.

For Christians, our confidence is not in ourselves but in God. The Bible teaches us to face life knowing He is able, and we are not. This is to establish trust in the One whose grace is sufficient. This is the way God calls us to live.

Now, hear me; Paul has confidence, but it's not confidence in himself. "I can do all things, through Christ who strengthens me" (Philippians 4:13). Paul also says he was confident of this. "He who began a good work in you will bring it to completion" (Philippians 1:6). Paul's confidence is based in "...Christ in you..." (Colossians 1:27). It's not rooted in his flesh.

In the context of this passage, Paul is especially referring to not putting spiritual confidence in the time he spends in prayer, the number of chapters of Scripture he reads, or the number of verses he's memorized. Paul doesn't put his confidence in his own ability to impress God with his spiritual credentials.

The Apostle Paul opened up the whole Western world to Christianity but refused to put confidence in his missionary endeavors. He wrote most of the New Testament but refused to put confidence in his ability to persuade people to turn to Christ. But Paul had much confidence because he was "in Christ" (2 Corinthians 5:17) and because "God was for him" (Romans 8:31).

Scripture testifies that we are to be bold and to see ourselves as "more than conquerors"(Romans 8:31). But remember, that confidence is not in the flesh but in "God who works in you" (Philippians 2:13).

In Philippians 3:12-14, Paul compares our Christian life to a race. He uses words like prize, goal, pressing on, and win. That's odd because in the earlier verses of chapter 3, he hasn't been talking about our own effort but what Christ has done for us. He even calls his own human achievement "rubbish." He emphasizes grace and now seems to stress our human efforts. How do we reconcile these two opposite things?

It's crucial to know that grace is a two-sided coin. Grace is unmerited favor that God gives us freely. But grace is also a power, a power to run the race of the Christian life and run it to win. Our lifewords today are from Titus 2:11-12. "For the grace of God has appeared to all men. It teaches us to say 'No' to ungodliness and worldly passions, and to live self-controlled, upright, and godly lives in this present age." Grace in this passage teaches us and empowers us to live a godly life. This two-sided grace shows up again in Paul's writings. "By the grace of God I am what I am, and his grace toward me was not in vain. On the contrary, I worked harder than any of them, though it was not I, but the grace of God that is with me" (1 Corinthians 15:10).

Yes, yes, yes, a thousand times yes. Grace is pardon—free pardon. But the biblical Christian also knows that grace is a power of the Holy Spirit working within us to help us mature in Christ. The grace of God is not only for sins forgiven in the past, but it's a power to live the Christian life now and in the future.

I can't sell grace short and simply claim mercy for forgiveness. I've got to believe God will empower me, through His grace, to press on, run, and win the prize.

Wisdom is the ability to make good choices. Wisdom is not something we're born with. Wisdom is gained year by year, experience by experience. You're not wise because your father is, although that may help. You're not wise because you have an advanced degree, although there's nothing wrong with that. Wisdom shows up in our daily lives in the choices we make. One choice that the Bible says is very wise is the choice to "shut up." You can't read the book of Proverbs without coming to that conclusion.

Today's lifeword comes from Proverbs 10:19: "He who holds his tongue is wise." A few times in my life I should have said something when I didn't. But countless times, I've gotten myself in trouble because I spoke when I should have kept my mouth closed. Some of my greatest accomplishments in life have been when I kept my mouth shut. Can you relate?

Proverbs 10:14 says, "A wise man holds his tongue. Only a fool blurts out everything he knows." Proverbs 17:27 says, "The one who has knowledge uses words with restraint..." The Bible says you can even deceive people into thinking you are wise. "Even fools are thought wise when they keep silent; with their mouths shut, they seem intelligent" (Proverbs 17:28).

While we can ask for forgiveness for the times we should have kept our mouths shut, the consequences remain. We'll even have to give account on Judgement Day for not keeping our mouth shut. Jesus says, "But I tell you that every careless word that people speak, they shall give an accounting for it in the day of judgment" (Matthew 12:36-37). Because we will give an account for the words we speak, we should be motivated to speak fewer of them.

So, put a sock in it, zip it, clam up, and shut up. Whatever you want to call it, just do it. It's a mark of wisdom.

We spoke yesterday of the wisdom of keeping quiet. There are many reasons it's wise to choose not to speak, but our lifewords today offers us a really good one. "The way of fools seems right to them, but the wise listen to advice" (Proverbs 12:15).

How many opportunities for gaining wisdom have we lost simply because we were talking too much? One biblical characteristic of the wise is the ability to listen. "Listen to advice and accept discipline, and at the end you will be counted among the wise" (Proverbs 19:20). The Bible says we listen to learn.

The New Testament encourages us to be quick to listen (James 1:19). You learn by listening—not by talking. We can learn from every person if we'll just stop talking and listen. Everyone knows something I don't.

Pride keeps me talking and robs me from learning from others. Pride makes me want to show you how much I know about the subject. Pride keeps us from listening and learning, all the while making us think we are wise.

When we listen, everything we hear will not be truth. We should be humble enough, and respect people enough, to listen and evaluate what they have to say. God will give us the grace to discern between what is worthy of taking to heart and what is not.

A willingness to listen is a mark of wisdom. Proverbs 1:5 says, "A wise man will hear and increase learning, and a man of understanding will attain wise counsel." The Hebrew word for learning in this verse means "a taking in." I can't "take in" unless I listen.

It's polite to listen. It's respectful to listen. I get along better with others when I choose not to speak but listen. All of those are good and socially acceptable reasons to listen. But the biggest advantage of listening is that I learn.

Yesterday, we spoke of the importance of listening to learn. While learning is the best consequence of listening, there's another that is crucial to us as Christians. One of the reasons we choose not to speak, one of the reasons we listen, is so we can hear the other person. Our lifewords are from Proverbs 18:13, "To answer before listening—that is folly and shame." They tell me if I answer before listening, that is "folly and shame." Holding my tongue and listening is an expression of love, respect, and value to the person who is talking. Nothing makes us feel more insignificant than trying to talk to someone when their mind is somewhere else and they're not listening. What happens when we listen? We express love.

Someone has said, "Seek first to understand, then to be understood." I don't know if the person who first said that was a Christian or not, but it sure is a Christian statement. Putting others first by making sure I understand them is a great way to work out Philippians 2:3. "Do nothing out of selfish ambition or vain conceit. Rather, in humility value others above yourselves." As I listen, really listen, I express love to the person I'm listening to.

Listening is a powerful form of acknowledgment. It's a great way to live out Romans 15:7: "Accept one another..." Listening conveys the message that I'm not judging you. Listening says you are worthy of my time. Listening tells the speaker they are important to me. 1 Corinthians 13:4 defines love as being patient and kind. Patience and kindness are both exhibited as we listen. I listen for a lot of reasons, but one of the best is to love.

Never forget this. When someone blesses us by intentionally listening, we feel loved.

I'm fascinated by the TV show *Storage Wars*. If you've never seen it, it's a reality program that features the auction of storage units. The buyers can observe the unit from the outside before the auction. They aren't allowed to enter the unit or open boxes. Because of this, buyers may end up with nothing of value. But sometimes, these bidders find hidden treasure, like a painting that was resold for $77,000!

Our lifeword today is from Matthew 13:44, and it speaks of a hidden treasure. "The kingdom of heaven is like treasure hidden in a field. When a man found it, he sold all he had and bought that field." I don't know about you, but I was taught that the hidden treasure was salvation, and we should give up everything, sell everything, so that we can get it. Salvation is so valuable, so precious, that it's worth any price, any sacrifice we have to make. While I will agree with that, I don't think that is what Jesus meant.

Do we have to give everything for Jesus to save us? That's not good theology! We're saved by grace. It is a gift of God; it's not of works (Ephesians 2:8-9). Do you know what the hidden treasure is? It's you! You are the treasure. You are the one Jesus gave everything for. He bought you with a price! The highest price anyone could pay. This is the only interpretation of the parable that makes theological sense.

I know you don't feel much like a treasure. But the truth of God's Word is that you are so valued that God sent His Son to die for you. I know you don't feel like you're worth much. But in God's eyes, you were worth His Son. It's an oft-used phrase, but it's true: God loves you. You're valuable to Him.

February 10th

Yesterday's devotional... You don't buy it, do you? Jesus knew you wouldn't, so after He tells the parable of the hidden treasure, He says, "Again..." (Matthew 13:45). It's like He knew He would need to repeat the truth again because you wouldn't grasp it. So, He says, "Again, the kingdom of heaven is like a merchant looking for fine pearls. When he found one of great value, he went away and sold everything he had and bought it" (Matthew 13:45,46). That's our lifeword for today.

Jesus repeats Himself in Matthew 13 and says the Kingdom of Heaven is not only like a hidden treasure; it's like a merchant looking for fine pearls. When he found one of great value, he sold everything he had and bought it. Do you know what the pearl is? It's you! You are the pearl. You are the one Jesus gave everything for. He bought you with a price, the price of His own life. No one could have paid higher. He gave up everything He had, even His place in Heaven and became like you and me. He eventually was denied by His most loyal follower. He was betrayed by another. All this He did so that He could have His pearl. God counted the cost and decided you were worth the life of the Son of God. You are the pearl of great price, and that's not my opinion; it's God's.

Okay, maybe you're starting to grasp this. If so, let me bring you back down to earth. If you're the pearl, that means that irritating person in your life is a pearl as well. We may not see them as very pearly, and they may not act very pearly, but God thinks they're pearls, just like He thinks you're one. So, forgive that pearl, love that pearl, accept that pearl, serve that pearl, and encourage that pearl.

In the Old Testament, there's a story of a man named Jonah who at first failed God by resisting His call upon his life. But the Bible says in Jonah 3:1 that the Word of the Lord came to Jonah a second time. God gives Jonah a second chance to become who He called him to be. A second chance to say yes to God. A second chance to receive His grace and wisdom. A second chance to open his eyes to the possibility of impacting people's lives.

Throughout God's Word, He is portrayed as the God of the second chance. For instance, Jacob failed God again and again. But God would not give up on him, even to the point of crippling his leg to get him to listen. God continued to give Jacob a second chance.

King David was also the recipient of a second chance from God. The Bible gives vivid details of David failing God. But God didn't give up on him and gave him a second chance. If He had not, we wouldn't have Psalm 51. Where would all of us who need second chances be without that Psalm?

And then, Simon Peter denied Jesus three times. Two precious words show up in Mark 16:7 that scream to us that God is the God of the second chance. The angel said "...Go, tell his disciples and Peter..." And Peter!! In those two words, God says, "I'll not give up on Peter no matter what he's done." God had much for Peter to do. He even preached the first sermon on the Day of Pentecost when 3,000 men came to Christ.

God gives us a second chance. And when I say second, I mean second upon second upon second. I stopped counting my second chances at 17. I'm way up in the hundreds now, I'm sure. The only thing we have to do to make these second chances operable in our lives is to be willing to try again. We'll have more about that in tomorrow's devotion.

God is the God of the second chance or 57th chance—whatever number you're up to. But the key is I have to try again. Jesus tells Peter to go fishing. Peter doesn't want to because he's been fishing all day and hasn't caught a thing. Finally, Peter gives in and says, "At your word, I will let down the net." That's our lifeword for today from Luke 5:5. He was saying, "I will try again."

Maybe you've blown it with your spouse, your child, your boss. All of us have. God is the God of a second chance, but we've got to want to give it another shot. Your failure was not fatal. Actually, failures are a prerequisite to success. Who succeeds the first time? I don't know anyone who does. The athlete who kicks the winning field goal, hits the home run in the bottom of the ninth, or hits the last-second shot at the buzzer all have one thing in common. They've missed last-second field goals, struck out in the bottom of the ninth, and air-balled the winning shot. The only thing fatal about failures is if they keep us from trying again.

Jesus' first attempt at ministry didn't go very well. He was in His hometown of Nazareth. The people in Nazareth were opposed to the work of Jesus. "They got up, drove him out of the town, and took him to the brow of the hill on which the town was built, in order to throw him off the cliff" (Luke 4:29). Not a real good start for Jesus.

So, you've failed. Big deal. Join the club. God is not standing behind you shaking His head disapprovingly because you blew it yesterday. He has another chance for you IF you will try again.

I love the movie *One Flew Over the Cuckoo's Nest*. It's filled with one great scene after another. One of my favorites is when R. P. McMurphy accepts the challenge to lift up the massive cement water fountain and throw it out the window so that he can escape. After he tried and failed, he said "At least I tried... at least I tried." In the Christian life, we need a whole lot of tryers. We ought to celebrate them, praise them, even in failure. When people try something for God and fail, let's honor them because at least they had the courage to try.

Our lifeword is from Matthew 14, where we have a story of a failure. It's the story of Peter who walked on water momentarily but then sank. I can hear the others who wouldn't leave the boat. They may have ridiculed him for trying something so unreasonable. Maybe Peter thought, "I tried, didn't I? At least I tried."

The words of Theodore Roosevelt fit well here: "It is not the critic who counts; not the man who points out how the strong man stumbles...The credit belongs to the man who is actually in the arena, whose face is marred by dust and sweat and blood; who strives valiantly; who errs, who comes short again and again...who spends himself in a worthy cause; who at the best knows in the end the triumph of high achievement, and who at the worst, if he fails, at least fails while daring greatly, so that his place shall never be with those cold and timid souls who neither know victory nor defeat."

"Cold and timid souls." Wow, I don't want to live my life like that. Trust Jesus and take a risk. Even if you fail, you tried... at least you tried.

February 14th

This is Valentine's Day. For many of us, it's a week to thank God for our spouse. If you're like me, you have no clue where you'd be today if God hadn't brought that special person into your life.

After many years in the ministry, I know this week does not bring out the best of emotions for all people. There are some out there who have given up on your marriage. It started well, but it's not the same as it used to be. He's done that, and she's done this. He said that, and she said this. He was wrong, and she was wrong. A whole lot of stuff has built up over the years. There's a lot of water under the bridge, right?

You are married but just existing together. You are living under the same roof but with little passion or feeling. May I encourage you today to give your marriage another shot? A second chance. But this time, do it God's way.

Our lifeword today is from 1 Corinthians 13:5, where the Bible defines love as keeping "no record of wrongs." Are you a record-keeper? It's impossible to love your spouse as God wants you to if you are keeping track of past wrongs. Wrongs will happen every single week, maybe every single day of your marriage. To have a great marriage, you must learn to deal with them.

Keeping records is the biggest obstacle to a great relationship with your husband / wife. Some marriages have stacks and stacks of wrongs that have piled up over the years. Piles of wrongs are almost impossible to get over. You must let them go and start again. As you eliminate the piles of wrongs, resolve not to let the stack get that big again. It's a lot easier to forgive when the stack is small. Keep short accounts. Be terrified to allow the wrongs to pile up again. If you do this, you are loving your spouse according to the Bible's definition of love.

How about giving your marriage another shot today? Give it a second chance. But this time do it God's way by keeping no record of wrongs. Don't allow the wrongs to pile up.

We've talked about how, in God's eyes, we are pearls and treasures. That certainly competes with all the other messages we tune into daily. Through TV, radio, books, Facebook, Instagram, and other people, our identity is shaped. But for the Christian, only one message about ourselves matters: You are who God says you are. You aren't what you think you are. You aren't who that little voice inside says you are. You aren't who your parents say you are. You aren't who your boss says you are. You aren't what your performance says you are. You are who God's Word says you are. This area of Christian teaching is called your identity in Christ.

When it comes to who you are, the most important issue is not what you think about yourself. Your thoughts can't be trusted! Jeremiah 17:9 says, "The heart is deceitful above all things, and desperately sick; who can understand it?" Bottom line, the only thing that matters is what God thinks about you. The only way we know that is through His Word.

If you are a follower of Christ, you are His own special possession, chosen by God (1 Peter 2:9). You are loved beyond compare (1 John 4:10, 19). You are adopted (Romans 8:15). You are His child (1 John 3:1). You are precious to Him (Isaiah 43:4). All of those verses will be our lifewords for today.

I could go on and on. When you see yourself as God sees you, others may as well. When you are comfortable and consistent in your identity in Him, your walk and your talk will express His desires for you.

Tune in to the biblical message of who God says you are and allow His thoughts about you to build your identity. You will discover a remarkably different thought pattern developing. It will be one that can embrace the truth that you are a treasure. You are a pearl!

Our names don't have much meaning. When you hear Mark Atherton, if you don't know me, it doesn't mean anything to you. But nicknames are another matter. There's a lot in a nickname. A nickname tends to focus on a certain aspect of one's personality or demeanor. Pete Rose was nicknamed "Charlie Hustle" because he hustled around the baseball diamond. Michael Jordan was nicknamed "Air Jordan" because of his ability to jump. Elvis was nicknamed "King" because he was the King of Rock and Roll. My nickname was "Fog." I'll leave that reason to your imagination.

Nicknames are even biblical. Jesus' apostles gave a man named Joseph a nickname. The Bible says they called him Barnabas, which means "son of encouragement" (Acts 4:36). If you are familiar with the book of Acts, you certainly remember the nickname Barnabas better than his given name Joseph. This man was such an encourager that this trait in his life overshadowed his real name.

Our lifeword today is from Romans 12:8. The Bible says if your gift is encouragement, "then give encouragement." The Greek word translated encouragement literally means to "come to one's aid." When someone is injured, we give them first aid. Likewise, when a friend is injured in spirit, we give them encouragement. Someone said encouragement is like oxygen to the human spirit. It's amazing to think that I could aid someone to such an extent that it's like giving them air to breathe.

For us to be encouragers, we need to be others-focused. There's no way I can come to another's aid if I'm only seeing my problems and my issues. Fifty-nine times the Bible mentions "one another." It's essential to the Christian life. Let's learn from Joseph, nicknamed Barnabas, as we focus on others by being an encourager.

It could be argued that the Apostle Paul was more important to Christianity than anyone except Jesus Himself. When you investigate the beginning of Paul's Christian life, it's fascinating to see that the followers of Jesus were terrified of him and wanted nothing to do with him.

The Scriptures say when Paul, then known as Saul, came to Jerusalem, the disciples did not really believe in his conversion. They must have thought he was trying to infiltrate their ranks to stamp out this new sect called Christianity. Acts 9:26 plainly says, "they were all afraid of him." Our lifeword today is Acts 9:27: "But Barnabas took him and brought him to the apostles. He told them how Saul on his journey had seen the Lord and that the Lord had spoken to him, and how in Damascus he had preached fearlessly in the name of Jesus."

Verse 27 starts with "But Barnabas..." Like Superman from a phone booth, Barnabas comes to the aid of Saul, giving encouragement and personally vouching for him in front of the disciples. If not for a lesser known person like Barnabas, the great Apostle may have never been accepted into the Christian ranks. If that had not happened, his impact on Christianity would have been much less.

I wonder, how did Barnabas know Saul needed his help? We have no clue. God's intervention, of course, is assumed here. He was behind the scenes orchestrating, directing, protecting, and making a way for the one who would eventually open up the whole Western world to Christianity.

God has his Barnabases stationed, ready to give aid. You may be one; if so, listen to God's direction. You may need one; if so, trust in the One who has promised to supply your needs. Barnabases are everywhere, coming to the aid of one in need of encouragement.

The Bible doesn't shy away from the problems in the Church. In Acts 15, we read of a time when Barnabas and Paul had a "sharp disagreement." Our lifeword today is from Acts 15:39. It says, "They had such a sharp disagreement that they parted company." They did not see eye to eye on what to do with John Mark. He had quit the ministry, and Barnabas wanted to give him another shot. But Paul had lost confidence in John Mark and no longer felt he could count on him.

In this disagreement, like in many others, there are two sides and maybe two rights. I say that Paul was right. He didn't want someone who put his hand to the plow and looked back (Luke 9:62). Paul was no doubt a driven man and didn't have time to deal with personnel problems when the word about Jesus needed to get out. To him, that mission was the most important thing.

Barnabas saw it from a different viewpoint. He was a people person, and while he knew of the importance of the mission, he saw potential in John Mark, and his heart must have gone out to him. Barnabas, the encourager, saw someone who needed a second chance. I say that Barnabas was right too.

It is important to note that it was in the will of God for Paul and Barnabas to separate. The work needed to increase. But it was not the will of God that they should be sharp in their disagreement. The Spirit of God may lead Christians to go in different directions. When this happens, we should do so while agreeing to disagree.

The Holy Spirit works through fallen, imperfect humans, so it's not surprising conflicts will arise. God is not as concerned with the disagreement as He is about how we disagree. If we focus on that, we can please and glorify God even in our conflict.

"Houston, we have a problem." Those words, or ones like them, were spoken by Apollo 13 astronaut Jack Swigert as he communicated the discovery of the explosion that crippled their spacecraft. The Apostle Paul may have been thinking something similar when he wrote our lifeword for today: "Be kind and compassionate to one another, forgiving each other, just as in Christ, God forgave you" (Ephesians 4:32).

God's forgiveness of us through Jesus' work on the cross is the cornerstone of the Christian life. We have no problem preaching and singing about it. But our forgiveness of others is another story. It's here we have a problem. C. S. Lewis wrote, "Everyone says forgiveness is a lovely idea, until they have something to forgive."

I wonder if Paul was addressing a problem in the Ephesian church? Were they having problems forgiving each other? If they were, they would be like many churches today, filled with folks struggling to let go. Filled with people who are holding on to past hurt and pain. To the Ephesians and to the modern-day church, Paul commands us to forgive each other, "just as in Christ, God forgave you" (Ephesians 4:32).

Let me speak plainly. The reason why some of you have a hard time letting go of hurt is you've never understood Christ's forgiveness of you. Or maybe, worse than that, you never received it. In Colossians 2, Paul writes of a marvelous truth. He says that God has forgiven all our sins. He has canceled the record that contained the charges against us. He took it and destroyed it by nailing it to Christ's cross.

I will never be asked to forgive anyone more than God has already forgiven me. Understanding that makes my forgiveness of others easier. If I don't understand that, if I don't see the depths of my sin, if I don't conceive of God's complete forgiveness of me, then my forgiveness of others will be a problem for me.

Being a person who can forgive others starts with accepting God's forgiveness of you. Have you done that? If you haven't, why not?

Yesterday, we looked at Ephesians 4:32. Let's go back there today. It says, "Be kind and compassionate to one another, forgiving each other, just as in Christ, God forgave you." Paul repeats here one of the great fundamentals of Christian living: we are to forgive those who offend us. Forgiveness is not an easy thing to do or to define. It's easier to talk about what forgiveness is not.

My forgiveness of others is not conditional. They don't earn it. They don't deserve it. Forgiveness is not based on their promise to never do it again. It's unconditional. If someone says, "I will forgive you, if...," that's not biblical forgiveness. In fact, that's bargaining. Something like, "If you do this, I'll do that." Putting conditions on forgiving others misses the whole point of what Scripture says over and over. The emphasis is always on forgiving freely and willingly... "seventy times seven" (Matthew 18:22). God, through His Word, always puts the emphasis on the attitude of the forgiver, not the conditions of the forgiveness.

Here's another thing forgiveness is not. Receiving forgiveness isn't saying "It's no big deal. Just forget about it." That actually cheapens forgiveness. If it wasn't a big deal, someone doesn't need to ask you to forgive them, or you don't need to offer it. When someone asks for forgiveness, and when it is granted, it's a big deal! So, don't cheapen it by pretending the offense didn't bother you.

In Scripture, when Jesus was sad, He cried (John 11:35). When He was angry, He let others know about it (John 2:15-16). If someone has hurt you, it's okay to be hurt. It's okay to accept someone's offer of forgiveness.

This Christian idea of forgiving others is not easy. It's very complicated. But as we work through it, please know that offering forgiveness is not conditional, and receiving it is not about pretending.

Our lifeword for today is from Colossians 3:13. Paul writes, "Bear with each other and forgive one another if any of you has a grievance against someone." That's an easy verse to memorize but a tough one to put into action, right? Forgiving others is something that people struggle with for years. It's not an easy thing to do or define. For some reason it seems easier to say what forgiveness is not.

Forgiveness isn't forgetting what happened. Forgive and forget. You've heard that a lot, haven't you? There's only one problem: you can't do it. You really can't forget a hurt. You will never forget it. In fact, you can't even try to forget it. When people say, "Have you forgotten it?", what happens? You remember the very thing you're trying to forget.

Often, forgetting a hurt is harmful. For instance, if a friend cannot keep a secret and has broken that trust many times, you're smart to remember that and be careful not to confide in that person again. When I remember, I will not be foolish and repeat the same mistake over and over. "As a dog returns to its vomit, so a fool repeats his folly" (Proverbs 26:11).

Forgiveness doesn't mean forgetting, but it does mean you won't bring it up again. To forgive means to promise not to hold it over a person's head. Even though your memory will go back to it, you will not dwell on it and allow it to make you angry all over again. The second it comes back to mind, you ask God for grace to lay it aside because it's in the past.

By the way, there's something better than forgetting. It's remembering the hurt and seeing how God has brought good out of it. As I see how God has healed it and brought restoration, I thank and praise Him. You can't thank God for things you forget.

In our discussion of forgiveness, you may be thinking, "What if my spouse, my parent, or my boss does something unforgiveable?" Jesus never said forgiving would be easy. But He did say it was very serious business. Read these sobering words, which will be our lifewords for today: "If you do not forgive men their sins, your Father will not forgive your sins" (Matthew 6:15). For those who are reluctant to extend forgiveness, read that verse again.

Some are slow to show mercy because they confuse trust and forgiveness. Forgiveness is about the past. Trust is about the future. Hear these words from Rick Warren: "Forgiveness must be immediate, whether or not a person asks for it. Trust must be rebuilt over time. Trust requires a track record. If someone hurts you repeatedly, you are commanded by God to forgive them instantly, but you are not expected to trust them immediately, and you are not expected to continue allowing them to hurt you." "Trust requires a track record."

Do you understand those words? After an offense, trust does not happen immediately. Remember, trust is about the future. Just because you forgive someone doesn't mean you allow them back into your life. If the offender shows remorse, trust may be possible eventually. How do you know they are remorseful or repentant? One way is that they make no excuses for their offense and accept complete responsibility for the sin and the consequences that have followed. Psalm 51 is a good guide to gauge the truly repentant person's heart. This person should be understanding of your need for time to see evidence of their trustworthiness.

For the last four days, we've looked at the serious business of forgiveness. We've said what it is and what it is not. Forgiveness is such a tough road to go down that many choose not to. But for those who do, they find burdens can be lifted and freedom can be enjoyed.

There are so many things I don't understand about the Christian life. As I get older, I feel the need less and less to have it all figured out. In fact, I'm comfortable saying there is great wisdom in admitting, "I don't know." Nowhere is this truer than in the area of pain and suffering. As I heard a chapel speaker at Asbury Seminary say, "I don't have all the answers, but I've learned to be at peace with the questions."

While not answering the unanswerable "why" question, the Bible does say that God wants to use our pain. It's through our pain and hurt that God can draw us closer to Him. It is God's desire that through hard times, we learn to trust and rely on Him more. When difficulty happens in our lives, we always have a choice. We can draw closer to God, or we can run away from Him.

How do you draw close to God in your pain?

Tell Him how you feel. Cry out to God. Battle it out in prayer. Draw close to Him in worship and through His Word.

Our lifeword today is from 2 Corinthians 1:8-9. Paul writes, "We do not want you to be uninformed about the troubles we experienced...we were under great pressure, far beyond our ability to endure...but this happened that we might not rely on ourselves but on God." In Paul's mind, it was obvious. God wanted to use pain to teach him to trust.

The unanswerable questions are not really the issue when we go through hard times. The issue is my choice. Do I choose to lean hard on a God whose ways I don't seem to understand? Or do I pull away from Him because I can't figure it all out? Do I choose to lean on my own understanding or leave it in my Father's hands and be at peace with the questions of life?

February 24th

When we go through the hard places of our lives, we are brought face to face with some important choices. One we spoke of yesterday was drawing closer to God. Another is drawing closer to other people.

God desires that we use our pain to draw closer to others. Our lifeword today is from Galatians 6:2: "Carry each other's burdens and in this way you fulfill the law of Christ." What is the law of Christ? Loving God *and* loving others, the Great Commandment. When we allow others to help us in our pain, we draw closer to each other and come closer to fulfilling God's greatest commandment.

It's very easy for us to allow pain and suffering to isolate us from each other. None of us likes to spoil the fun because we just don't feel up to it. But we testify to God's grace when we let others see His strength in our weakness. God is glorified when we don't pretend to have it all together but confess God's goodness amidst the mess we're going through.

Those who are presently going through suffering or have just come out of it can love others by comforting them in ways only a fellow sufferer can. According to Scripture, it is God's desire to comfort the suffering through the ministry of a fellow-sufferer. Paul writes, "Blessed be the God and Father of our Lord Jesus Christ, the Father of mercies and God of all comfort, who comforts us in all our affliction, so that we may be able to comfort those who are in any affliction, with the comfort with which we ourselves are comforted by God" (2 Corinthians 1:3-4).

God promises in Romans 8:28 that good will come from our hard times in life. Some of that good happens when we choose to draw closer to others by allowing them to minister to us. More good comes when we choose to minister to others as only a fellow-sufferer can.

It's hard to talk biblically about pain and suffering without talking about Paul's thorn in the flesh from 2 Corinthians 12. From Paul's viewpoint, his thorn was not a good thing because he refers to it as a "messenger from Satan." Paul says it was sent to "torment him," and he "pleads" that it be taken away. We don't know what this was. Many biblical scholars have speculated, but that's all it is… speculation. The Bible simply doesn't tell us. But it does tell us why he had it: "to keep him from being conceited." Evidently, God allowed Paul to be hindered in some way for a greater purpose. God used pain and suffering in Paul's life. God chose not to remove the thorn but simply used these words to respond to Paul's pleading: "My grace is sufficient for you." Those are our lifewords for today from 2 Corinthians 12:9.

In the original language of the Bible, those words are actually ordered "Sufficient for you is the grace of Me." God doesn't give us grace dose by dose—a couple of teaspoons here and a couple there. He is always with us, and He is the grace. He's not like a doctor who gives us what we need and then goes to the next patient. He comes to stay. He promises, "I am with you always, even unto the end of the world" (Matthew 28:20).

The word sufficient means "enough." It doesn't mean overflowing. It doesn't mean I will be flooded with His grace. It's simply enough. It will get me through. The pain will still be felt, and the suffering will be real. But Jesus, the Alpha and Omega, will be with me. Jesus, the King of Kings and the Lord of Lords, will be there. "Sufficient for you is the grace of Me."

Many people have been helped by what C. S. Lewis wrote on pain and suffering. Lewis was a fellow sufferer. His mother died of cancer when Lewis was 9. His dad emotionally deserted him. Lewis was wounded in World War I and saw his wife die when she was 45 years old. In his book, *The Problem of Pain,* he wrote these words: "Pain insists upon being attended to. God whispers to us in our pleasures, speaks in our conscience, but shouts in our pain: it is His megaphone to rouse a deaf world."

We are very sensitive to God's power in our suffering. It is then we become aware of how vulnerable and weak we really are. If we choose to, it's in that moment of weakness we experience God's power. Our lifeword today is from 2 Corinthians 12:9, where God tells Paul, "my power is made perfect in weakness." In our pain, unlike other times in our lives, we sense His power. It's in our pain we learn that His grace is sufficient in our lives. God uses pain as a megaphone to teach us that He is sufficient to meet our deepest needs.

God uses our pain to speak to those around us. It's here that the megaphone imagery makes most sense. The paraplegic who has joy in the midst of suffering shouts loudly to a watching world. Who cannot be amazed by the parents who bury their child while still professing faith in our good God?

If you are a fellow sufferer, your pain gives you a voice, a voice to speak to others who are looking for ways to deal with the tragedies of life. God uses our pain, and He uses us to minister in ways no one else can. We didn't ask for this megaphone. Life has a way of handing us things we did not want. Will we use it to attest to God's grace in the midst of weakness?

God is in control. Theologically, we call this the sovereignty of God. This is seen all through the Bible but especially in our lifeword for today from Romans 8:28: "And we know that for those who love God all things work together for good, for those who are called according to his purpose."

As we try to get a handle on pain and suffering in our lives, the following statement is true and helps me be at peace with questions I can't answer: **Everything that happens to me has been filtered through the love and wisdom of my Father in Heaven.** Whatever occurs has been sovereignly approved. The happenings of my life are no accident to Him. He has seen fit to allow this to occur.

That doesn't mean that all things that happen are His design and come from His will. There are consequences for being a fallen person who lives in a fallen world. But the promise of our lifeword today is that He will use all things for good for those that love Him. Read it again. It doesn't say all things are good. It also doesn't say that He will use them for *my* good. God is the governor of the universe, and He's working for the overall good of His creation.

I attended a funeral today of a friend of mine who battled cancer for 7 years. The cancer was not good. The suffering was not good. The fact that her husband is now without his wife is not good. But God promises to take that which is not good and use it for good. I believe that promise by faith without knowing the particulars of when and how He will fulfill it.

Nothing happens to me that catches God off guard. Nothing happens that He has not allowed. Not caused, but allowed. There is no telling how much bad God has filtered out and sovereignly saved me from. But for all that He allowed, good will come from it.

Our lifeword today is from Proverbs 6:16. The Bible says, "There are six things the Lord hates. Seven that are detestable to Him." We have a hard time thinking about God hating anything. After all, the Bible tells us He is love. Love is not something He does; it is something He is. Love for us is a verb. In God's grammar, it's a noun. If the very essence of who He is can be defined by His loving nature, how can the Bible say that God detests or hates anything?

One's capacity to love is defined by one's capacity to hate. The more you love something or someone, the more you will hate anything that threatens what you love. No one has a deeper capacity to love than God. Thus, no one has a deeper capacity to hate than He does. When we humans hate, it's most likely a sinful action. But God hates without sinful intent. He hates what keeps us from being who He created us to be: people who love Him and love other people.

Man's hatred and God's hatred are extremely different. God hates without sinful intent. Though man's hatred is most often characterized by sin, it doesn't have to be that way. I can love something so much that I hate anything that comes in opposition to that.

As Christians, we should love what God loves and hate what He hates. Some things He hates are listed in Proverbs 6: proud eyes, hands that shed innocent blood, a lying tongue, a man who stirs up dissension. I don't know about you, but I hate those things in other people. I'm quick to condemn it and judge it as sin. But why is it easier to hate those things in others than it is to hate them in myself? Maybe one reason the Bible lists what God hates is so that we will see them in ourselves and hate them as well.

When you miss a putt on the golf course, do you enlarge the hole so that it will be easier to make the next time? When we get caught speeding on the interstate, do we start a campaign to up the speed limit to 75? Of course we don't, but that's exactly what many people do with God's Word. Because His standard is high, we decide to lower it to make us feel better about not living up to it. We say we're only human, and after all, it's a 2,000-year-old book that surely must be brought up to date.

God's call for our lives is very high. There's no question it's difficult to attain. It's tempting to lower the bar so that we will feel better about ourselves. God calls us to keep aiming high for the life He wants for us (Philippians 3:14). When we fall short, embrace the forgiveness provided by Jesus and keep aiming toward the high calling of God.

The distance between where I fall short and God's desires for me leaves a GAP. What do we do with it? Do we feel condemned? It's easy to feel that way when we read that God's standard is high. I mean, love my enemies, turn the other cheek? Wow! The difference between what God calls me to and the reality in my life can be vast. There's a huge GAP there!

I used to feel guilty about that GAP, but one day, I realized that's why Jesus died. God knew His people would not always live up to His call for them. God knew there would be a GAP. So, He sent Jesus to die for the GAP. Our lifeword today is from Revelation 13:8. It says, "Jesus was the Lamb who was slain from the creation of the world." Even from the beginning, God knew there would be a need for a Savior because there was going to be a GAP. Don't allow the enemy to remind you how big the GAP is. Remind him that God knew about that eons ago and made plans to send Jesus to die for your GAP and mine.

March 1st

My 16-year-old son told me a few days ago, "Dad, I don't want to grow up. I don't want to have to get a job and be responsible." While I sympathized with him not wanting the responsibilities of getting older, my response was, "Sorry Son, it just doesn't work that way." That's sort of what Paul says in Ephesians 4:15,16. I summarize it this way: we are not meant to remain as children, but we are to grow up in every way into Christ. Those are our lifewords for today.

The goal for any child is to grow up. If the child stays a child, physically or emotionally, something is definitely wrong. The same is true of the Christian. We are not meant to remain as children (Ephesians 4:14). The goal for the Christian is to mature or, as these verses say, to grow up. When we are new Christians, the Bible calls us infants, or babes in Christ who are not ready for solid food. Infants need milk as Paul says in 1 Corinthians 3.

Growing up as a Christian is like growing up as a human. It happens little by little, day by day, week by week, and month by month. This process takes time, and it can't be rushed. If you are a new believer, be patient with yourself. Give yourself a break. Growing into maturity as a Christian takes one step at a time.

If you are a mature Christian, let's not get impatient with new believers because they are infants. Just like little babies, they will make messes all the time. We don't expect much from babies, so let's not expect much from babes in Christ either. Allow them time to grow up. They are learning just like you and I had to learn. Let's allow the Holy Spirit to bring them along in His way and in His time.

How tragic to see an adult who has developmental disabilities. Many of them struggle with tasks that little children do without thinking. Our hearts go out to them and their families. Something has gone wrong. If we look at stunted mental or physical development as tragic, what must God think when He looks at Christians who have not developed... have not grown up?

Growing up is NOT automatic. Allow me to paraphrase the writer of Hebrews, "You have been Christians a long while, and you should be teaching others. Instead, you need someone to teach you again and again the same ole things a beginner must learn about the Christian life. You are like babies who drink only milk and cannot handle solid food. And a person who lives only on milk isn't very mature. He doesn't know much about doing what is right" (Hebrews 5:12-13). Peter writes, "Continue to grow in the grace and knowledge of our Lord and Savior, Jesus Christ" (2 Peter 3:18). That verse is our lifeword today, and it assumes a process. Growing as a Christian is step by step. It's intentional and certainly not instantaneous.

I was a high school math teacher for six years. To calculate how far someone had traveled, we needed to know the rate of travel and how long they had been moving. Rate x Time = Distance. Let me restate it as a formula for spiritual growth. Desire x Time = Spiritual Growth.

The Christian must have the desire to grow up. It is not automatic. It is intentional. There is no shortcut to spiritual growth. No sermon, no CD, no radio program, no seminar, no church can provide a way around the time needed to grow.

If your heart is right, you will have the desire. If you have the desire and put in the time, God will grant the desires of your heart and grow you up as a Christian.

The last two days, we've been talking about growing up as a Christian. The obvious question is, "How do you grow up?" You grow as your faith and trust in God increases. The Bible says it's by faith that we please God (Hebrews 11:6). As I mature and learn to lean not on my own understanding but on God and His Word, I mature spiritually. Romans 10:17 is our lifeword today, and it says, "Faith comes by hearing, and hearing by the Word of God." When we hear God's Word and believe it, trust it, and stand on His promises, we grow as Christians. Are you hearing on a regular basis? One way is through consistent church attendance. Although this won't guarantee your spiritual growth, a lack of it will guarantee spiritual immaturity. But if you attend with a heart that desires to grow as a Christian, watch out! Maturing will happen, step by step.

I like to play solitaire, but being a solitary Christian can be very detrimental to my growth. The biblical faith is communal. We grow as we love one another, encourage one another, pray for one another, and accept one another. Hebrews 10:24 says we should "spur one another on toward love and good deeds." To spur means to motivate or encourage. Immediately following this verse, we are told "not to give up meeting together." (Hebrews 10:25).

Your faith will grow as you are in the company of other growing disciples. Friendships with believers through church attendance and small group opportunities will increase your capacity to trust God. It's sad to see huge attendance on Easter Sunday, followed by a significant drop the following week. This happens because too many people think, "I was just there last week!"

Please hear me again. Consistent church attendance will not guarantee spiritual growth, but *a lack of it will guarantee spiritual immaturity.* Gather together with other believers who desire to grow just as you do. If your heart is right, God will take your desire, add His grace to it, and you'll find yourself growing up as a Christian.

Ephesians 4:15 commands us not to remain as children, but to grow up as Christians. Yesterday, we said we grow up as our faith increases. One way our faith increases is through hearing (Romans 10:17). Faith also increases as we exercise it. Just like physical exercise increases our strength and stamina, spiritual exercise increases our faith. A biblical faith takes action. Faith is not just a mental assent to some truths. It's taking it out of your head and putting it in your life. Your faith is developed as you practice what you believe.

The Bible condemns a faith that is in your head only. Hear our lifewords for today: "What good is it, my brothers and sisters, if someone claims to have faith but has no deeds? Can such faith save them? Suppose a brother or a sister is without clothes and daily food. If one of you says to them, 'Go in peace; keep warm and well fed,' but does nothing about their physical needs, what good is it?" (James 2:14-16).

What haunting words..."What good is it?" The Bible knows nothing of a faith that doesn't work itself out in tangible ways in our lives. The Bible is clear: faith without action is dead (James 2:17). Biblical faith is not just made up of spiritual things, but also the basic needs of life. When we see needs arise, faith prays and then helps. I have to admit, there have been times in my life when I used prayer as a substitute for action. I was too heavenly minded and thus, no earthly good.

Faith is meant for the streets, not just for the sanctuary. Every Sunday, as our service closes, I say something like, "it's time to scatter and put into practice what we've heard as we've gathered." I'm basically saying, "Go and exercise your faith." That's one sure way to grow up as a Christian.

"Then we will no longer be infants, tossed back and forth by the waves, and blown here and there by every wind of teaching and by the cunning and craftiness of people in their deceitful scheming" (Ephesians 4:14). These are our lifewords today. Here, Paul lists two things that define a Christian who needs to grow up.

Immaturity

"Then we will no longer be infants." In the language of the New Testament, that word translated here as "infants" literally means stupid. "Then we will no longer be stupid." We start the Christian journey as a child, an infant. Children have their minds on childish things. There's nothing wrong with that unless we continue in childish ways as we enter the teenage years. Paul says of himself, "When I was a child, I talked like a child, I reasoned like a child. But when I became a man [spiritually mature] I put away childish things" (1 Corinthians 13:11).

Instability

Paul describes those needing to grow up as "tossed back and forth by the waves, and blown here and there by every wind of teaching" (Ephesians 4:14). The Christian who believes *this* one day and *that* the next day is not stable. They lack the discernment to distinguish between truth and error. They jump from church to church looking for the key to the spiritual life. They think that some new teaching will be the answer to their spiritual troubles. I once saw a vial of holy water from the Jordan River advertised on a Christian TV station. For only $9.99, you can be anointed with the same water that Jesus was baptized in. Just think how that will jump start your Christian life! I'm sure some spiritually immature people bought a vial or two!

Grown-up Christians may have a child-like faith, but they aren't childish. Grown-up Christians don't look for a new and improved Christianity; they rely on the faith that's been passed down for generations.

We hear a lot of teaching and preaching about the first sin, the taking of the fruit from the tree in the garden. Our first parents, Adam and Eve, disobeyed God and did the one thing He told them not to. My preaching professor at Asbury Seminary, Ellsworth Kalas, called this next part the second sin. It's the sin that Adam committed when God asked him about the first. Adam said, "This woman....she made me eat it." That's our lifeword for today from Genesis 3:12. Adam didn't own up to his sin; he deflected blame and made an excuse. That's the second sin. There's marvelous forgiveness for the first, no matter what it may be. But I know of no forgiveness for the second sin. If we don't take responsibility for our actions, there is no hope for us. There is no plan of salvation for the one who won't admit their own guilt.

Sin will not destroy us. While the consequences from sin aren't pleasant and are serious, they won't destroy us either. What destroys is the passing of the buck. What destroys is not coming to grips with my own actions. What destroys is the inability to say, "I was wrong," and confess that it was my fault.

I was a school teacher for eight years. There is great hope in life for the ones who will learn from their mistakes, own up to past failures, and seek to correct their behavior. The ones who make the most of their schooling are the ones who are most teachable. A huge part of being teachable is admitting that you don't know it all... admitting that you need help.

In the spiritual realm, admitting you need help equates to asking God to forgive your past sin and set you on a new path in life. But it's not only forgiveness; its repentance as well. Psalm 51 is our guide. King David could recover from horrendous sin in his life because he repented... he admitted. He didn't commit the second sin. That sin, the sin of not accepting responsibility, is deadly. You cannot recover from it.

Yesterday, we looked at the famous passage of when temptation entered our world. Our first parents didn't respond very well. The Apostle Paul wrote to some in the church at Corinth who may not have dealt with temptation well either. Paul reminds them that what they experienced is common. The same is true for you. Whatever the temptation, others are going through the same thing. Our lifeword for today comes from 1 Corinthians 10:13. The Bible says, "No temptation has seized you except what is common to man." Though we don't know this for sure, maybe some Corinthians thought their temptation was more powerful than what the Ephesians or Galatians were going through.

This verse says whatever was tempting them was not unique to them. The enemy of your soul wants you to think that no one else deals with this. No one will understand, and no one will care. Hear the truth: you are not the only one going through it. Our verse says, "No temptation has seized you except what is common to man."

Some may doubt if anyone else besides them has bad thoughts or continues to struggle with the lure of sin. This can leave them feeling alone, isolated, and unsure of their own salvation. After over 23 years in the ministry, the things I have heard in the pastor's office are "common to man." The enemy is not very creative. It's the same thing over and over again.

Temptation can make us feel dirty and unworthy. But remember, temptation, by itself, is not sin. Even Jesus was tempted. Scripture says in Hebrews 4:15 "...because Jesus was tempted, He is able to help us in our temptation." Jesus understands how tempting sin can be. You don't need to confess it to Him because it's not sin. Just talk to Him about it. Don't hide it from Him. He already knows about it anyway.

Also, don't hide it from others. Share it with a close friend who will keep their mouth shut. Don't be surprised if they struggle with the same temptations. After all, temptations are "common to man."

I remember when I was the pastor of a small church. I'd see all the larger churches and wish I could pastor one of those. Now, I'm one of those larger church pastors, and think how cool it would be not to have all the responsibilities that come with a bigger church. Contentment is an elusive thing.

The Apostle Paul writes in Philippians 4:12, "I know what it is to be in need, and I know what it is to have plenty. I have learned the secret of being content in any and every situation, whether well fed or hungry, whether living in plenty or in want." That's our lifeword for today. Paul says he's been hungry, and he's been well fed. He's been needy, and he's had plenty. In all of these situations, he has been content. Paul knows that contentment is not about what you have; it's about Who has you. By the way, Paul wrote this in a Roman jail. No one will ever convince me that he didn't want out of there. But even though he didn't have all his wants, he was still content.

Do you ever feel like you would be content if your circumstances were different? Of course you do; we all do. But let's not live by our feelings. Let's live by the truth. In Philippians 4:11, Paul says, "I have learned in whatever situation I am, to be content." The person who is biblically content doesn't ride the roller coaster of life's circumstances. That's because contentment is not about what you have; it's about Who has you.

Contentment is an inside job that can't be touched by life's ups and downs. It's out of trouble's reach. It can't be stolen by sickness or poverty. Biblical contentment is NOT rooted in circumstances or material things. Paul says that no matter the circumstance, "I can do all this through him who gives me strength" (Philippians 4:13).

Lack of contentment is reflected in many ways. We aren't content to live within our means, so we go into debt to live above our means. Our discontentment shows up in our high rate of mobility. People seem to be on the move, looking for a bigger house, a better job, and a nicer community in which to live and raise a family. It's as if we think we will be satisfied when we find the right living situation. Could discontentment be at the root of our high divorce rate? We trade mates and find we have the same issues as before. In over 23 years of ministry, I've seen people jump from church to church to church. What are they looking for?

Can I tell you a secret about human nature? Getting more and different stuff will not bring you satisfaction in life. In fact, the Bible says satisfaction is not in what you have... it's in Who has you. Our lifeword is from Hebrews 13:5: "Don't love money; be satisfied with what you have. For God has said, 'I will never leave you. I will never forsake you.'" Literally in the Greek, Hebrews 13:5 says, "I will never, never, never, never leave you or forsake you." Never raised to the power of 4! This verse says our contentment comes from God and not from our stuff. No matter what we have, where we live, or what is happening, good or bad, God is with us and on our side. That is enough.

It is because God is with us always that we can say, "I have found satisfaction." David writes, "The Lord is my shepherd; I shall not want" (Psalm 23:1). Satisfaction in life is a function of knowing the Lord is my Shepherd. May I repeat? It's not about what you have; it's about Who has you.

If you're like me, many times you allow your circumstances to determine your feelings. If life is going smoothly, then we feel good about life and about ourselves. But when life gets hard, we feel bad. However, we don't have to allow our feelings to be dictated by our circumstances. We will never find contentment in life if we live by our circumstances.

Contentment means accepting things the way they are—and knowing, "I can do all things through Christ who strengthens me." That's our lifeword from Philippians 4:13. No matter my circumstances... no matter my feelings... no matter what I have or have not, I can be content because I have a can-do attitude that comes from leaning on Christ. When we respond to life with this kind of thinking, we move beyond living by circumstances or feelings to living by the truth. It's then that contentment becomes possible.

It's important to leave Philippians 4:13 in the context that Paul uses. In the two preceding verses, Paul is talking about how he has learned to be content, no matter the circumstance. So, Paul's aim here is contentment, not achievement. Too many times, we use this verse for motivation to accomplish some task. Remember, Paul is in prison as he writes this. He's not trying to accomplish anything. He's trying to endure something. This verse is not about what we can achieve because God is on our side.

So, when we lose the game, don't get the job, or fail to get that new client, that's when this verse becomes precious. Christ enables me to be content in Him, even though the achievement didn't happen. Likewise, when we win the game, get the job, or get the new client, I know I don't need these achievements to be content. After all, it's not about what I have but Who has me.

Paul says we can be content no matter the circumstance. That's because we have something greater than circumstance on our side. We have the strength of Christ living in us.

In Philippians 4:11, Paul wrote, "I have learned in whatever situation I am… to be content." That's our lifeword for today. Paul said he **learned** to be content in all of life's circumstances. That means Paul was not always content. It is not something he, or we, are born with. No one is blessed with the gift of contentment. It is a learned condition. Part of this learning is understanding a new definition of contentment. Most of us start life with a definition of contentment that's something like having what we want. Somewhere along the line, Paul learned to be content with what he had and to accept things as they are.

For us to learn contentment, we must avoid comparisons. As humans, we want to know how we stack up in comparison to others. This is as old as Cain comparing himself to Abel. When we compare ourselves to others, we either want what they have or think we're better than they are. Comparisons lead to discontentment. When the disciples started to play this game, Jesus said not to worry about the other guy. "You follow me" (John 21:22).

As a pastor, it's easy to compare my church with others. I read books and go to conferences that tell me how to succeed in ministry. In all of them, I'm tempted to compare. Jesus says to me as a pastor, "You follow Me." Comparison is the enemy of contentment.

Contentment starts with our choices. Choose to believe the "Lord is my Shepherd. I shall not want" (Psalm 23:1). Choose to believe that no matter what others have, Jesus simply says, "You follow Me." When we make those choices and make them repeatedly, we create a lifestyle. It won't happen overnight. But choice after choice, it will happen. Don't get frustrated with your discontentment. Be patient with yourself. Contentment is a learned behavior. One day, you will thank God that you've learned that it's not about what you have. It's about Who has you.

Yesterday, we spoke of one of the enemies of contentment... comparison. Little in life will erode our sense of contentment faster than comparing my life with those around me. It can lead to resentment, anger, envy, discouragement, and pride.

The often-overlooked consequence of comparison is anger and resentment toward God. If I'm focused on my neighbor and what he has that I don't, I'm close to questioning the goodness of my heavenly Father. Instead of praising God from whom all blessings flow, I become dissatisfied and ungrateful. I begin to think I deserve more and that God is holding out on me. That's not an exaggerated picture of what comparison can do to me. Comparison can create envy. The Bible says envy was a motivator in the crucifixion of Christ. In Mark 15, Pilate says, "'Do you want me to release to you the King of the Jews?' Pilate said this because he knew that the chief priest had handed Him over because of envy."

When we compare ourselves to someone else's situation, we take our focus off God's plan for our life. Our lifeword today is from Hebrews 12:1: "run with endurance the race that is set before us." God has a race only you can run. He hasn't called you to keep up with runners ahead of you. Run your own race. Contentment is running your own race to the best of your ability and leaving the results up to God. Remember, in the Christian life, the reward is not for the one who finishes first. It's for the one who remained faithful while running the race marked out for them.

Don't compare your race to others. God doesn't give you grace to run someone else's race, but His grace is sufficient for running yours. Your race has its own challenges and hardships. It also has its own victories and pleasures. If you run the race God has sovereignly marked out for you, contentment is possible.

Who is Jesus? The way one answers that question tells us a lot about their relationship with Him. Most people around the world would have good things to say about Jesus. Many of those comments would center around the fact that He was a good teacher and taught us how to love one another. There's no question He was a teacher, but He was infinitely more than that.

Our lifeword today comes from the angel's words in Matthew 1:21: "She will give birth to a son, and you are to give him the name Jesus, because he will save his people from their sins." When Joseph was told to name the child Jesus, it wasn't just because all children must have a name. The name was chosen because it described the eventual purpose of His life. Jesus is the Greek form of the Jewish name Joshua, which means "the Lord is salvation."

The angel pointed out to Joseph that Jesus was God's answer to sin. Never let it be misunderstood that He came because we are sinners, and we need saving. We don't face our sins easily. It's much easier for us to say that Jesus was a model that showed us how every human should live. It's much harder to admit that I am a person who needs Him, simply because He is the Savior.

God did not want us to forget this about ourselves or about His Son. Every time we say the name Jesus, we are saying, "the Lord is salvation" or, "God saves." Jesus asked us to remember Him in this way (Luke 22:19). The bread and cup of communion are symbols of His death, which paved the way for our salvation. When He said, "Do this in remembrance of me," He was forever etching into our minds how He wants us to think of Him. Through the Lord's Supper, we remember Him through His broken body and shed blood. Both are reminders of His death on a cross for our sins.

So, who is Jesus? The Bible teaches us He's the Savior of the world. That statement, though true, is incomplete. There must come a day I define Him as *my* savior.

Who is Jesus? That's the million-dollar question, isn't it? No question has more significance than this. Every person must one day have an answer. No one will escape this question. You may pretend you didn't hear it. You may avoid it or delay it. But everyone must eventually answer it.

"Jesus asked His followers one day, 'Who do people say I am?' They replied, 'Some say John the Baptist; others say Elijah; and still others, one of the prophets'" (Mark 8:27-28). Then Jesus got to the core of the matter. "'But what about you?' he asked. 'Who do you say I am?'" (Mark 8:29). Peter answered with our lifeword for today. "You are the Christ, the son of the living God" (Matthew 16:16).

"Christ" is not the last name of Jesus. "Christ" is a title, as in "Jesus the Christ." The word "Christ" can be translated as "the Messiah." A similar title would also be "the anointed One." In biblical times, people were anointed as they began their service for God. This was a sign of God's calling. To call Jesus "the Christ" means He's God's promised Deliverer. Rich Mullins wrote "My Deliverer is Coming." It speaks to the heart of the Hebrew people who were waiting for their promised Messiah. At Christmas, when we sing, "Come, Thou Long-Expected Jesus," we are singing of this truth. I can't imagine the anticipation of a long-suffering people waiting for their "Christ." When He came, unfortunately, most missed Him. They weren't expecting him to come as a baby.

Philippians 2:9-11 says that a day is coming when every knee will bow and every tongue will confess that Jesus is who He says He is. On that day, there will be two classifications of people. One group will be those who had believed Jesus was their Messiah and Christ. On that day, they will confess with joy. But there will be another group who finally realized too late who Jesus was. They will confess Him, but in humiliation as they meet their Judge. It's not too late for you to still choose: what group you will be in?

Who is Jesus? Jesus means savior, and Christ means anointed one. To get a more complete understanding of the person of Jesus, we look to Acts 2:36: "God has made this same Jesus whom you have crucified both Lord and Christ." Those words, spoken by Peter, will be our lifewords for today.

Jesus is Lord. The Greek word is "kurios." It was a common word that means "sir" and was a polite way of referring to another man. It also carries the connotation of "authority" or "absolute ruler." This is how it is used in reference to Jesus. The Bible presents Jesus as "King of kings and Lord of lords"(Revelation 19:16). "Lord" means that He has authority of the universe, and He answers to no one.

The most radical thing early Christians could do was confess "Jesus is Lord." When they did that, they were saying Jesus was emperor. This clashed with the politics of the day. Emperors of Rome were called Caesars, and Romans were to confess "Caesar is Lord." New Testament Christians had to make a choice. Either Jesus was Lord or Caesar was. The wrong choice could mean persecution or death.

Rome did not care that Christians believed in the deity of Christ, that He was the Messiah, or that Jesus died and rose the third day. Those were religious beliefs that did not threaten the political structure. But the declaration "Jesus is Lord" attacked the Roman Empire and was punishable by death. Declaring "Jesus is Lord" was saying that He has the supreme authority, and Caesar does not.

Today, in the spiritual realm, it's still a matter of life and death. Romans 10:9 says, "If you declare with your mouth, 'Jesus is Lord,' and believe in your heart that God raised him from the dead, you will be saved." Jesus seemed to think it was more than a simple confession from your mouth. "Why do you call me, 'Lord, Lord,' and do not do what I say?" (Luke 6:46). Confessing "Jesus is Lord" today is about our intention to do as He says. More about this tomorrow.

Who is Jesus? One answer to that question would be "Jesus is Lord!" This is the earliest Christian creed. This statement of faith is basic Christianity, but it can get lost in our culture. We go to church, where we focus on Christ. We then return to our everyday lives until we can get our next dose of Jesus. This is not a biblical understanding of the lordship of Christ. To say "Jesus is Lord" means He invades every part of our lives. He's at the center of all because He is Lord of all.

A prayer of a fifth century Irish monk went like this, "...Christ with me, Christ before me, Christ behind me, Christ in me, Christ beneath me, Christ above me, Christ on my right, Christ on my left, Christ when I lie down, Christ when I sit, Christ when I stand..."

For me to confess "Jesus is Lord," I must first repent of my own lordship. I came out of the womb wanting to be the center of my life. This is the deepest problem of humanity. The battle between the Father's will and our will is epic. On the cross, Jesus said, "...not my will, but Yours be done" (Matthew 26:39). The prayer that Jesus taught His disciples to pray included, "Thy will be done" (Matthew 6:10).

The Apostle Paul struggled with his own will. "I do not understand what I do. For what I want to do, I do not do, but what I hate I do...For I know that good itself does not dwell in me, that is, in my sinful nature. For I have the desire to do what is good, but I cannot carry it out" (Romans 7:15,18). What Paul describes as the sinful nature is nothing more than "self" wanting control or lordship of his life.

Who is Jesus? He is Lord, which means I am not. Though none of us works out Christ's lordship perfectly in our lives, this confession is not to be taken lightly. It is a statement that I am wholly governed by Christ. "Jesus is Lord" is central to any Christian creed. The expression of it is central to the Christian life.

Who is Jesus? These are some of the things Jesus said about Himself. "I and the Father are one" (John 10:30). "He who sees me sees the One who sent me" (John 12:45). "I am the way, and the truth, and the life; no one comes to the Father but through me" (John 14:6). "Truly, truly, I say to you, before Abraham was, I am" (John 8:58). Those verses will be our lifewords for today.

What are the implications of these radical statements? I'll let one much wiser than I answer that. In his book, *Mere Christianity*, C. S. Lewis writes, "I am trying here to prevent anyone saying the really foolish thing that people often say about Him: I'm ready to accept Jesus as a great moral teacher, but I don't accept his claim to be God. That is the one thing we must not say. A man who was merely a man and said the sort of things Jesus said would not be a great moral teacher. He would either be a lunatic — on the level with the man who says he is a poached egg — or else he would be the Devil of Hell. You must make your choice. Either this man was, and is, the Son of God, or else a madman or something worse. You can shut him up for a fool, you can spit at him and kill him as a demon, or you can fall at his feet and call him Lord and God, but let us not come with any patronizing nonsense about his being a great human teacher. He has not left that open to us. He did not intend to."

Who is Jesus? We need to go no further than what He said about Himself. The claims that Jesus made back us into a corner. He either was who He said He was, or He was, as Lewis said, a lunatic. Jesus' claims about Himself force us to make a decision. That decision will then govern our lives.

I feel weird transitioning from devotions about the person of Christ to devotions on money. To me, it feels too secular… kind of worldly. While it may feel awkward to me, it must not have felt that way to Jesus. He talked more about money than Heaven and Hell combined! One out of every seven verses in Luke's Gospel spoke of money. Overall, the Bible discusses money and possessions three times more than love, seven times more than prayer, and eight times more than belief. Money comprises 15% of the Bible.

Maybe one of the reasons for this is that money occupies our lives. We need money for food, shelter, clothes, and a host of other things we need and want in this life. We do a lot of thinking, planning, and worrying about money.

Jesus teaches about everyday issues that affect me. He is not a "pie in the sky, Heaven by and by" kind of Savior. He's a "rubber meets the road, down to earth, real life" Messiah. That's the kind of Christ I need.

Here are two of Jesus' practical teachings about money: "Give to the one who asks you, and do not turn away from the one who wants to borrow from you" (Matthew 5:42). It's our lifeword for today. All through Scripture, the Bible asks us to get our eyes on other people and not only on ourselves.

When we give, we are not to make a show of our giving. "When you give to the needy, sound no trumpet before you, as the hypocrites do in the synagogues and in the streets, that they may be praised by others" (Matthew 6:2). My giving should come from a heart that wants to help, not one that wants to be noticed.

Wanting to be noticed… here Jesus gets to where we live. He uses the topic of money to get very personal. If things always center around me, what I do and what I give, it shows I'm living for myself and not for God. Our use of money can shine a light on our true selves and our true desires. Maybe that's why Jesus talked about it so much.

Many criticize pastors for preaching about money. While it's true that this is sometimes used for the personal gain of the pastor, history shows the saints of the ages did not avoid this topic. In the 1500s, Protestant Reformer Martin Luther said, "There are three conversions a person needs to experience: The conversion of the head, the conversion of the heart, and the conversion of the pocketbook."

Our lifeword today comes from the story of Zacchaeus' conversion. When that happened, he declared that he would give half his possessions to the poor and would pay back four times the amount he had overcharged anyone on their taxes (Luke 19:8). Three days ago, our devotion was on the lordship of Christ. Zacchaeus understood that his conversion was linked to the totality of his life. For a rich man—a tax collector—this especially meant his thoughts and usage of money.

For most of us, this "third conversion" comes sometime after we have been saved. When we accept Christ, we are babes (1 Corinthians 3:1). We know very little about the Christian life. But week after week and month after month of Christian teaching brings new light to our life. A light that says this Christian life is more than having our sins forgiven. Jesus wants us—all of us—lock, stock, and barrel. Paul prays for the believers that they would be sanctified wholly, or entirely (1Thessalonians 5:23). Part of that entire sanctification is what Luther is speaking of. This includes a total conversion of our head, heart, and pocketbook.

I had the pleasure of baptizing Merrill Thornton when he was in his 80s. He wanted to be baptized with his wallet in his back pocket. Martin Luther was somewhere up in Heaven, and I bet he was smiling.

The book of Proverbs is filled with practical, everyday thoughts about life, many of them dealing with money. Proverbs 11:24-25 say, "One person gives freely, yet gains even more; another withholds unduly, but comes to poverty. A generous person will prosper; whoever refreshes others will be refreshed." This is our lifeword for today.

So, Solomon, the wisest man who ever lived, says when you treat others generously, you will be treated in like manner. The principle is that giving doesn't help God; giving helps you. God does not need a dime of your money. This is not about bringing in more money for the church. This needs to be taught without apology because it's your spiritual welfare at stake. Giving is for our benefit.

Jesus agrees with Solomon in Luke 6:38: "Give, and it will be given to you. Good measure, pressed down, shaken together and running over, will be put into your lap. For with the measure you use it will be measured to you." While this verse is certainly applicable to money, the context is in giving mercy and forgiveness. Give mercy, give forgiveness, and it will be given back to you. So, this concept of being a generous person extends far past our finances.

Paul agrees with both Jesus and Solomon. "Whoever sows sparingly will also reap sparingly, and whoever sows generously will also reap generously" (2 Corinthians 9:6). This is repeated negatively in the book of Job. "As I have observed, those who plow evil and those who sow trouble, reap it" (Job 4:8).

God is a generous God, and He's trying to make us generous people. Don't forget, money is just a part of generosity. Paul writes "...if a man's gift is serving, let him serve; if it is teaching, let him teach; if it is encouraging, let him encourage; if it is contributing to the needs of others, let him give generously; if it is leadership, let him govern diligently; if it is showing mercy, let him do it cheerfully" (Romans 12:5-8). Remember our lifeword for today: "A generous person will prosper; whoever refreshes others will be refreshed."

There are 880 verses of wisdom in the book of Proverbs. There are at least 101 that refer to money in some way. Let's take a look at some of those today.

Proverbs 19:1: "Better the poor whose walk is blameless than a fool whose lips are perverse." Money is important. We have to pay our bills and put food on the table. This verse tells us it's not as important as our integrity. Proverbs 22:1 echoes the same theme when it says, "A good name is more desirable than riches."

Proverbs 17:1: "Better a dry crust with peace and quiet, than a house full of feasting, with strife." As we make choices with our money, remember that harmony in our homes is something you just can't buy. Put money in its proper place... behind peace and unity in our families.

Proverbs 11:4: "Wealth is worthless in the day of wrath but righteousness delivers from death." As we stand before God, wealth is worthless. The only thing that matters on that day is the righteousness that comes from God through faith in Jesus Christ (Philippians 3:9).

Proverbs 11:28: "Whoever trusts in riches will fall." Wealth merely for the sake of wealth will not bring true prosperity. If, however, money is a means to an end, and its purpose is to accomplish good things, God will honor your wealth as you honor Him in the use of it.

Proverbs 14:20: "The poor are despised even by their neighbors, while the rich have many friends." This verse says we can be tempted to choose our friends by how much money they have. A better choice is found in verse 21: "Blessed is he who is kind to the needy."

We all think life would be better if we could change a few things. Who among us needs to change nothing about our lives? So, in an effort to change, we move from one house to another or one city to another, we buy a new car, get a haircut, go to a new church, start a new diet, begin a workout program, or buy a new outfit. Those are not wrong and may be needed, but they are outward changes. Most of us have learned that the outward stuff doesn't promote real change in our lives. It's inward change we need. I can make all the above changes, but I'll still carry the "same ole me" on the inside. More than likely, the "same ole me" is the thing that needs changing.

Our lifeword today comes from Romans 12:2: "Do not conform to the pattern of this world but be transformed by the renewing of your mind." This verse says real change comes when we change our thinking patterns. For many of us, it's not our behavior that needs to change; it's our thinking. After all, the thought is the father of the deed. If you want to change the way you act, you start by changing the way you think. By some act of discipline, you may change behavior temporarily. But long-term change comes from renewing your mind.

We've all heard someone say, "It's all in your head." God would agree. He knows that our thinking determines our actions. That's why in His Word, He says, "The truth will set you free" (John 8:32). As we renew our minds with the truth of God's Word, our behavior will change.

One way to renew your mind is to guard it. God tells us, "I want you to be wise about what is good, and innocent about what is evil" (Romans 16:19). Guarding your mind means being cautious about what goes in it. This has to do with what you watch on TV, what you read, the music you listen to, and the conversations you take part in. Change happens as you filter what goes into your mind. That's because your behavior flows from what's in your head.

Caterpillars can't fly although they were born to fly. Sound silly? No, it's metamorphosis! You remember that word from seventh grade science. It's the process of transformation from an immature form to an adult form. When the caterpillar has been changed into a butterfly, it becomes what God always intended it to be. Metamorphosis reveals whatever was put there by God.

The Greek word for "transformed" in Romans 12:2 is related to the English word metamorphosis. God, through the renewing of your mind, wants you to turn into what He intended you to be. Think of it this way: You will never be what God wants you to be unless your mind is changed, renewed, and transformed. Jesus said to love God with "... all your heart and with all your soul and with all your mind" (Mark 12:30). A Christian whose heart is right toward God is good, but not good enough.

Yesterday, our lifeword was "...be transformed by the renewing of your mind" (Romans 12:2). A major way this happens is by what the Bible calls "setting our minds." Our lifeword today is "Set your minds on things above, not on earthly things" (Colossians 3:2). This verse could be translated, "Fix your thoughts on things above" or, "Choose to focus on things above" or, "Intentionally think on things above." The original language indicates a choice made with the mind not the emotions.

Today, whether or not you feel like it, deliberately put your mind on *things* above. Eternal *things,* like people, or *things* that God desires, like peace and unity. This means seeing *things* from God's viewpoint, like His values about money and work. Paul says, "Whatever is true, whatever is noble, whatever is right, whatever is pure, whatever is lovely, whatever is admirable—if anything is excellent or praiseworthy—think about such things" (Philippians 4:8).

As we "set our minds on things above," we start to be transformed. As we make a choice to renew our minds, the new "you" will be revealed. The "you" that God has intended all along. Don't be surprised if it's a very different you. Almost as different as a caterpillar and a butterfly.

Our lifeword today gives us the biblical blueprint to change our lives. "Do not conform to the pattern of this world..." (Romans 12:2). How often do we allow others to shape our lives? God doesn't want you to be like the crowd; experience tells me that the crowd is seldom right. Don't copy, don't conform, especially to the crowd, or as our text says, "the pattern of this world." Don't be afraid to be different.

In this context, worldliness means buying into the notion that this world is all there is or will ever be. The old beer commercial said, "Go for the gusto." In some ways, that can be very right. Giving it all you have and leaving nothing for tomorrow serves you well in some areas of life. But living like there's no tomorrow is what Paul commands we **don't** do. If this world is all there is, then "go for the gusto!" After all, Paul says if Christ has not been raised from the dead, "Eat, drink and be merry. For tomorrow we die" (1 Corinthians 15:32). But if you think there's another world to live for, live today in light of the next world. The old song expresses Paul's sentiment well: "This world is not my home, I'm just passing through."

Today's lifeword gives us the secret to real change in our lives. It starts with the phrase, "Do not conform..." In the original language, do not conform conveys the sense of "Stop doing this!" Paul implies they were already allowing themselves to be poured into the mold of the world. Stop it! Do it no longer! Make the choice today to be different.

How about you? What should you stop doing today? Are there people you should no longer hang out with? Are there attitudes that you should drop today?

The Bible commands Christians to stop conforming. Don't be afraid to stand out from the crowd. Christians are different. A quote by rock and roll artist Alice Cooper fits well here: "Drinking beer is easy. Trashing your hotel room is easy. But being a Christian, that's tough. That's rebellion." Be a rebel. Be a Christian.

Somewhere along the line, you may have heard some preacher say, "You gotta get rid of that stinkin' thinkin' and start thinkin' godly." The text for that sermon may have been the verse we've been discussing: "Do not conform to the pattern of this world but be transformed by the renewing of your mind" (Romans 12:2). Let's look today at some "stinkin thinkin" and how we can renew our mind with "godly thinkin."

Stinkin' Thinkin' #1 - God will forgive me so I can do this and do that. Renew your mind with one of my favorite verses: "I do not set aside the grace of God, for if righteousness could be gained through the law, Christ died for nothing!" (Galatians 2:21).

Stinkin' Thinkin' #2 - No one understands the way I feel. Renew your mind with Psalm 139:1-4: "You know when I sit and when I rise; you perceive my thoughts from afar. You discern my going out and my lying down; you are familiar with all my ways. Before a word is on my tongue, you, Lord, know it completely."

Stinkin' Thinkin' #3 - Something's wrong with me. Christians don't get depressed like this. Renew your mind with the Apostle Paul's words. He seemed pretty down – even depressed. "We do not want you to be uninformed about the troubles we experienced…We were under great pressure, far beyond our ability to endure, so that we despaired of life itself. Indeed, we felt we had received the sentence of death" (2 Corinthians 1:8-9).

Taking out the stinkin' thinkin' and putting in the godly thinkin' reminds me a lot of what Paul says in Ephesians 4:22-24: "…put off your old self, which belongs to your former manner of life…and be renewed in the spirit of your minds, and put on the new self, created after the likeness of God in true righteousness and holiness." Those are our lifewords for today.

The love of God is something many of us have heard preached, taught, and sung about for decades. One of the first Bible verses we memorized told us how much God loved the world (John 3:16). A loving God is assumed in our theology, so much so that we may be guilty of taking this truth for granted. Teachings on this subject may not excite us because its "an old hat." While we may not say this, we think it. Something like, "Okay, yeah, I get it. God loves me. Let's go on to something deeper."

The Apostle John didn't seem to tire of this truth. As a 70+ year-old Christian, he writes these words: "See what great love the Father has lavished on us, that we should be called children of God!" That's from 1 John 3:1, and it's our lifeword for today. The Message Bible translates it this way: "What marvelous love the Father has extended to us! Just look at it— we're called children of God!" We used to sing, "Behold what manner of love the Father has given unto us." John was amazed by the love of God.

John begins with the Greek word "eido," which means, "Hey listen up! Stop and think this through." John then uses the word "potapos," which conveys amazement and wonder. It was used by a disciple of Jesus after seeing Him calming the storm. "The men were amazed, and said, 'What kind of a man is this, that even the winds and the sea obey him?'"(Matthew 8:27). Do you get the idea? God's love spawned a sense of wonder, awe, and amazement in John. He uses a word that expresses that something is foreign. He's so astonished by the love of the Father that he wonders from what country it came!

God's love should astonish us as well. Songwriters say, *"Amazing Love, how can it be?", "The Wonder of it all", "Oh, how He loves you and me."* And as a verse of the old hymn, *"Such Love"* says, "Did ever human tongue find nobler theme than love divine that ransomed me?" God loves you. Don't ever get used to that truth. As I've written this, I have tears in my eyes. I hope you do as well.

Let me be honest. I'm pretty much ignorant of the book of Zephaniah. I know it's in the Old Testament, but I don't know if it's after Hosea or before Nahum. I know he is one of the "minor prophets," whatever that means. I can't teach you what his book is about or even quote one verse from it. So, I'm shocked that I'm including a lifeword from Zephaniah 3:17. I found it as I was looking up verses on God's love. "The Lord your God is in your midst, a mighty one who will save; He will rejoice over you with gladness; He will quiet you by His love; He will exult over you with loud singing."

There's one phrase I want to focus on. "He will quiet you by His love." I need quieting today. I'm on a sabbatical. I'm supposed to be spending time relaxing, renewing, and refocusing. But I'm not because of the stuff of life. Husband stuff, father stuff, son of an aging mother stuff, pastor stuff. I'm not wanting you to feel sorry for me. We all have stuff.

I need this quieting, but I don't think I really understand what it means. I do know there is something inside me that wants it, needs it. "Lord, please quiet me with Your love."

I have too much loud in my life, even on sabbatical. I feel pressure to get this book finished. That pressure is loud. I have a 16-year-old whom I need to teach how to drive. Man, that is loud! I'm 60, and I don't have enough money saved for retirement. That's loud too. No one in Washington seems to have any answers for the problems of our nation. I worry about that, and it causes loudness. Even though it's my sabbatical, there is a situation going on at church that only I can deal with. More loudness. "Lord, please quiet me with Your love."

We all need to be quieted at times. I will admit there are lots of ways to do that. Some are more productive than others. But I desire a quietness that comes from knowing God and His unfailing love for me. So, "Lord, please quiet me with Your love."

I really like author Brennan Manning. He's a Catholic, so I don't agree with all of his teachings, but I'm a better Christian today because of his writing. By better, I don't mean better than others, I mean I more deeply rely on God's grace because of Brennan's teachings.

I like him because he's honest. We Christians aren't the most honest bunch, you know? We have to keep up appearances. Especially me; I'm a pastor! Keeping up those appearances forces us to lie sometimes. I find myself wanting people to think I'm a better Christian than I really am.

One of my favorite quotes of his is "My deepest awareness of myself is that I am deeply loved by Jesus Christ and I have done nothing to earn it or deserve it." That's not Scripture, but it will serve as our lifeword for today. It's a very simple statement but extremely profound. It's easy to say that, but I wonder if it's true for me. I really hope it is.

What's your deepest awareness of yourself? Is it something that you've earned or deserved? If you lose it because you are no longer deserving, you have to find a whole new identity. It's better to allow your self-worth to be in something that you didn't earn or deserve. Let it be that you are deeply loved by Jesus, and then shape your life as a response to that love.

Here's another quote by Brennan that is closely related: "Do you believe that the God of Jesus loves you beyond worthiness and unworthiness, beyond fidelity and infidelity—that He loves you in the morning sun and in the evening rain—that He loves you when your intellect denies it, your emotions refuse it, your whole being rejects it? Do you believe that God loves without condition or reservation and loves you this moment as you are and not as you should be?"

Do you believe that? If you do, would you respond to His love by accepting His gift to you? His gift of eternal life. This comes to all who believe... not in their own worthiness, but in the worthiness of Jesus Christ.

In your estimation, what is the most important verse in the Bible? Pretty tough to choose, right? John 3:16? It's hard to argue against that. Someone may say, "Love God and love your neighbor" from Matthew 22:37-39. It's difficult to argue against what Jesus said was the greatest commandment. If I was an Orthodox Jew, I may vote for Deuteronomy 6:4. It's repeated in every synagogue on every Sabbath. "Hear, O Israel: the Lord, our God, the LORD is one." Your choice depends on how you were raised, your theological convictions, even the church or denomination in which you were raised. We could go on and on, but I'd like to recommend to you Genesis 1:1. It's our lifeword for today. "In the beginning God created the heavens and the earth."

Much of the Book of Genesis will look like folly if you do not believe this verse. Adam would not be the first man. He would simply be a symbol of mankind. The serpent would represent the reality of evil, and certainly wouldn't be evil himself. The fall of man in Genesis 3 would be a mere parable of man's brokenness. The flood and the tower of Babel would be nice ways to describe deep truths.

Genesis 1:1 opens the floodgate to the rest of the miracles in the Bible. If I believe this verse, it's an easy jump to believe in a God who can flood the earth (Genesis 7:11-12) or part the Red Sea (Exodus 14:21). A God leading a people out of Egyptian bondage is child's play for a God who created the world (Exodus 6:6). I can believe that a donkey can talk if there is a Creator who is sovereign over His creation (Numbers 22:28). How about Jonah in the belly of a whale? (Jonah 1:17). No big deal for a God that said this far shall the oceans come and no farther.

If Genesis 1:1 is true, it's a game changer. I only believe this verse by faith; it can never be proved to me. "By faith we understand that the universe was formed at God's command, so that what is seen was not made out of what was visible" (Hebrews 11:3). That's another reason Genesis 1:1 is crucial. It introduces faith, a major component to life with God, in the Old or New Testament.

Let's pick up where we left off yesterday. Genesis 1:1 is our lifeword today. If that verse is true, it really helps my prayer life. Our lifeword says God created a world where there was no world. If He can do that, He can create love where there is no love. Peace where there is no peace. Unity where there is no unity. Hope where there is no hope. Asking God for love, peace, unity, and hope requires no faith if I have the faith to believe Genesis 1:1.

If I open my mind to a God who is not subject to the natural laws of this world, it's easy to pray that He can give rain so that the farmer's crops can grow. Or, for that matter, that He can stop rain if what the corn needs is sunshine. If He is not limited by the natural laws of this world, I can pray for cancer to be healed. If He created man and woman with will, drives, and emotions, I can pray for hearts to be softened and wills to be changed so that marriages can be restored.

Genesis 1:1 says God is not part of nature. He's distinct from nature. Not part of the natural realm. If that is true, He can be here and there at the same time. Time would not even be an issue for the One who created time. This dramatically affects my prayer life. I can pray for God's presence and intervention for my missionary friends in Papua New Guinea and for my children in Xenia, Ohio. God doesn't have to travel to PNG to help out, and then to Ohio. He is not limited by time. For that matter, if Genesis 1:1 is right, He's not limited by anything. Who wants a God who is limited? How can you worship a God who is limited?

If Genesis 1:1 is true, I can pray for whatever I choose. He is not limited. "His arm is not shortened" (Isaiah 59:1). "With God, all things are possible" (Matthew 19:26). There is no person He can't save, no sickness He can't heal, no need He can't meet. So, pray Church. Pray to your creator God.

Harriette Thompson, at the age of 92, ran and finished the San Diego Rock 'n' Roll Marathon in 7:24:36. Running a marathon at the age of 92 is beyond the limitations of 99.99% of humanity. That's why this story is so hard to believe. Humanity has limits, but God does not. As we said yesterday, Genesis 1:1 communicates this to us. Limited people like you and me need a God who will not wear out or run down. We sing, "He was and is and is to come." There's only One like that... the "eternal" or "everlasting" God of Israel. Our lifeword today is from Isaiah 40:28: "Do you not know? Have you not heard? The LORD is the everlasting God, the Creator of the ends of the earth. He will not grow tired or weary, and his understanding no one can fathom."

If Genesis 1:1 is true, God simply "is." E. V. Hill preached a great sermon on the two words, "God is." If God just "is," He has no beginning, requires no assistance, and has no limitations. "Before the mountains were born or you brought forth the earth and the world, from everlasting to everlasting you are God" (Psalm 90:2). The "is-ness" of God means He never began, does not experience growth, and will always be.

Theologians call this the eternality of God. It speaks to His timeless nature... a God with no beginning and no end. This is a foundational belief of Christianity. In the mystery of the Trinity, God the Son, Jesus Christ, spoke of this in John 17:5: "And now, Father, glorify me in Your presence with the glory I had with You before the world began." If God had a beginning, then He would have been created. Then, we would need to find out who created God and worship that Being. Take away this truth in God's eternity, and Christianity is futile.

Because God is eternal, I can face an uncertain future with the confidence that God will be there... indeed, already is there. Because God is eternal, He is outside of time. Not being bound to time, He can be in my future orchestrating events for good. Because God is eternal, He can grant eternal life to you and me. Because God is eternal, He is worthy of worship. It all starts in Genesis 1:1, the most important verse in the Bible.

It's fascinating that God makes no argument for Himself in Scripture. An assumption the Bible makes is that God exists. You would think that the Bible would start off with an argument for the existence of God. But you won't find a word of Scripture used to convince us that God exists. God is simply assumed.

Maybe that's why Psalm 14:1 calls atheists fools. "The fool says in his heart, 'There is no God.'" Part of Scripture's assumption of God is because His existence is plain to all through creation. "For since the creation of the world God's invisible qualities—His eternal power and divine nature—have been clearly seen, being understood from what has been made, so that people are without excuse" (Romans 1:20). This is our lifeword for today.

The natural world must have an explanation, and the only adequate one is God. Though there are some who have not been exposed to the Scriptures, all mankind has been given a revelation of God through nature. The Bible contends that the proof of God's existence stares us in the face every day. Maybe that's why no argument for God is ever found in His Word. He is simply assumed.

Dr. William Leonard Rowe was a professor of philosophy at Purdue University. He was also an atheist. He is quoted as saying, "I cannot reject God by reason alone, for there is too much evidence of His existence." Then why would Dr. Rowe be an atheist? The unbeliever doesn't want to open the door to a creator God. If that door is opened, the door to judgment and a standard of right or wrong is opened as well. If there is a Creator, then we are His creation. He has ownership of us, and the secular world knows that has consequences.

"The heavens declare the glory of God; the skies proclaim the work of His hands" (Psalm 19:1). The Bible assumes God because of all we can see through His creation. Our lifeword today says God is so evident through creation that we will be without excuse on Judgment Day (Romans 1:20). Yet another reason why Genesis 1:1 is the most important verse in all of God's Word.

How big is the universe? So big that scientists really don't know how big it is. Here's an illustration that may help us grasp the vastness of space. The nearest star to Earth is the sun, which is 93 million miles away. I've traveled to Papua New Guinea twice, and it was a loooong plane ride. It was a total of 25 hours in the air, not counting layovers. And that's just one way! That trip was only 10,000 miles, and the sun is 93 million miles away. To get to the sun riding in an airplane going 500 mph, it would take 21 years of continuous flying. And I thought I had jet lag coming back from Papua New Guinea!

Trying to get your mind around God's creation is difficult. The sheer size of it makes it tough to explain. How do you explain the infinite? Simply thinking about it makes us amazed at the greatness of God. On Christmas Eve 1968, the crew of Apollo 8 read in turn from Genesis 1:1-10. As they orbited the Moon, it seemed like no other reading would be appropriate. But an equally good choice would have been Psalm 8:3: "When I consider Your heavens, the work of Your fingers, the moon and the stars, which You have set in place, what is man that You are mindful of him, and the son of man that You care for him?"

The story of God's creation has powerful implications for evangelism. Children are fascinated by outer space, the moon and the stars. It's through verses like Genesis 1:1, Psalm 8, and many others that we introduce our kids to the Christian faith. None of us start with the cross of Christ. We start with God as creator. Even toddlers can grasp that. I don't know how much a 3 or 4-year-old can understand about Jesus dying on the cross for their sins. But they sure can understand that God made the mountains and the sea. They can understand that God gave them blue eyes and blond hair. It's through teaching God as creator that our kids enter the door of Christianity and, as they mature, make it to the cross of Christ. Yet another reason that Genesis 1:1 is the most important verse in the Bible.

For the last five days, we've been looking at Genesis 1:1: "In the beginning, God created the heavens and the earth." In the Bible, the word translated here as "created" is only used in reference to God. When man creates something, a different Hebrew word is chosen. Also, the Bible seems to indicate that God created out of nothing. The old preacher said that God didn't only create the heavens and the earth from scratch: He created the scratch too! So, He took nothing and made the universe and everything in it. That's why we say He breathed this world into existence. When He said "Let," the sun and the moon appeared. When He said "Let," the stars fell into place. Only God could create like that.

I cannot comprehend how someone can take wires, silicone, aluminum, plastic, and other things, and make the computer I'm typing on. But to think that Someone created everything from nothing... only God could create like that.

If God can create the entire universe, can't He create something out of my life? The Bible answers that with an emphatic *Yes*! God can take what I give him, which isn't much by the way, and turn it into something brand new (2 Corinthians 5:17). Only God can create like that.

God took Paul, a man who was so hostile to Jesus that he killed Christians, and turned him into the man who opened up the whole Western world to Christianity. God took Peter, an uneducated fisherman, and turned him into a great leader in the early church. Only God can create like that.

We could talk about Abraham, Noah, Moses, David, and on and on. But the real issue is you and me. Have we allowed God to come in and do what only He can do? Education can improve and sophistication can polish, but only God can create something brand new.

A lot of people come to Genesis 1 looking for who, what, when, where, and how. Many want to know when God created. Others want to know how God created. Some would like to know where. The Bible simply talks about the "Who."

Questions abound when it comes to Genesis 1. Was this the beginning of time or merely the beginning of recorded history? Was that 6,000 or 6 million years ago? How in the world did God create? The answers are left up to our speculation because they aren't "Who" questions. Not much is spoken of in Genesis 1 other than the "Who."

The "Who" is mentioned 38 times in 31 verses. The "Who," of course, is God. That's what the writer of Genesis is stressing to us. God did something. God created. God is on the move. The whys and the hows don't matter much. It's the "Who" that counts.

Dr. Dennis Kinlaw tried to teach me that God is the center of Genesis 1. All the other questions are nice and thought-provoking, but the center of the first chapter is God. Don't miss this. If you do, you'll live your life for the margins. The "Who" is the center. All else is in the margins.

Much of the Christian life is this way. We debate about modes of baptism. Is it sprinkling, pouring, or immersion? This debate is about margins. The center is God at work in the life of a person, and it's like they are brand new... as if they've been washed clean. We debate about music. Is it traditional, modern, or blended? This debate is about the margins. The center is God, who inhabits the praises of His people, and that has nothing to do with guitars or pianos.

As we close our look at Genesis 1, let's not miss what it's all about. Let's not miss the center because we're focused on the margin. And that's a good rule for the rest of the Bible as well. The Bible is about God revealing Himself through the person of Jesus Christ. It's the "Who" that counts.

April 5th

I imagine none of you know a high school science professor from Cleveland, Ohio by the name of Roy Hinkley. But those my age will remember him as the professor on Gilligan's Island. We knew him only by the name Professor, and he, along with the other castaways, took a "three-hour cruise."

I was amazed by his ability to invent something out of the stuff he found on the island. Somehow, he created a hot air balloon, a sewing machine, and a stove. On one episode, he even took a pineapple shell and scrap metal and constructed a battery charger for the island's radio. How could he spend his time coming up with all these amazing inventions, but couldn't fix the hole in the boat? The Professor didn't have his priorities straight. He spent his time on the wrong things. If he had spent half as much time fixing that boat as he did making fudge out of algae, they would have been off the island within the first few episodes.

Jesus tells His disciples to get their priorities straight. Or better yet, drop their priorities and adopt His. Matthew 6:33 says, "But seek first His kingdom and His righteousness, and all these things will be given to you as well." That's our lifeword for today. We all are seekers. We come out of the womb seeking comfort, food, and warmth. We are seekers by nature. Some people seek money; others seek pleasure. Some may seek a husband or a wife. Others may seek a new job, new friends, or a new church. Jesus wants us seeking the right things.

Seeking is about keeping the main thing the main thing. My dad always said there's a way to know what's important in someone's life. Look at their calendar and their checkbook. Those two places will show you their priorities in life.

How about you? What do you seek? What do you want? The old saying goes, "Be careful what you want because you just might get it." It would be awful to get to the end of our life, after seeking after so many things, only to discover the boat still has a hole in it. "Seek first the Kingdom of God."

Responsible people are concerned about providing for their family. This means food, shelter, clothes, money, education, and so forth. *These things* (Matthew 6:33) and others are needs that are universal no matter if one is black or white, rich or poor, Christian or unbeliever.

What does God's Word have to say about *these things*? In Matthew 6:31, Jesus says not to worry about them. Now, He can't mean *these things* aren't important to Him. One verse later, Jesus says, "...your heavenly Father knows that you need all *these things*" (Matthew 6:32, emphasis added). God cares about *these things*. Just don't worry about them. The Scripture doesn't say this, but it implies that if you're going to worry about something, worry about getting first things first. Matthew 6:33 says, "...seek first His kingdom and His righteousness, and all *these things* will be added to you as well" (emphasis added). That's our lifeword for today. Don't focus on *these things*. Focus on seeking God, and the promise is "all *these things* will be added to you as well."

God knows your needs, and He has promised to provide (Philippians 4:19). He wants us to put our focus on higher things, heavenly things, eternal things. Our priority should not be on the *"these things"* of this world. Sure, we go to work, pay our bills, shop for clothes, and pay the mortgage, but *these things* are not to cause us worry. God's got this. Trust Him for them.

Being a good provider is a very Christian thing. Paul writes, "Anyone who does not provide for their relatives, and especially for their own household, has denied the faith and is worse than an unbeliever" (1Timothy 5:8). The text implies even unbelievers are responsible enough to make sure *these things* are present. The subtle difference is the focus. The unbeliever is focused on *"these things."* The Christian should be focused on seeking God.

Our lifeword today is from Matthew 6:31-33. "So do not worry, saying, 'What shall we eat?' or 'What shall we drink?' or 'What shall we wear?' For the pagans run after all these things, and your heavenly Father knows that you need them. But seek first His kingdom and His righteousness, and all these things will be given to you as well."

Look at these verses carefully again. Jesus didn't tell the disciples to stop worrying. He told them to replace worry. Replace worry with a desire for God's rule and reign in your life. Be so preoccupied with seeking God first that worry has no place in your mind. So, in the context of our lifeword from Matthew 6, we replace worry with giving. Giving without worry or concern about who sees you. Give because you trust God sees (Matthew 6:1-4).

We also replace worry with:

- Prayer, knowing your Father knows what you need before you ask Him (Matthew 6:5-8).
- A concern for others that is exhibited by our forgiveness of those who have offended us (Matthew 6:14).
- Spiritual disciplines, like fasting (Matthew 6:15-18).
- A desire to store up treasures for eternity, not just for use here on earth (Matthew 6:19-21).
- Healthy eyes that are being trained to focus on things that please God (Matthew 6:22-23).
- Service to the only Master in your life (Matthew 6:24).
- Faith and trust that if the Father cares for the birds of the air, how much more He will care for us (Matthew 6:25-26).

God is the Creator. He made our minds, and He knows they need to be occupied with something. Take care to make sure it's not worry. Replace that worry with a preoccupation with the Kingdom of God and His righteousness.

One of the great blessings of my life is to be on the receiving end of some great preaching. A good sermon has a good story or two that will drill home whatever point the preacher is making. As we continue to look at seeking God first, let's look at some stories I remember that cemented that truth in my heart.

This first one I've probably heard 50 times. A butcher was asked what difference it made in his life when he became a Christian. He replied, "I stopped weighing my thumb." He then told how he used to put meat on the scales in such a way that his thumb could not be seen. As he put his thumb on the scale, along with the meat, the meat weighed more. He was cheating his customers. But after he was saved, he stopped weighing his thumb! Now when he weighed meat for customers whom he had cheated, he added more meat to make up for the past. Praise God for such a experience in Him that we stop weighing our thumbs! Praise God for the grace to stop seeking our own kingdoms and start seeking God's.

In 1875, John Wanamaker opened the first department store in Philadelphia and one of the first in the United States. It was very successful and stayed that way through his death. Operating his store wasn't Wanamaker's only job. In 1889, Wanamaker began the First Penny Savings Bank. In the same year, President Benjamin Harrison named him Postmaster General of the United States. If that was not enough, he served as Sunday School superintendent at Bethany Presbyterian Church. When asked how he could hold all those positions at once, he explained. "As a child I read, 'Seek ye first the kingdom of God, and His righteousness, and all these things shall be added unto you.' The Sunday school is my business, all the rest are the things."

Yes, I know as these stories are told over and over, they get added to and probably exaggerated. Still, the points can't be missed. The butcher discovered that when we seek God first, we take our thumb off the scale. John Wanamaker learned there's no telling what we can accomplish when we seek God first.

In the phrase, "Seek first the kingdom of God," the word "seek" is filled with meaning. The Greek verb tense here doesn't mean to start seeking. It means to "keep on seeking." It always implies a continual strong-minded pursuit. The idea is to "continue to set your heart on." It's not written to people who aren't seeking. It's written to people who are and need the encouragement to stay at it.

The thought here is determination, hanging tough even when you feel like hanging it up. Little is as important to the seeking Christian as stubborn determination. I'm to *seek* first the kingdom of God. Do it when it's easy and when it's hard. Do it in the morning and in the evening. Do it when things are good at work and when things are bad. Do it when you're up; do it when you're down. Do it when it rains and when the sun shines. Do it when the preaching's good and when the preaching is not so good. Do it when the music is great and when it's not so great. Just keep on doing it; keep seeking. In fact, "keep seeking" is a good translation of the word translated "seek." I know you are seeking now, but stay at it! That's determination!

The reason this takes determination is that it's hard to keep putting God first in our lives. Many things detour us from seeking first the Kingdom of God. Our lives are filled with so many things that try to push into the center... into first place. Marriage, kids, career, education, sports, and lots more. All of those are really good things, but they're not to be first. To seek means to continue to keep the first things first.

This is one of the reasons you attend church. It refocuses you. It recalibrates you. It brings you back to the center... to the most important thing. Each Sunday, God speaks through His Spirit and encourages us to keep seeking. The gentle nudge of God says, "Hang in there. Keep at it. Don't give up."

April 10th

This is Good Friday, and it's a very solemn day. It's the day we remember the death of Jesus. This day is holy and deserves our reverence. As Christian parents, we need to pass on the seriousness of Good Friday to our children. Of course, we don't only want to pass that on. God's Word says it's our responsibility to pass on the faith to our kids.

Our lifeword today is from Deuteronomy 6:4-7: "Hear, O Israel: The Lord our God, the Lord is one. Love the Lord your God with all your heart and with all your soul and with all your strength. These commandments that I give you today are to be on your hearts. Impress them on your children. Talk about them when you sit at home and when you walk along the road, when you lie down and when you get up."

We have a lot of churches, don't we? Methodist, Baptist, Presbyterian, just to name a few. But the most important church is not any of these. It's the one that you pastor, Moms and Dads, the church that meets in your home. No church is more important than that one. No church, no children's or youth pastor, and no vacation Bible school has more influence than you do, Mom and Dad.

We've been talking about seeking for the last five days. Where do our children learn to seek? It's in the home, of course. It's here that "seeking first the kingdom of God" begins. Our lifeword says, "These commandments that I give you today are to be on your hearts. Impress them on your children." Before we can impress them on our children, they have to be impressed on our hearts.

I really hope you worship with other believers this Sunday. It's critically important to gather with other believers. Your children need that. But I hope it doesn't take the place of the most important church services. These happen in your home… everyday… not just on Sunday.

Proverbs 2:3 is our lifeword for today. The Bible says, "If you call out for insight and cry aloud for understanding, and if you look for it as for silver and search for it as for hidden treasure, then you will understand the fear of the Lord and find the knowledge of God."

Did you read all those action verbs? Call out for insight. Cry aloud for understanding. Look for it as for silver. Search for it as for hidden treasure. All through Scripture, we are told to be seekers after God. One of the most well-known verses is 2 Chronicles 7:14: "If my people, who are called by my name, will humble themselves and pray and seek my face and turn from their wicked ways, then I will hear from heaven, and I will forgive their sin and will heal their land." God calls men and women to seek Him.

In the face of all this seeking, it's not surprising we hear talk of "finding God." We are promised that if we seek, we will find (Matthew 7:7). The phrase "finding God" is synonymous with accepting Jesus, being saved, and being born again. It's common in an evangelistic endeavor to ask if one has "found God."

Finding God is not the result of some divine "hide and seek" game. God is not hiding from us. He loves to be found. In fact, God is revealed to us in Scripture as One who is seeking us. He certainly was in the earliest chapters of the Bible. Adam and Eve went astray, and God found them. The greatest example of seeking is the Christmas story. God takes on human flesh and visits a wayward people.

So seek. Seek first. As you do that, know that God is not hiding and that He delights to be found. Zacchaeus was a seeker in the New Testament. He went as far as climbing a sycamore tree to see Jesus. To this seeker, Jesus said, "For the Son of Man has come to seek and to save the lost" (Luke 19:10). That leads us to a great truth of Scripture: When we seek after God, we find out He's been seeking after us.

Today is Easter, and you need to know that Easter changes everything. It's the very cornerstone of Christianity. Without a resurrection, there is no Christian faith. I remember being asked in a theology class that if the bones of Jesus were found today, and it was proved beyond a shadow of a doubt that these were Jesus' bones, would I still be a Christian? Several of us "gung-ho" young seminarians in the class said, "Yes, sure, we would." The professor responded, "Well, you're all fools."

Obviously, he was trying to make a point, and it's a biblical point, by the way. The professor was simply repeating what 1 Corinthians 15:19 teaches us: "If only for this life we have hope in Christ, we are of all people most to be pitied." Those are our lifewords for today.

Easter changes everything, and that's what Paul is trying to tell us in chapter 15 of his Corinthians letter. This letter was written mainly because the church at Corinth was incredibly messed up. They seemed to have everything wrong, and evidently, they were really struggling with the truth of the resurrection.

1 Corinthians 15:12 says, "...if it is preached that Christ has been raised from the dead, how can some of you say there is no resurrection of the dead? If there is no resurrection of the dead then not even Christ has been raised. And if Christ has not been raised, our preaching is useless and so is your faith."

Wow, Paul says here that if Christ has not been raised, what I've dedicated the last 24 years of my life to is useless. It's been done in vain. Furthermore, verse 17 says my faith is futile, and I'm still in my sins. Easter changes everything!

The death of Christ is essential to our faith, but without the resurrection, Jesus would have been just another martyr. But when God raised Him from the dead, God showed Jesus to be the Son of God. Easter changes everything!

Without Easter, there would be no such thing as Christianity. It's really as simple as that, and that's what Paul is arguing in 1 Corinthians 15:17. If there is no resurrection, "you are still in your sins." There can be no forgiveness of sins without Jesus' resurrection. In verse 18, Paul goes on to say that without the resurrection, even those who have died with hope in Christ are lost.

I attend a lot of funerals. There is usually a funeral register there to sign, and I sign my name like everyone else does, but I also write "I Corinthians 15:19." "If only for this life we have hope in Christ, we are of all people most to be pitied."

Paul continues to ram home his point with a very strong statement in 1 Corinthians 15:32: "If the dead are not raised, let us eat and drink, for tomorrow we die." Those are our lifewords for today. Without hope after the grave, Paul tells his readers he would give up his ministry. He would "go for the gusto" and live for the moment if he was convinced nothing came after. Easter changes everything!

Easter changed a Friday that was filled with discouragement, despair, and disillusionment. On that Friday, all hope was lost. Easter took that Friday and made it Good Friday. It's now a day that's remembered as a "good" day. All because of Easter.

The cross was a symbol of torture, execution, and death. Easter took this symbol and made it a universal symbol of hope. Churches have huge crosses in the front of their buildings, and people even wear them around their necks. Easter took a borrowed grave from Joseph of Arimathea. It was a common, everyday grave. Easter made it the empty tomb.

I'm trying to tell you that Easter changes everything. But the only really important question for you and me is... has Easter changed us?

May I say it again? Easter changes everything. Easter took a man named Peter who was so afraid of a little servant girl that he denied Christ. Easter took this fisherman, this fearful, ashamed man, and turned him into a man who preached the message of Pentecost that birthed the Church of Jesus Christ.

Easter took a doubting Thomas who said, "Unless I see the nail marks in his hands and put my finger where the nails were, and put my hand into his side, I will not believe" (John 20:25). Easter took this man and turned him into a man who fell at the feet of Jesus and made a startling theological pronouncement when he said, "My Lord and my God" (John 20:28).

Easter changed the Sabbath day to the Lord's day. Can you even imagine the magnitude of that? Jews worshipped for thousands of years from 6pm Friday night to 6pm Saturday night. What could have happened that made those Jews change their day of worship? Let's think about that in modern-day terms. What drastic thing would have to happen for us to change our worship day from Sunday to Tuesday? You see, Easter changes everything.

Easter took 11 men who were locked in a room in fear of the Jews and the Roman soldiers. The sight of the resurrected Christ changed these men so that they went out boldly and literally started something that has changed the world.

Because of Easter, everything has changed for the Christian. We know that life is stronger than death. Love is stronger than hatred. Hope is stronger than despair. We know that Christ has risen and is with us. We know how much God loves us. We know what it means to experience new life—even in small ways—in our daily lives. And we know that nothing is ever beyond the power of God's grace. Have I convinced you that Easter changes everything?

Have you figured out my goal this week? I'm trying to convince you that Easter changes everything. Easter changes the way we look at death. Ask any funeral director. They cannot deny there is something vastly different about the funeral of a believer. It's not only what is read and sung. You can see it and feel it in the attitude of the people there.

Easter allowed me to sit with my dying dad and talk about his funeral in a matter-of-fact way. He told me of the songs he wanted sung and the Scriptures he wanted read. He even gave me three points he wanted the preacher to preach! Dad and I could sit there and have that discussion in a very lucid manner without tears because Easter changes everything.

I could sit there by his bed in the last weeks of his life when we were transitioning him from the hospital hospice room to a nursing home. I spent the last night in the hospital room with him. I prayed that God would take him that night because I didn't want to put him in a nursing home. I prayed that my dad would die. Easter changes everything.

My mom, my brother, and I were around Dad's death bed there at the nursing home in Ripley, Ohio. We saw him breathe his last breath. I grabbed my brother's hand and my mother's hand, and we prayed a prayer of thanksgiving for Dad's life. Were we nuts... or does Easter change everything?

Hours later, I picked up the phone and called Dad's best friend, Ed Pollack. Ed was instrumental in Dad's life. He helped disciple him. I told him of Dad's death, and Ed responded, "Praise Jesus, hallelujah to the Lamb!"

"O death, where is your sting? O grave, where is your victory?" Those are our lifewords today from 1 Corinthians 15:55. They shout to us that Easter changes everything.

Our lifewords today come from 2 Corinthians 4:16-5:1: "Therefore we do not lose heart. Though outwardly we are wasting away, yet inwardly we are being renewed day by day. For our light and momentary troubles are achieving for us an eternal glory that far outweighs them all. So we fix our eyes not on what is seen, but on what is unseen, since what is seen is temporary, but what is unseen is eternal. For we know that if the earthly tent we live in is destroyed, we have a building from God, an eternal house in heaven, not built by human hands."

I've read those words beside many a deathbed and at many funerals. Those verses would be meaningless without the truth of Easter.

Winston Churchill was Prime Minister of England during World War II. He left instructions concerning his funeral. He said after all was said, read, prayed, and sung, six military officers were going to come prepare his coffin. They would close it and drape the flag over it. As that was going on, he wanted "Taps" to be played. That's the military call that signifies night is here; go to bed. But as the coffin was lifted and carried down the aisle, out of that cathedral in London, Churchill wanted the buglers to play "Reveille." Of course, it's chiefly used to wake military personnel at sunrise. It comes from a French word that means "wake up." Time to get up!! Jesus has risen!

1 Peter 1:3 says, "Praise be to the God and Father of our Lord Jesus Christ! In his great mercy he has given us new birth into a living hope through the resurrection of Jesus Christ from the dead." John 14:19 teaches us that because He lives, we will live also.

Dr. Billy Graham once said, "If I were an enemy of Christianity, I would aim right at the Resurrection, because that is the heart of Christianity."

Easter changes everything!

If there is no Easter, how would we deal with the injustice, evil, and suffering in this world? How could we make sense of that? Dr. Jerry Walls was my Philosophy of Religion professor at Asbury Seminary. One day, Dr. Walls arrived and walked to the front of the class. Before he started to speak, he simply stood there for what seemed like two or three minutes. He could not speak, and I could tell he was choked up. It seemed like the longest time. When he finally gained his composure, he said, "This thing makes no sense apart from the resurrection." After that, he went on with his lecture for the day.

We found out about a week later that Dr. Walls' wife had left him that very morning he was choked up. As he stood before us young seminarians, the first words out of his mouth concerned the resurrection. Without it, life and Christianity make no sense.

Knowing this world is temporary and that there is an eternal home where all things will be made right helps us deal with the injustices of life. This world is marred by sin, and things are not as they should be. We await a new home where we will have a new body. The stuff of this world will be gone and seem small in the light of eternity. "For our light and momentary troubles are achieving for us an eternal glory that far outweighs them all" (2 Corinthians 4:17). Those are our lifewords for today.

God has not promised us an easy passage in this life, but He has promised a safe landing. As Bill and Gloria Gaither sung, "We'll soon be done with troubles and trials...yes in that home on the other side...shake glad hands with the elders...tell my kindred good morning...sit down beside my Jesus...sit down and rest a little while.

Without Easter, that song would be meaningless. Easter changes everything.

The resurrection of Jesus Christ changes your tomorrow, but it changes your today as well. Not only do we have hope for eternity; we have hope for today. The Apostle Paul prays that we can understand and believe that. He writes in Ephesians 1:19-20, "I also pray that you will understand the incredible greatness of God's power for us who believe Him. This is the same mighty power that raised Christ from the dead and seated Him in the place of honor at God's right hand..." Those are our lifewords for today.

Many people feel powerless. Their lives feel out of control. Our lifewords today ask us to believe that we have the same power inside of us that raised Jesus from the dead. That's enough power to change a bad situation. That's enough power to correct a bad habit. That's enough power to save that relationship. That's enough power to get out of debt. That's enough power to break that addiction. That's enough power to help you deal with whatever today will bring you. Resurrection power! Easter changes everything!

Jeremy Camp recorded a song that speaks to this truth. "The same power that rose Jesus from the grave. The same power that commands the dead to wake, lives in us, lives in us. The same power that moves mountains when He speaks. The same power that can calm a raging sea, lives in us, lives in us."

Jesus' resurrection power lives in us! Because of that, we can face whatever life throws at us. Paul wrote that God's grace will be sufficient to deal with the myriad of life's difficulties (2 Corinthians 12:9).

Too many times, we preach the good news as forgiveness only. It's not only that but a power that lives in us to allow us to face the storms of life and to live a life pleasing to God. Do you believe that? If you do, Easter changes everything.

Psalm 1 answers the question, "What kind of person does God bless?" He blesses the person who…

Marches to the beat of a different drummer (Psalm 1:1). The Christian hears a different beat that comes from a different drummer. The Christian is out of step in the eyes of the world. God's Word tells us this in 1 Corinthians 2:14: "The person without the Spirit does not accept the things that come from the Spirit of God but considers them foolishness, and cannot understand them because they are discerned only through the Spirit." The beat we hear comes from God's Holy Spirit. The world hears the beat from that drummer, but they can't understand it.

Believes in truth (Psalm 1:2). As I write this, I've just watched the 2019 General Conference of the United Methodist Church. The denomination is deeply divided on the authority of Scripture. Some people think the church should stay united for "love's" sake. They feel unity is more important than matters of truth. Others believe that God has spoken through His Word and that any unity must be centered around that truth. One speaker just made this statement: "It's better to be divided by truth than united in error." I say Amen, but if we must be divided by truth, that division should be as gracious and loving as the Holy Spirit will allow.

Has deep roots. This is more of a consequence than a characteristic. Because of the commitment to truth, the person God blesses is anchored. Hear our lifewords for today: "That person is like a tree planted by streams of water, which yields its fruit in season and whose leaf does not wither— whatever they do prospers. Not so the wicked! They are like chaff that the wind blows away" (Psalm 1:3-4). These deep roots hold when the winds of life blow. Ephesians 6:13 comes to mind: "Therefore put on the full armor of God, so that when the day of evil comes, you may be able to stand your ground, and after you have done everything, to stand."

God's blessing is reserved for those who hear a different drummer. A drummer the world does not understand. To the Christ-follower, the drumbeats are the sound of truth.

Our lifeword for today comes from Psalm 1:1: "Blessed is the one who does not walk in step with the wicked..." "The wicked" of Psalm 1 are those who desire to live on their own, independent of God and His Word. They have only a human perspective on life. They live according to the standards of the world. Another word for the wicked is the "crowd."

Do you hear the crowd talking? I sure do. I hear them saying if you're unhappy in your marriage, "Get a divorce." If you have an unwanted pregnancy, "Get an abortion." If you're facing temptation, the crowd says, "Everyone does it." The crowd says to a husband, "It's just one little text from an old girlfriend; it's not a big deal." If you want the blessing of God in your life, let the crowd pass you by.

Consider the progression in this verse. "Blessed is the one who does not walk in step with the wicked or stand in the way that sinners take or sit in the company of mockers." Walk... Stand... Sit. What starts innocently can lead to something you never anticipated. What starts casually may lead to closeness.

An old basketball coach of mine said, "If you sleep, eat, run, and hang out with the crowd, don't be surprised when you smell, sound, and look like them." The crowd has an impact on us. Many have thought they were strong enough to resist the crowd's pull, but in the end found out they weren't. "Therefore let anyone who thinks that he stands take heed lest he fall" (1 Corinthians 10:12).

While God calls us to have an impact and influence in the lives of unbelievers, He never calls us to live like them. "In the world but not of the world" can be reworded to say "in the crowd but not of the crowd."

The Bible calls Solomon the "wisest man who ever lived" (1 Kings 4:30-31). He was also a father. Hear the words of Proverbs 1:10, the words of a father to his son: "My son, if sinful men entice you, do not give in to them."

Psalm 1 describes the blessed person as one who refuses to follow the path of least resistance and give in to the thinking of the day. The blessed person chooses a different path, one that leads to blessing and prosperity.

Our lifeword today is from Psalm 1:1: "Blessed is the one who does not walk in step with the wicked or take the path (or way) that sinners take." Most of us, when given the choice, will take the path of least resistance, won't we? Robert Frost said he "took the path less traveled and that has made all the difference." This is the path of the blessed person. Jesus spoke of it in the Sermon on the Mount, where He described a person who takes a different path in life.

"Blessed are the poor in spirit…blessed are those who mourn…blessed are the meek…blessed are those who hunger and thirst for righteousness…blessed are the merciful…the pure in heart…the peacemakers…those who are persecuted." (Matthew 5:3-10). This does not describe the path of the average person. Jesus knew this, because at the end of His sermon, He said not many people will be on this path. He said it was narrow and that few will find it (Matthew 7:14).

The blessed life is not for the ones who choose to "go with the flow." The blessed person seems to be going against the current. The path they are on is not well-worn, but Jesus said it is the path to life (Matthew 7:14).

Our lifeword today is the Old Testament equivalent of Romans 12:2: "Do not be conformed to the pattern of this world." In the New Testament, James says that being friends with the world makes us enemies of God (James 4:4). John says that loving the world means that the love of God is not in us (1 John 2:15). The world-the crowd-is on the wrong path. Though their path is well-worn, it does not lead to life. That path is well-worn because it's crowded.

As always, Jesus allows us to choose. Well-worn or less traveled path, broad or narrow path? The right choice leads to a blessed life.

Where would we be without the grace of God? We would be left trying to be good enough to earn God's favor. How would we ever know if we've done enough good? How would I know if I'm saved or not? How could I have assurance of Heaven? Are my sins forgiven? I would have no clue were it not for the grace of God. As Paul says in 1 Corinthians 15:10, "...By the grace of God I am what I am."

Psalm 1 says that we are blessed if our "delight is in the law of the Lord, and...meditate on His law day and night" (Psalm 1:2). Those will be our lifewords for today. The word translated here as meditate is used to describe the way animals eat something they have just killed. Meditation here is not sitting on the floor and closing your eyes. In this case, meditation is really getting into a good meal of God's Word.

When David speaks of his love for "the law of the Lord," he doesn't speak of it as a way we prove our goodness to God. He speaks of God's directions to us, which are meant to show where we can find the blessings of God. These blessings are often a consequence of living the life God has called us to live. God's law is meant to protect us, to lead us away from the dangers of living life void of it.

God's law is a loving and gracious fence that keeps us from straying into areas where we will find hazards. It warns us of trouble on the other side. God's law is a school where we learn how to walk with Him. Without the law, we would be left to our own devices as we attempt to please Him. God's law is a mirror that shows us our need for grace. When we know we are sinners, we can seek the Savior.

Please hear me. Following the law will not gain anyone salvation. "If righteousness came through the law, why did Jesus die?" (Galatians 2:20). Salvation is by grace, apart from the law (Romans 3:21). The law simply points me to and teaches me about the abundant life God has for all His children. I'm thankful God has plainly shown me the life He desires for me.

I'd love to see the giant Sequoia tree known as the "The General Sherman Tree." It's in Sequoia National Park in California and is one of the largest trees on earth. The General Sherman is close to 300 feet tall. The diameter of the trunk is more than 40 feet. These trees can weigh 2 million pounds and can be 3,000 years old.

David wasn't thinking about Sequoias when he wrote Psalm 1:3, but he certainly didn't have an average tree in mind. The blessed person is compared to a special kind of tree. "He is like a tree planted by streams of water which yields its fruit in season, and whose leaf does not wither. In all that he does, he prospers."

Water in the Middle East is seasonal, and when it's dry, most things wither and die. So, the tree that is carefully planted has the best chance of life. This is not a wild tree but one that has been intentionally planted at the most advantageous spot. It is not planted by just one stream. The text says it is planted by streams... plural. The King James Version says "rivers of water." The picture here is a place that has been chosen because of the abundant supply of water.

Remember now, this tree delights in God's Word and feeds on truth (Psalm 1:2). The consequence of a lifetime of interaction with the truth of God's Word is the healthy tree described above. The consequence of a head and heart filled with the Word of God is a tree that thrives in rainy season or dry. Jeremiah picks up this same thought in Jeremiah 17:7-8: "Blessed is the man who trusts in the LORD...He is like a tree planted by water, that sends out its roots by the stream, and does not fear when heat comes, for its leaves remain green, and is not anxious in the year of drought, for it does not cease to bear fruit."

Jesus changes the imagery when He says those who hear His words and put them into practice build their house on a rock. The winds and rains will come, but that house will stand (Matthew 7:24-25). Trees, rocks, whatever the comparison, good things come to those who value God's Word (law) and apply it to their lives.

Our lifeword today is from Luke 15. Here we find three parables. The word "parable" is the combination of two Greek words. One means to "come alongside." The other means to "see" with. So, a parable is, literally, something that comes alongside to help us see something. The best modern-day example would be an illustration. That's a story a speaker tells that helps you better understand what they're saying. Jesus' parables were teaching aids, something like an analogy or a comparison.

In Luke 15, there are three parables. We'll focus on two of them today. We learn of a lost sheep and a lost coin. One common denominator of both is that they are being sought. The shepherd leaves 99 sheep to find the one who had wandered off. The woman turns the house upside down until she finds the lost coin.

Both of these parables teach us something about God. Here, it's plain that God is a seeker of what is lost. He sought Adam and Eve after they sinned. He didn't give up on them but sought them out. He comes to us today as well. If we have strayed from the path, He reminds us of that. It's called conviction of sin, and it's one of God's great gifts of love to us. God may seek through a Bible verse, through a preacher's message, through a song, or through the gentle rebuke of a friend.

Francis Thompson, an English poet, was so taken by this concept that he saw God as the "Hound of Heaven." His poem captured his religious experience: "I fled Him, down the nights and down the days; I fled Him, down the arches of the years; I fled Him, down the labyrinthine ways; Of my own mind; and in the mist of tears, I hid from Him…"

Just like a bloodhound goes after a rabbit, Thompson gives us the image of God seeking us, following us, drawing near with His grace. The Bible is not a record of man's pursuit of God; it is a record of God's pursuit of us. Jesus said of Himself in Luke 19:10, "The Son of Man has come to seek and save the lost."

Isaiah 49:16 is an amazing verse. God says, "See, I have engraved you on the palms of my hands..." I cannot get my mind wrapped around the fact that God, the one who breathed this world into existence, tries over and over in Scripture to convince me of my worth to Him. In Psalm 139:13-16, God says "He knew me when I was created in the secret place."

I have a hard time comprehending Matthew 10:29-31. "Are not two sparrows sold for a penny? Yet not one of them will fall to the ground apart from the will of your Father. And even the very hairs of your head are all numbered. So don't be afraid; you are worth more than many sparrows." God knows the number of hairs on my head? Some say this can't be true. They say God has a lot more important things going on than counting hairs. Okay, let's accept that. Even if it's not true, God is still trying to put into words how valuable we are to Him. He's trying to convince you and me that we matter to Him. By the way, don't be shocked one day in Heaven when an angel gives us a note that says, "92,762."

All of this goes well with Luke 15. That's our lifeword for today. Here we have three parables about one sheep, one coin, and one son. We all know that God so loved the WORLD that He gave His only Son, but hear me today: He loves YOU. We would all do better if we took God's love out of the context of the world and brought it home to us. There was one sheep, one coin, and one son.

While I'm on that subject, Jesus went to one man's house (Zacchaeus'). He met with one woman at the well, and He met with one religious man (Nicodemus). With all that was on His mind on the cross, Jesus turned to one man and said, "Today, you will be with me in Paradise" (Luke 23:43).

You matter to God. No matter what you did last night or are planning to do today, God loves you. He sees you. He knows you. He wants the best for you. He sent His Son, Jesus, to die for you. Yes, you.

Luke made an amazing observation when he said, "sinners drew near to Him" (Luke 15:1). That's our lifeword for today. Jesus was the type of person sinners wanted to be around. They didn't run from Him. They didn't ridicule His teachings. Sinners, who heard Jesus tell them to "go and sin no more," wanted to be around Jesus. Think about that for a moment.

Why were sinners hanging out with Jesus? I think it has something to do with the words in John 1:14. Jesus was "full of grace and truth." They must have known His words were truth. But they sensed it was different than the truth of the Pharisees and scribes. Jesus' truth was combined with grace. In Luke 4:22, we learn the crowd "...marveled at the gracious words which proceeded out of his mouth." He was full of truth. He didn't compromise the seriousness of sin, but He must have spoken truth in a gracious manner. Paul later wrote to the Romans, "God's kindness is intended to lead you to repentance" (Romans 2:4).

Jesus didn't beat people over the head with truth. He used truth in a gracious way. As the religious people complained and murmured, "This man receives sinners and eats with them" (Luke 15:2), Jesus spoke of God as a loving shepherd who leaves the 99 to go find that one lost sheep. Through this parable, He was helping them see God's love and His joy when even one sinner repents.

Jesus didn't come to earth to condemn sinners. He didn't come to catch them in their sin. It's the law that condemns, and it's Jesus who saves (John 3:17). Jesus came to seek and save sinners. He came to make a way for sinners to be freed and forgiven of their sin. Jesus came to die.

Possibly, the sinners sensed this, and that's why they "drew near to Him" (Luke 15:1). Maybe, if sinners sensed grace and truth from us, there would be more sinners hanging around us. Also, if they heard this message of grace and truth from our pulpits, we would have more sinners coming to our churches.

President Barack Obama said this in a Father's Day speech in 2008: "Of all the rocks upon which we build our lives, we are reminded today that family is most important. And we are called to recognize and honor how critical every father is to that foundation. They are teachers and coaches. But if we are honest with ourselves, we'll admit that what too many fathers also are is missing. They have abandoned their responsibilities, acting like boys instead of men."

Democrats and Republicans can agree that one of the biggest problems in our society is fatherlessness. Let's define that as "fathers who refuse to be dads." The word father is a biological term. Any man can become a father, but being a dad is a commitment. "Dad" is a relational term. Fathers aren't automatically dads.

Our lifeword for today is from Luke 15:20. A son left his father's house and went out into the world. He wasted all of his money and hit rock bottom. This son was longing for the food the pigs ate. That's really low. Here the Bible tells us the son had enough. "When he came to his senses, he said, 'I will set out and go back to my father and say to him: Father, I have sinned against heaven and against you. I am no longer worthy to be called your son; make me like one of your hired servants.' So he got up and went to his father" (Luke 15:17-20). Our lifeword is that last phrase, "So he got up and went to his father." Even though the son wandered far from home, he remembered he wasn't fatherless. He remembered he had a loving Father who would forgive him and welcome him back home. The text then says the father saw him a long way off and ran to greet him.

I don't know about your earthly father, but your heavenly Father is there for you. You are not fatherless. You have a Father who is looking, waiting, and longing for you to "come to your senses." He's the best father anyone could ever have. Fatherlessness is an earthly problem—a big problem. But it's not a spiritual problem. You have a heavenly Father. You are not fatherless.

One of the tools that stores use to bring in new customers is a generous return policy. The Lands' End return policy is short and sweet. If you aren't happy with a product, return it at any time for a refund or exchange. It doesn't get much better than this. At IKEA, shoppers get a full year to return their purchase. At Kohl's, you can return any item, at any time, even without a receipt. WOW! The only catch is you must have used their store credit card. Each of these stores hope that the more lenient the return policy, the more customers they will acquire.

Returning to God is a common refrain in the Bible. In the Old Testament, the prophets speak often of God's people not returning to Him. In Joel 2:12-13, the prophet relays God's invitation: "'Even now', declares the Lord, return to me with all your heart with fasting and weeping and mourning'. "Return to the Lord your God, for He is gracious and compassionate, slow to anger and abounding in love, and He relents from sending calamity".

Zechariah 1:3 says, "'Return to me,' declares the Lord Almighty, and I will return to you." Malachi 3:7 says, "'Ever since the time of your ancestors you have turned away from my decrees and have not kept them. Return to me, and I will return to you,' says the Lord Almighty." For centuries, God's people have left Him. The call to return to God suggests that someone has turned away.

The father of the prodigal son was looking for the son's return. The text says when the son was still a long way off, the father saw him (Luke 15:20). This pictures a father who is looking for the son's return. The Scripture also says that upon seeing his son, the father "ran to his son" (Luke 15:20). That's our lifeword for today.

I'm not sure you can find a return policy more attractive than this one. The only "catch" is you have to come to your senses. That means you realize what you've done is wrong and have a Father waiting for your return. The arms of God are open wide to accept the return. And not only that, but He runs to greet the one returning! In God's Kingdom, returns are accepted, any time, any place.

We love to write about and tell the story of the younger brother in Luke 15. He's the one who left, took his part of the money, wasted it, repented, and came home. But there was another son... the elder brother. By all accounts, he's a good person. He does what he's supposed to do. I imagine he shows up on time and does a good job. The problem wasn't his behavior; it was his attitude. Underneath that good, hard-working son lay an ungrateful and bitter person.

The older brother speaks in Luke 15:29: "All these years I've been slaving for you." We learn a lot about him in those words. He had the heart of one who saw his work as duty and obligation. He saw himself not as a son but as a household slave. He also refers to his younger brother as "This son of yours" (Luke 15:30). It's almost as if he has disowned his brother.

Earlier in the story, we learn that the younger brother went off to a "far country" (Luke 15:13). By the older son's words, we learn that he was in a far country of his own. His heart was far from his father's. In his heart, he may have been more lost than his brother. A bad thing about a good, older brother is thinking you're good enough. These "good enough" folks are blinded to their need for forgiveness. This is called self-righteousness. It's the biggest obstacle to accepting the righteousness of God through Jesus Christ.

Jesus came to deliver both the prodigals and the older brothers from their far countries. It takes no more of a miracle to be delivered from sinful self-righteousness than it does from an obviously sinful lifestyle.

Jesus uses older brothers. In fact, Paul, certainly had older brother tendencies until God got ahold of him on the Damascus Road. In Philippians 3, we read of how much of an older brother he was. God chose this well-behaved, good person to proclaim the riches of His love and grace. The story of the prodigal son highlights that all of us need the grace of God. Sometimes, it's easier for the younger brothers to realize that. Through this story, may all you older brothers and sisters know you need God's mercy and grace as much as your younger siblings.

We transition today from a well-known passage of Scripture, Luke 15, the story of the prodigal son, to a lesser known passage that speaks of an obscure biblical character, Tabitha. The Bible says she was always doing "good works and acts of charity." These are our lifewords today from Acts 9:36. Tabitha was a seamstress. In those days, this would have been a tedious and labor-intensive endeavor. She willingly gave of her time and effort to help others. She was well-known in Joppa for this, and when her name is brought up, that's how people remember her. Tabitha used what God gave her to become known for "good works and charity."

God is not impressed with the big things on your resume. Those things carry weight in the world's eyes but not in His. Through Tabitha's simple acts of service, which amounted to making dresses for widows, she became endeared to the people of Joppa. God is looking for little things done from a heart of compassion.

God honored Tabitha's life of service, and when she died, there was much grieving in Joppa. The Apostle Peter arrived and the widows showed Peter the garments that she had made for them and told him of her many good deeds (Acts 9:39). God then used Peter to do the miraculous. In response to Peter's prayer, God raised Tabitha from the dead. Afterward, this miracle "... became known throughout all Joppa and many believed on the Lord" (Acts 9:42). God used a compassionate woman that could sew. God took her gift and her willingness to serve and used it. Since her good works were known, especially among the widows, God used her notoriety to spread the word about Jesus.

God will make use of the gifts we have if we make them available to Him. Does the ability to sew seem small to you? Maybe it is in the eyes of the world, but God can take that and use it as a means to spread the good news about Jesus Christ.

Yesterday, we learned of Tabitha who had a heart for people and hands that could sew. We said God can take a small thing, like the ability to sew, and use it to further the gospel. I'm reminded of Zechariah 4:10: "Who despises the day of small things?" If the truth be known, plenty of us do.

How many times have we heard someone say something like, "God has bigger plans for you." This sometimes comes at times of discouragement when something smaller has not gone well. Once when I was pastoring a small church, someone after the service said, "God has bigger things planned for you than this." These may seem to be harmless bits of encouragement, but it gives the impression that God cares more about the big things than He does the lesser. I want to tell you He values the small things going on in your life.

The truth that small things matter is evident in Luke 21:1-2: "As Jesus looked up, he saw the rich putting their gifts into the temple treasury. He also saw a poor widow put in two very small copper coins." These are our lifewords for today. While in the temple, Jesus saw a widow. He noticed an inconsequential woman doing a small thing... at least, small in the eyes of the world. Jesus said, "This poor widow has put in more than all the others. All these people gave their gifts out of their wealth; but she out of her poverty put in all she had to live on" (Luke 21:3-4).

This is an important concept. What we do today is big in the eyes of God. In fact, if we're not faithful in the small things of today, there will not be any bigger things of tomorrow (Luke 16:10). If we get caught up in the "greater things tomorrow" type of thinking, we may miss the routine and daily opportunities to serve Him. Remember the widow whose "two very small coins" were a big deal in the eyes of the Lord.

Today's devotion is taken from the Bible verse, "God helps those who help themselves." That's in 1 Obligations 12:22. Turn to that now.... Didn't find it, did you? Look again. You'll find it right next to, "To thine own self be true." Struck out again, huh? Can't even find 1 Obligations? Well, neither of these statements, as well as 1st or 2nd Obligations, are found in the Bible. They may align with popular culture, but that doesn't make them biblical. No doubt many of you have heard someone quote, "God helps those who help themselves," as if it was biblical. That's not in God's Word either.

You can find it in *Poor Richard's Almanac*, the 1757 edition. You can also find it in *Aesop's Fables* dated 600 B.C. It's in the Quran. "Indeed Allah will not change the conditions of a population until they change what is in themselves" (Ar-Ra'd 13:11). So, Allah promises his help after we change ourselves. But, God helping those who help themselves is not a biblical teaching. Although 2 Thessalonians 3:10 and James 4:8 *seem* to teach this, the Bible as a whole teaches the opposite.

All we receive from God is grace. God doesn't owe me anything just because I did something to help myself. A better saying would be, "God helps those who position themselves to receive His grace." Our lifeword today is from Mark 10, where we have the story of Bartimaeus who received great help from God. Bartimaeus was blind, but he heard that Jesus was coming to his town, so somehow, he positioned himself by the roadside. He positioned himself to receive grace. He got to a place where Jesus was coming by.

How about you? Do you get by the roadside? Do you go to a place where grace can reach you? Remember the biblical principle from this story and others: God helps those who position themselves to receive His grace. We'll dig deeper into this tomorrow.

If you thought that "God helps those who help themselves" is in the Bible, don't feel bad. You're certainly not alone. Polls show that 75% of Americans and 40% of Christians believe this is a Bible verse. Believing this statement puts the pressure on me and on you to first make a change before God will help us. But God wants the pressure on Him, and He says His grace is sufficient for us (2 Corinthians 12:9).

Illustrating God's grace is difficult, but let me take a shot at it. As I plug in my laptop computer, I realize I don't provide the electricity. As I turn on the power button, I know I have very little to do with making the computer compute. I tap some buttons, but I don't make the computations. There's nothing in response to me plugging it in and turning it on without someone else's work. That's a very incomplete and insufficient explanation of God's grace.

Our spiritual lives are lifeless without the empowerment of His grace. While I don't have control over it, and can't make it flow over me, God has given us ways to plug in and connect to His grace. This is what I mean by God helping those who position themselves to receive His grace. He seems to have places where His grace flows often and frequently. It seems it would be common sense for us to put ourselves in these places.

Bartimaeus did this in our Scripture today. He was blind and needed help from God. He could have sat at home, but when he heard Jesus was coming by, he must have thought that Jesus could help him. He somehow got "by the roadside." That's our lifeword for today from Mark 10:46. He got to a place where Jesus was coming by. He positioned himself to receive the grace of God.

Do you need help from God today? That help is called grace. You can't demand it. You can't insist upon it. You can't name it and claim it. You can't make it flow to you. It is a free gift. But you can position yourself to receive. Where do I find the grace of God? We'll dive into that tomorrow.

God's work of grace in our lives is not magical. He doesn't wave His wand or hit us over the head with His holy baseball bat, and we're miraculously changed. Instead, God has specific ways He has chosen to bring grace into our lives. These are like the hoses that firemen carry to put out a fire. The hose isn't the water, but it does carry the water. In the same way, God uses specific means to carry the grace that works in our lives.

These paths that God uses are called "means of grace." By "means" we mean the instrument that is used to bring about a desired result. For example, the football team arrived at the game by means of a bus. The bus was the instrument used to bring about the result desired... to get to the game. The "means of grace" function as a path or a channel to bring us the grace we need. So, if I need help from God, I need to use the various ways God has ordained to help (grace) me. Hence our principle of the last two days, "God helps those who position themselves to receive His grace."

These means are the everyday stuff Christianity is made of. They are not magical or mystical. At times, they may seem routine, but God uses them in a powerful way. Saints down through the ages have put these means of God's grace into three broad categories... Word, prayer, and fellowship.

We will talk about these in the coming days, but one thing is important to note here. Simply knowing the means of grace will help you about as much as Bartimaeus knowing that Jesus was coming to his town but refusing to get "by the roadside" (Mark 10:46). If he had not placed himself in the way of God's grace, he would have missed the grace of Jesus in his life.

Paul put it this way, and it will be our lifeword for today: "By the grace of God I am what I am, and His grace to me was not without effect. I worked harder than all of them, yet it was not I, but the grace of God that was with me" (1 Corinthians 15:10).

This illustration may help you understand this concept of God's "means of grace." If I'm the captain of a sailboat, I am in charge of putting up the sails. I don't make the wind blow, but if I never put up the sails, I'm going nowhere. I put the sails up because I know the wind usually blows this way. God has provided a way of locomotion on the water. It's called wind. If I make use of what He provides, He'll move me across the water.

Remember, the three means of grace from yesterday? Word, prayer, and fellowship. Let's start with prayer today. Prayer is nothing more than dependence on God. Through prayer, I confess to God that I'm not sailing solo, I need the wind. Admitting my dependence is also stating that He is able. I'm confessing to Him that I believe in His strength and power. "Now to him who is able to do immeasurably more than all we ask or imagine…" (Ephesians 3:20).

Bartimaeus did this in our story of his healing in Mark 10. He heard Jesus was coming by. He positioned himself "by the roadside" (Mark 10:46). When he saw his opportunity, he cried out, "Jesus, Son of David, have mercy on me!" (Mark 10:47). He must have made something of a scene because the disciples told him to quiet down. "Many rebuked him and told him to be quiet, but he shouted all the more, 'Son of David, have mercy on me!'" (Mark 10:48).

That was a prayer if I ever heard one. Prayer is not only something you say with your hands folded reverently. Many times, it's a cry of desperation, as it was for Bartimaeus. He shouted out his dependence on God's grace. The ear of God is inclined to such cries for mercy. Our text says that upon hearing Bartimaeus' prayer, "Jesus…stopped and said, 'Call him.'" (Mark 10:49)

God helps those who help themselves? No. God helps those who position themselves to receive His grace. His grace flows to those who pray, admitting their need for His mercy in their life.

I'll admit it. Prayer is hard for me. I'm short on discipline, and prayer takes discipline. In fact, some call the means of grace "spiritual disciplines." Maybe for some, prayer comes easy. I've heard people talk of prayer as if angels descended on them when they prayed. But it's not like that for me.

Most things in life that are meaningful take discipline. Because of that, prayer doesn't come natural to most Christians. It's important to admit this. Let's not put up a good face and let our friends think prayer is a piece of cake. Being honest will help them fight the battle of persevering in prayer. Yes, prayer is a battle; one the devil is fighting as well. The enemy of our souls fights us in prayer and will discourage our efforts any way he can.

Remember, prayer is an expression of our need for God. Maybe that's one of the reasons it's so hard. Our sinful nature doesn't take kindly to our neediness. In prayer, we are admitting to God that we are dependent upon Him for all that He provides. When He tells us to ask (Matthew 7:7), it's not that God is a divine vending machine. God wants us to ask because it's then that we are reminded of our need for Him.

Prayer is a continual dialog with God. Our lifeword today is, "Pray without ceasing" (1 Thessalonians 5:17). Prayer can take place any time and any place. I always laugh when someone speaks of "banning prayer in schools." No one can ban prayer. It happens without permission. In fact, private prayer, prayer that is genuine, is what God calls for (Matthew 6:5-8). Now, we cannot pray every moment, but it is possible to carry Him with us wherever we go. Prayer is not only an action but an attitude that places Jesus, and our dependence on Him, at the focal point of our life.

Prayer is hard. Pray anyway. Prayer takes discipline. Pray anyway. Prayer may be routine. Pray anyway. God's grace flows generously to those who pray. He is worshipped when we admit our need for Him. God helps those who pray.

The last few days, we've said that God has "means" or "pathways" that He uses to channel grace to us. This is how God helps us. We've said He doesn't help those who help themselves, but He helps those who position themselves to receive His grace.

We put ourselves in the flow of the Lord's grace and receive His help through very ordinary means. They are not mystical. They are not heavenly. In fact, they are very earthly. Spending time in prayer, time in His Word, and time in fellowship with other Christians is the prescription for accessing the grace of God.

Time spent reading, meditating, and listening to God's Word is vital to receiving help from God. For this to happen, we don't read the Bible merely for information, but with a desire for transformation. We must truly believe that "the truth will set us free" (John 8:32). Grace flows freely to us if our heart's desire is to know God... not just know about Him.

As you read the Scriptures, you'll find a clear admonition to trust God and His Word. This is where application comes in. As we take God at His word and apply it to our lives, we trust. The more we trust, the more God gives grace. The more grace He gives, the more we grow.

As you read God's Word, you are hearing Him. He's talking to you, and grace is coming your way. As you listen to sermons, you are hearing His voice and receiving His grace. That's why it's vital you attend a Bible preaching and teaching church.

Our lifeword today is from 2 Timothy 3:16-17: "All Scripture is God-breathed and is useful for teaching, rebuking, correcting, and training in righteousness, that the servant of God may be thoroughly equipped for every good work." The purpose of the Bible is that we "may be thoroughly equipped for every good work." That certainly sounds like a "means of grace" to me.

For the last few days, we've focused on ways we get help from God. It's not by helping ourselves, but it comes by positioning ourselves to receive His grace. Today, let's see how God's grace comes to us through Christian fellowship.

When we get together for fellowship, it's much more than a potluck supper. There's nothing wrong with that unless that's all the fellowship one experiences. Christian fellowship can be defined as relationships between Christians that can't be found with those outside the faith. We gather together not just for good food but because of our faith in Christ. Scripture records that those first believers "...devoted themselves to the apostles' teaching and to fellowship, to the breaking of bread and to prayer" (Acts 2:42). Those are our lifewords for today. Christians have always sensed the need to gather together for support and encouragement. As a Christian, your beliefs are counter to many around you. The desire for fellowship with like-minded people is natural because it's God-given.

Hebrews 10:24-25 says, "Let us consider how to spur one another on to love and good works, not neglecting to meet together, as is the habit of some, but encouraging one another..." It's in Christian fellowship that we hear God's Word preached (2 Timothy 4:2), that we pray together (Acts 4:24), that we lift our voices to God in song (Colossians 3:16), that we bear each other's burdens (Galatians 6:2), speak truth to one another (Ephesians 4:25), and encourage one another (1 Thessalonians 5:11). It's in the fellowship of believers that we celebrate the Lord's Supper and Baptism. The Bible knows nothing of "lone ranger Christians."

We were created to be in relationship because we are created in God's image (Genesis 1:26). In the mystery of the Trinity, God is a relationship... Father, Son, and Holy Spirit. No one is complete in and of themselves. Paul makes it clear that we need one another if we're serious about being Jesus' followers (1 Corinthians 12). To neglect this is to sabotage our Christian growth and maturity.

As Christians, we are called to share the good news about Jesus. For most believers, this does not come naturally. We don't want to offend or be pushy. Some don't feel equipped to handle the questions an unbeliever might ask. One of the reasons we hesitate is because we have a wrong view of evangelism. The Bible describes it as a natural process that happens in the context of relationships.

Our lifeword today is from Colossians 4:5-6: "Walk in wisdom toward outsiders, making the best use of the time. Let your speech always be gracious, seasoned with salt, so that you may know how you ought to answer each person." That last phrase tells us that a one-size-fits-all approach to sharing the gospel is not biblical because it is impersonal and makes you feel like a project. Maybe a Jehovah's Witness or Mormon knocked on your door, and you felt like they were giving a rehearsed speech.

Paul says, we need to know how we ought to answer each person. How can I do this if I don't get to know the person, listen to them, and have a relationship with them? The recipient of our evangelistic efforts should feel loved, accepted, and respected. Someone has said that if he had an hour to spend with a non-Christian, he would "listen for fifty-five minutes, and then, I would know what to say."

When Jesus approached the woman at the well in Samaria, He asked her a question. Evangelism is not a monologue; it's a dialogue. Ask people about themselves and, as they talk, listen. Don't forget to listen. Be sure to avoid arguments. You may win the argument and lose the person. No one is ever argued into the Kingdom of God.

More than anything else, relax. If you're nervous, your friend will be as well. That doesn't make for a good dialogue. Don't feel pressure to convert your friend. The converting is up to God. All He asks us to do is share.

If you desire to make an impact for Christ among unbelievers, you must grasp this truth: Evangelism is more about process than decision. Our lifeword yesterday and today tells us, "Walk in wisdom toward outsiders, making the best use of the time. Let your speech always be gracious, seasoned with salt, so that you may know how you ought to answer each person" (Colossians 4:5-6). Let's investigate the first words of this verse, "Walk in wisdom toward outsiders..."

Paul tells us to evangelize with wisdom. Wisdom is more than knowledge. Knowledge is having the facts and the correct information. Wisdom combines understanding and knowledge. Knowing what to do with the knowledge is wisdom. In the context of our lifeword, it's using the knowledge with grace, respect, and love. This comes with spiritual maturity and through prayer.

Walking in wisdom means seeing evangelism as a long-term endeavor. Listening, loving, and respecting takes time. Conversions are a process. People need time to work through their doubts and skepticism. This process ends in a decision, but that decision is not the result of a single encounter.

Walking in wisdom also means knowing how much information to give. Our lifeword says, "Let your speech always be gracious, seasoned with salt..." Too much salt ruins a meal. Too much truth ruins a gospel presentation. Wisdom has the understanding to know how much information to give.

Remember, wisdom combines knowledge of the truth of the gospel with understanding the moment. This wisdom comes through prayer. Through prayer, God gives us discernment on time and place... whether we move forward now or later. Through prayer, God can give us wisdom to know how much salt to give. Pray that God will allow you to walk in wisdom toward outsiders.

Yesterday, we talked about being wise in our evangelistic efforts. Paul says in Colossians 4:5, "Walk in wisdom toward outsiders...." Then, he proceeds to say that one way to be wise is in the choice of our words. "Let your speech always be gracious, seasoned with salt, so that you may know how you ought to answer each person" (Colossians 4:6). Our speech, the words we use, is critical to the success of our evangelistic efforts.

As Christians, we must use the language of the listener. On the Day of Pentecost, God did a miraculous thing. Though people were there from different countries, all heard the disciples "speaking in his own language" (Acts 2:6). People could not understand and respond to the good news unless it was in a language they knew. What was true over 2,000 years ago is true today. We need to use words that unchurched people understand. Whether we know it or not, church folks speak a foreign language. Let's call it Christianese. The world does not understand all this Christian talk. We must speak the greatest news of all time in everyday language.

Paul chastises those speaking in tongues publicly because there was not an interpreter present (1 Corinthians 14:16). He says, for the sake of the outsider, speak words people can understand. He also tells us to follow him as he becomes all things to all people that some might be saved (1 Corinthian 9:22).

We wouldn't confuse our neighbor with a foreign language when we told them how to fix their washing machine. We don't speak insider words when discussing the upcoming election. Why would we do it as we share the gospel? The only stumbling block to our neighbor should be the message itself (1 Corinthians 1:23).

Would you pray and ask God to show you how your speech can be "gracious, seasoned with salt, so that you may know how you ought to answer each person" (Colossians 4:6)? As on the Day of Pentecost, may the gospel be heard in the people's own language. Their eternal destiny may be riding on it.

Evangelism is a team effort. Sometimes, you will hear someone say, "I led Sue to Christ," or "I brought Mike to the Lord." Someone accepting Christ is never an "I" event. Whenever anyone becomes a Christian, there were many people involved in the victory. And behind the scenes, there was One who was guiding and directing the process. Paul writes in 1 Corinthians 3:6, "I planted the seed, Apollos watered it, but God has been making it grow." That's our lifeword for today.

To grasp this team concept, it may help to change the way we think of evangelism. When most hear that word, they think of leading a person to Christ. The biblical word for that is harvesting. But before there can be a harvest, someone must cultivate, plant, and water. Jesus says: "One sows and another reaps...I sent you to reap what you have not worked for. Others have done the hard work, and you have reaped the benefits of their labor" (John 4:37-38).

According to Jesus, there are reapers and sowers, harvesters and gardeners. All play a role in leading people to Jesus. Jesus tells His disciples that they will reap where they did not sow. Others were at work here. Some planted, and some watered. Jesus calls that the "hard work" (John 4:38). So, it's a team working together, and each team member has different roles.

Our evangelistic efforts can seem fruitless at times. This is because we will not always see the immediate fruit of our labor. These verses today encourage us to keep at it. Someone has to cultivate. Someone has to sow, and someone has to water. All don't get the pleasure of harvesting.

If you do have an opportunity to harvest, remember it was a team effort. A lot of work has gone into this person before you ever showed up. By far, the most important work was done by God. God has more time invested in this person than anyone else does. Evangelism is not an "I" event.

Episcopal priest Sam Shoemaker spent his life helping people find new life in Jesus Christ. He served as the rector of Calvary Episcopal Church in New York City. He played a critical role in the founding of Alcoholics Anonymous. He was an ambassador for Jesus Christ. Our lifeword today is taken from 2 Corinthians 5:20: "We are therefore Christ's ambassadors, as though God were making his appeal through us. We implore you on Christ's behalf: Be reconciled to God." Toward the end of his life, Shoemaker sat down to write his philosophy of ministry. This work has become famous in evangelistic circles. It's titled, *I Stand By the Door.* I include it here in edited form. You can Google it and find the whole work.

"I stand by the door. I neither go too far in, nor stay too far out. The door is the most important door in the world. It is the door through which people walk when they find God. There's no use my going way inside, and staying there, when so many are still outside, and they, as much as I, crave to know where the door is.

"The most tremendous thing in the world is for people to find that door—the door to God. The most important thing anyone can do is to take hold of one of those blind, groping hands, and put it on the latch—the latch that only clicks and opens to one's own touch. Nothing else matters compared to helping them find it, and open it, and walk in, and find Him... so I stand by the door.

"I admire the people who go way in. But I wish they would not forget how it was before they got in. Then they would be able to help the people who have not even found the door, or the people who want to run away again from God. You can go in too deeply, and stay in too long, and forget the people outside the door. As for me, I shall take my old accustomed place, near enough to God to hear Him, and know He is there, but not so far from people as not to hear them, and remember they are there too. Where? Outside the door—thousands of them, millions of them. But—more important for me—one of them, two of them, ten of them, whose hands I am intended to put on the latch, so I shall stand by the door."

If you've been a Christian for very long, you no doubt have heard a teaching on your identity in Christ. This is defined in terms of what Christ does to us and the relationship He creates with us and the future Christ has for us. As Christians, our identity is not in ourselves or what we have done. It's in Christ. I am an adopted child of God, forgiven, His heir, and made in His image. We could go on and on about our identities as Christians. But one I want to focus on is found in 2 Corinthians 5:20. It's our lifeword for today. "We are therefore Christ's ambassadors, as though God were making his appeal through us". I am an ambassador of Jesus Christ.

In biblical times and in today's world, the word ambassador means the same thing. An ambassador is defined as: a person sent to a foreign country to represent the ruler or country that sent them. God's Word says you are His delegate- His envoy- His representative to Planet Earth. This means we have authorization to speak and act on behalf of the King who sent us—Jesus Christ. Do you see yourself this way? If you do, evangelism becomes a whole new ball game. Evangelism is not something you do. An evangelist—an ambassador—is something you are.

As a Christian, I know your occupation. You're not a factory worker. You're an ambassador of Christ disguised as a factory worker. You're not a teacher. You're an ambassador of Christ disguised as a teacher. You're not even a mother or a father. You're an ambassador of Christ disguised as a mom or dad. All of the roles you play in life are important. But your primary role, your primary identity, is that of an ambassador.

So, when you go here and there, you are a representative of Jesus Christ. Representing Jesus is not something you do; it's who you are. Being His ambassador is your identity. It's how you see yourself and how you get your self-worth. If this is true for you, you can't help but be an evangelist.

As Christians, we all have a story to tell of how Christ has worked in our lives. Telling that story is one of the best ways to be an evangelist. It was said of the woman at the well, "Many of the Samaritans from that town believed in him because of the woman's testimony..." (John 4:39). God will take all you've been through—the good, the bad, and the ugly—and use it to transform the lives of those around you. When you tell your story, you are really telling His story!

The Apostle Paul models this for us in Acts 26. It's our lifeword for today. Paul tells his story to King Agrippa. It breaks down into a simple outline: a) his life before Christ, b) his conversion to Christ, and c) his life after meeting Christ.

Paul first tells of his life before Christ in Acts 26:1-11. Paul is truthful and doesn't hide the embarrassing parts. "I too was convinced that I ought to do all that was possible to oppose the name of Jesus...And that is just what I did in Jerusalem...I put many of the Lord's people in prison, and when they were put to death, I cast my vote against them...I was so obsessed with persecuting them that I even hunted them down in foreign cities." Our story won't be as dramatic as that, but we can tell of our life before meeting Christ.

Paul goes on to tell of how he was saved in Acts 26:12-18. All of our conversion stories will be different. None are better than another. God works in many ways. However God got ahold of you, that's your story. Tell it with joy. Paul finishes as he tells of the difference Christ has made in his life in Acts 26:19-23. "...I was not disobedient to the vision from heaven...I preached they should repent and turn to God and demonstrate their repentance by their deeds." (Acts 26:19-20)

Since biblical times, Christians have used this simple formula to tell their story- before Christ, meeting Christ, and after Christ. Practice yours, maybe even write it out. Obviously, don't read it, but internalize it so that when God gives you the opportunity, it'll be on the tip of your tongue.

We used to have a day in junior high that we called inside-out day. We all would wear our clothes inside out. What if we could do that to our lives? What if what was on the inside was seen on the outside? What if people saw what was really in our heart? What if they saw what we were really thinking? That's kind of scary, isn't it? Inside out living is rather intimidating.

Jesus talked a lot about this. Now, He knows we all have weird things that flash through our minds that other people don't need to know about. There are things inside of us that ought to stay inside. That's part of being human. This is not what Jesus means by living inside out.

When Jesus preached the Sermon on the Mount, He taught very plainly that it's what is on the inside that matters. I like to say, "The heart of the matter is the matter of the heart." Those were lyrics from a band called Brother's Keeper.

Jesus was critical of the scribes and Pharisees because they had external behavior without the internal motivation. They cleaned the outside of the cup while leaving the inside dirty. That's our lifeword today from Matthew 23:25. Christianity can be faked. We can put on an act. We can fool our friends and family. We can fool the people in our church, but we can't fool God. God looks on the heart. We are a biblical Christian when we have a new heart that motivates external behavior.

The chorus of the song I referred to above goes like this: "The heart of the matter is the matter of the heart. To save a world that's dying it's the only place to start. We can sway one's opinion, turn their point of view. But only 'til the heart is changed can the old become the new."

Don't settle for looking good on the outside. Ask God to do deep work in your life. It's a great burden to continue to keep up the Christian act. It's much easier to allow God to change your heart so that you can stop *trying* to be Christian and just *be* Christian. The Christian life is lived from the inside out.

The Pharisee should have known better. He invited Jesus to dinner (Luke 11:37). When Jesus comes to your house for dinner, it won't just be any old dinner. Jesus did what He wanted and said what He wanted. The Pharisee should have known there wouldn't be normal dinner table conversation. Jesus didn't seem to engage in polite chit-chat, and He certainly wasn't a nice dinner guest on this occasion.

The Pharisee is surprised when Jesus sits down without washing His hands. This was not a hygiene issue. The Pharisees lived under a religious system that hoped to sanctify the common things of life, even eating. They desired to add a religious dimension to all things. There's nothing wrong with any of this; in fact, there's a lot good with it. But Jesus criticizes the Pharisees. He doesn't like the gap between the Pharisees' external religious practice and their internal belief. They had plenty of outward signs of piety, but the inward motivation was more important to Jesus.

So, Jesus, the invited guest, avoids niceties and addresses the issue. He then speaks our lifewords for today: "You Pharisees clean the outside of the cup and dish, but inside you are full of greed and wickedness" (Luke 11:39). Jesus gives a teaching that ruins dinner. The Pharisee should have known better.

Jesus told them they were more concerned about the rules that were important to them than what was important to God (Luke 11:42). Jesus said they were meticulous about tithing but were not treating people right. They were concerned about keeping parts of the Law but not others. They paid attention to the commands they wanted to keep but ignored ones they didn't.

Do we do that? Are there parts of God's Word that we keep while ignoring others? Some of the Christian life comes easier to us than other parts. Do we ask God for grace to help us in areas where we are weak? These are tough questions because they get to the heart of our faith. I'm sure they were tough for the Pharisee, but he had it coming. He should have known better than to ask Jesus to dinner!

When we talk about an "inside-out" type of Christianity, we are speaking of motivation. Jesus not only wants us to do something, He wants to know why we do it. He wants us to do it for the right reason. That makes Christianity a matter of the heart. That means we can't leave the inside of the cup dirty (Luke 11:39).

Jesus said that we have "dirty cup" Christianity when we love to be seen by others. "Woe to you Pharisees, because you love the most important seats in the synagogues and respectful greetings in the marketplaces" (Luke 11:43). The Pharisees wanted everyone to know they were righteous. They sought attention and desired for people to notice their spiritual accomplishments. Jesus condemned this because it's the wrong motivation. Remember, He's concerned about why you do what you do.

Jesus said in Matthew 6:4 that the reward that God gives should be enough. But the Pharisees wanted an earthly reward of people patting them on the back. They wanted the earthly reward of being known as a pious person. If we let people know what we are doing, we have received our reward. We have not obeyed for the love of the Lord.

Check your motivation! Why do you do what you do? You don't have to go up to others and tell them about it. Just do it and do it quietly. If the cup is clean on the inside, our focus will be on Jesus. This may not be a very spiritual question to ask, but I'm going to ask it anyway. Do you want God to reward you or do you want some human to reward you? What will be the bigger reward? I know the reward is not the reason we should obey, but it's something to think about.

Christianity is not merely a standard of behavior. It's not simply doing these things and not doing those. A Christian is one who has had a heart change and the internal motivations are not what they once were. It's about the "why." Jesus said, "Blessed are the pure in heart" (Matthew 5:8). Jesus knows if your heart is right, your talk and your walk will take care of themselves.

I saw a Dennis the Menace cartoon the other day. His mother had set him in the corner for misbehavior. She asked from the kitchen, "Dennis, are you sitting down?" He said, "Yes, but I'm standing up on the inside!"

Jesus has great patience and compassion with human failure, but He detested hypocrisy. He said, "Isaiah was right when he prophesied about you hypocrites; as it is written: 'These people honor me with their lips, but their hearts are far from me. They worship me in vain; their teachings are but rules taught by men.' You have let go of the commands of God and are holding on to the traditions of men" (Mark 7:6-8). These are our lifewords for today.

I wonder how often we may appear to be outwardly complying with God's commandments and living a Christian life, but we are "standing up on the inside." It's dangerous to be engrossed in religious formality and the traditions of men while neglecting the deeper things of God.

As parents, we don't want our children to obey us in deed only. If they do what we want, but do it with a bad attitude and a sour look on their face, we get after them. Wouldn't it be the same with our heavenly Father? As parents, we want more than outward obedience. Our heavenly Parent does as well.

Change is great on the outside, but real change comes from the inside out. It's not merely cosmetic. It's not simply a skinnier version of the same old you. God wants you to be new from the inside out – spirit, soul, and body. "May the God who gives us peace sanctify us through and through. May your whole spirit, soul, and body be kept free from every fault at the coming of our Lord Jesus Christ" (1 Thessalonians 5:23).

Outside-in Christianity is counterfeit. It leaves you "standing up on the inside." At the judgment, outside-in Christians will hear Jesus say, "Depart from me, I never knew you" (Matthew 7:23). Ask God today to do a deep work in your heart that changes you from the inside out.

It's been my observation as a pastor that people can change on the outside without an inside change. But an inside change ALWAYS shows up on the outside. Christianity is inside out. Outwardly, people can pray, respond to an altar call, be generous in their giving, conform to a standard of behavior, even teach Sunday School, but still not have the heart change that defines a Christian. That's fundamental to our faith. Using a baseball analogy, it's getting to first base.

During the seventh game of the 1924 World Series, a player hit a home run but failed to touch first base. Touching first base is fundamental in baseball and in Christianity as well. Unfortunately, some never get to first base when it comes to faith in Christ. They've never been born again. That's first base for the Christian.

Jesus told Nicodemeus that he would not see the Kingdom of God unless he was "born again" (John 3:3). That's our lifeword for today. Nicodemus was a respected member of the Sanhedrin, which was the ruling body among the Jewish people. The Bible says he came to Jesus "by night" (John 3:2). No doubt, he didn't want to be seen because of his respected position. He was the best religion could produce. And to this good man, Jesus said (in my paraphrase), "Something deeper must happen to you." He hadn't touched first base yet.

This is so hard for people to understand, especially good people. They've been raised in the church and have a lot of religious trappings about them, but Jesus said it's not enough. Nicodemus had a hard time grasping this. He responded to Jesus' teaching on this in John 3:9: "How can this be?"

Remember, one can participate in all the outward practices of the faith, without touching first base. These people have a "form of godliness," but they "deny its power" to transform their lives (2 Timothy 3:5). That power comes from a life that's been born again. That is Christianity 101... kind of like touching first base in baseball.

If your tongue gives you trouble, Jesus said it's not a tongue issue. He said it's what is on the inside that counts. "Make a tree good and its fruit will be good, or make a tree bad and its fruit will be bad…" (Matthew 12:33). The fruit depends on the tree. A tongue issue is the result of a heart problem. You've heard people say, "Let's get to the root of the issue." If the root is bad, the fruit will be. Jesus said, "…the mouth speaks what the heart is full of" (Matthew 12:34).

Our lifeword today is from Psalm 19:14: "Let the words of my mouth and the meditation of my heart be acceptable in your sight, O LORD, my Rock and my Redeemer." The Psalmist says the mouth and the heart work together. It's not an "either-or" thing. The words from a mouth are tied to what's in one's heart. When our words are harsh, we can work on those words and that may help some, but our time would be better spent getting to the root of the problem… our hearts. Ask God to change your heart and watch what happens to your tongue.

Jesus harped on this inside-out living time and time again. Jesus called the Pharisees "whitewashed tombs" because they looked good on the outside, yet on their inside they were full of "dead men's bones" (Matthew 23:27-28).

Because inside-out living is the very core of Christianity, it's crucial we follow Solomon's command to guard our hearts: "Above all else, guard your heart, for everything you do flows from it" (Proverbs 4:23). Because we live in the world, we are exposed to things that can pollute our hearts. Things we see and hear will affect our hearts and show up in our speech. Therefore, guarding your heart is the same as guarding your tongue. Remember Matthew 5:8 from a few days ago? "Blessed are the pure in heart." If your heart is right, your tongue will follow.

Apples don't come from peach trees. Peaches don't come from apple trees. If we want a certain fruit, we must start with the root… the tree. The same is true of our speech. If we want certain words to come out of our mouths, we must start with the root… the heart.

As we conclude our week of devotions concerning inside-out living, let's say the same thing again, but in another way. As we read the Bible, Old Testament and New, we see a lot of "do's." Do this... do that... don't do this... don't do that. It's easy to come to the conclusion that the Christian life is about our behavior. It is, of course... but it's not about our behavior first. It is first and foremost about what's going on inside. Yes, the Christian life is about doing. But it's about being first. Being before doing.

Well-meaning Christians can get so focused on what God wants us to do that we lose sight of the fact that He calls us first to "be." Jesus said we are salt and light (Matthew 5:13-16). Since that's who we are, we don't have to go around "doing salt" and "doing light"; we just have to "be" those things. As the text says, "Let your light shine." Just be who you are. Being before doing.

In the Old Testament, Ezra was a priest who led Jewish exiles from captivity in Babylon to Jerusalem. As a priest, he led the people spiritually. One verse in the book of Ezra shows his priorities. "For Ezra had prepared his heart to seek the Law of the LORD, and to do it, and to teach statutes and ordinances in Israel" (Ezra 7:10). Being before doing.

Ezra "prepared his heart to seek the law of the Lord." He first got his heart right. Ezra then did what was in his heart. "Ezra prepared his heart to seek the Law of the Lord and to do it..." Behavior is part and parcel to the life of God's people, but it flows from a prepared heart. Finally, Ezra taught "statutes and ordinances in Israel." Any good teacher knows that you can only teach what you have.

It's a terrible yoke around our neck to try to do things without the internal drive or compulsion. Our lifeword today is Jesus saying, "Come to me, all you who are weary and burdened, and I will give you rest. Take my yoke upon you and learn from me, for I am gentle and humble in heart, and you will find rest for your souls" (Matthew 11:28-29). If the Christian life is a burden to you, come to Jesus and allow Him to turn you inside out. Then you can be... before you do.

The Bible is a very practical book. Much of its teaching is down to earth and very useful in our day-to-day life. Even an atheist can find the Bible helpful in living a successful life. For instance, who can deny the practicality of Scripture's definition of love? "Love is patient, love is kind. It does not envy, it does not boast, it is not proud. It does not dishonor others, it is not self-seeking, it is not easily angered, it keeps no record of wrongs. Love does not delight in evil but rejoices with the truth. It always protects, always trusts, always hopes, always perseveres. Love never fails" (1 Corinthians 13:4-8). Even an atheist is a better spouse if those words are taken to heart.

Everyone, saint and sinner alike, needs to internalize Romans 12:18. It's our lifeword for today. "If it is possible, as much as it depends upon you, live at peace with all men." It's fascinating to me to see what the verse doesn't say. It doesn't say live at peace with all men. That sounds like something the Bible may say. It certainly sounds spiritual. But our lifeword says, "If it is possible, live at peace with all men." God knows there are some people it's not possible to live peacefully with. No matter how deeply devoted to Jesus you are, no matter how many times you turn the other cheek (Matthew 5:39, some people are nuts! Can I say that and still be a Christian? I hope so, because it's true. Another truth is: there are people who think I'm nuts!

Some people won't allow you to live at peace with them no matter how hard you try. Have you learned this yet? There are some people who, no matter what you do, will just not like you. It doesn't have anything to do with you. It has to do with their pain and their hurt. If that's the case, realize it's not about you. Then, move on. Don't beat yourself up. God knows, and He understands.

If my dad said this to me once, he said it to me a hundred times: "Better to keep your mouth shut and be thought a fool, than open it and remove all doubt." Mark Twain is credited with this proverb, but it's actually from the Bible. Proverbs 17:28 says, "Even a fool who keeps silent is considered wise; When he closes his lips, he is deemed intelligent." Mark Twain is not remembered as a Christian, but he must have gone around quoting the Bible. That's because Scripture is full of good advice for living that anyone, believer or unbeliever, can benefit from.

Our lifeword for today is very practical and is good advice even if you're an atheist. "If it is possible, as much as it depends upon you, live at peace with all men" (Romans 12:18). When I read this, I'm reminded of Jesus' words from the Sermon on the Mount: "Blessed are the peacemakers…" (Matthew 5:9). Peacemakers are blessed, but I need to tell you another truth. Peacemaking and peace-achieving aren't the same thing. It takes two to tango and two to make peace. Both parties must want peace for peace-achieving to happen. You must try, as the verse says. But you, and you alone, can't make peace.

You're blessed if your heart desires peacemaking. Don't feel you've failed if you don't achieve peace. The verse says, "As much as it depends upon you." The Apostle Paul is so practical here. He acknowledges that you are not responsible for the choices of others. You are responsible for you. You are not responsible for the other person. If you're not at peace with someone, it should not be caused by you. There may be times when peace cannot be achieved. If that happens, it should be because of the decisions and attitudes of others. But as for you, seek peace!

So, how do we react if peace is not possible? Right here in Romans 12, Paul gives us directions: "Be devoted to one another in love. Honor one another above yourselves…Be joyful in hope, patient in affliction, faithful in prayer…Bless those who persecute you; bless and do not curse…Do not repay anyone evil for evil…Do not take revenge…" (Romans 12:10-19).

This week, we've said the Bible can be very practical, even for an unbeliever. A lot of down to earth, rubber meets the road, kind of things are found in God's Word. Saints and sinners alike would better their lives by following it. One of the most usable verses is found in Romans 12:18, and it's our lifeword for today: "If it is possible, as much as it depends upon you, live at peace with all men."

There are two words in this verse that make it very hard, almost unreasonable. Paul said, "all men." The Greek words that Paul chooses are used to describe all of mankind. Paul chose an all-encompassing phrase. It is inclusive of the whole human race, not just my family and friends. I'm to live at peace with "all men."

No one faced more opposition in his ministry than Paul. Many of his letters were written because of conflict in churches over his teachings. There were also individuals who sought to undermine his leadership. Sometimes, the opposition came in the form of false accusations and unfair criticisms. Yet, through this verse, he teaches to do everything we can to live at peace with "all men."

Seeking peace does not mean denying the truth or sticking my head in the sand because of differences I may have with others. Paul did not compromise biblical truth in an effort to make peace. He confronted Peter and told him his conduct was wrong. (Galatians 2:12). Peace at the expense of truth is a fake peace. There are times when we need to stand firm.

The phrase "all men" probably brings a difficult person to mind. Negotiating with this person will not always be fruitful. You may be exhausted from trying to fix something that can't be fixed. Remember, through this verse, the Holy Spirit isn't saying you have to agree with "all men" or condone what "all men" do. It simply means you choose not to hold a grudge, or resent the person, or have bitterness in your heart. The Christian's heart's desire should be peace. As much as it depends on you, may God give you the grace to live at peace with "all men."

We've said for the last three days that Romans 12:18 is right down where the rubber meets the road. "If it is possible, as much as it depends on you, live at peace with all men." So, in an effort to be practical, let's look at some very doable steps that help us "live at peace with all men."

1) Take the initiative. In Matthew 5:23-24, Jesus said, "If you are offering your gift at the altar and there remember that your brother has something against you, leave your gift there in front of the altar. First go and be reconciled to your brother; then come and offer your gift." In times of conflict, it doesn't matter if you're the offended or the offender, you make the first move.

2) Get face to face. The scripture above says "Go." Emails, texts, and phone calls are not good enough. Most of communication is body language. I must read theirs, and they must read mine for us to communicate properly.

3) Pray before, during, and after the meeting. If the person is a Christian, pray together. "Pray without ceasing" (1 Thessalonians 5:17).

4) Put yourself in the other person's shoes. Philippians 2:4 says, "Each of you should look not only to your own interests, but also to the interests of others." Someone said, "Seek first to understand and then to be understood."

5) Talk about it... don't argue about it. Proverbs 15:1 says, "A gentle answer turns away wrath, but a harsh word stirs up anger." It takes two to have an argument. Choose not to argue and calmly deal with the issues.

6) Reconciliation of the relationship is the goal. You don't have to get your way. You don't have to come out on top. A "win" is for the relationship to be restored.

As we seek to "live at peace with all men," the way we choose to communicate is vitally important. In fact, few things in life are as important to us as this skill. Almost all areas of our lives suffer if we don't continually improve our ability to communicate. Our lifeword today comes from James 1:19: "Be quick to listen, slow to speak and slow to become angry."

Your friends and family will be amazed at how much better you communicate if you simply close your mouth and listen. Listening is hard work. Listening and hearing are not the same thing. Hearing is passive, and listening is active. If I'm not actively listening, it's easy for my mind to wander, and I end up pretending that I'm listening. A good question someone asked me years ago has dramatically improved my skills in this area. "Are you listening with the intent to listen, or are you listening with the intent of speaking?" Unfortunately, so many times, I find myself waiting for someone to stop talking so that I can talk. That's the opposite of listening. "If one gives an answer before he hears, that is his folly and shame" (Proverbs 18:13).

As a pastor, I've had many people in my office complaining of marriage trouble. Many times, I hear the same things. "He doesn't listen to me!" "Oh yeah, you never listen to me!" Much conflict comes in a marriage when you don't feel like you're being heard. You see, when we are quick to listen, we give the speaker respect. It's a way we show we value them. We give them weight in our lives by simply listening. Husbands, wives, dads, moms, employees, and employers, a crucial part of communication is looking people right in the eye and NOT being quick to speak, but being quick to listen.

As we seek to "live at peace with all men," the more we listen, the better chance we have for peace. Listening creates acceptance and openness. It conveys the message that you are not judging them. Also, listening promotes being heard. People are more likely to listen to you if you've listened to them. Listening isn't loving, but it's pretty close.

Our lifeword again today comes from James 1:19. The Bible says we should "be quick to listen, slow to speak, and slow to become angry." Wisdom begins when I listen more than I talk. A quickness to listen is a trait of a humble person. Paul says in Philippians 2:3, "Do nothing out of selfish ambition or vain conceit. Rather, in humility value others above yourselves." I obey that verse when I listen. Listening means that I don't view myself as wise in my own eyes (Proverbs 12:15).

When I'm slow to speak, I'm not only practicing good communication skills; I'm being wise as well. Proverbs 10:19 says, "When words are many, sin is not absent. But he who holds his tongue is wise." The Bible says love is patient (1 Corinthians 13:4). So, waiting before I respond is a loving response. Speaking quickly can be foolish. "Do you see someone who speaks in haste? There is more hope for a fool than for them" (Proverbs 29:20). When I'm slow to speak, I'm more likely to think about what I'm going to say.

Our lifeword says I should be "slow to become angry." If I'm not, I'm throwing a stick of dynamite into the communication process. As soon as emotion and anger enter, communication ceases. Proverbs 29:11 says, "A fool gives full vent to his anger but a wise man keeps himself under control." You are a better communicator if you keep yourself under control. By the way, self-control is a fruit of the Spirit.

When I speak, it is so important that my words "benefit those who listen." Other translations say, "Give grace to those who hear" (Ephesians 4:29). Gracious words may be tender or tough, depending on the situation. But they are always thought out and measured. Also, when fewer words are spoken, when your words are concise, there is less chance for misunderstanding.

Our lifeword today is full of wisdom for those who want to "live at peace with all men." It's very difficult to pursue peace in our lives if we turn a blind eye to God's instructions about how to communicate effectively.

Proverbs come from all walks of life, not just the Bible. You will find many secular proverbs that agree with the wisdom written down by King Solomon in the Book of Proverbs. Here's an example: "Write insults in sand, kindness in stone." This is very similar to the counsel found in Proverbs 12:16: "Fools show their annoyance at once, but the prudent overlook an insult." Those are our lifewords for today.

If I'm going to be a peacemaker, this verse is of paramount importance to me. Life is full of little offenses and maybe some not so little. A fool flies off the handle at these irritations. The wise person allows them to roll off their back. Jesus said, "Blessed are the meek, for they will inherit the earth" (Matthew 5:5). He also spoke of turning the other cheek (Matthew 5:39). No doubt Jesus had in mind our lifeword for today when He spoke these words.

We've got a problem in today's society. It's almost a badge of honor to get offended. It is way too easy to say something that offends this group or that organization. Someone is always getting bent out of shape about something. That's 180 degrees opposite from biblical teaching.

As Christians, we are followers of Christ. He was laughed at and about. He was misunderstood. He was cursed, and He was spat upon. Please hear me, the enemy of your souls wants you to get offended. He wants you to have your toes stepped on. He loves it when you have your feathers ruffled because of some little irritation or offense. For you to pursue peace with others, you first have to be at peace yourself. One of the ways that can happen is to overlook an insult.

One of the most basic questions anyone could be asked about our faith is, "What is the gospel?" I was watching a video the other day, and someone answered this question by saying, "The golden rule, do to others as you would have them do to you." The dictionary says the gospel is the teaching of Jesus recorded for us in the first four books of the New Testament. It's crucial we know what the gospel is because Paul says, "By this gospel you are saved" (1 Corinthians 15:2). He also says the gospel "is the power of God that brings salvation to everyone who believes: first to the Jew, then to the Gentile" (Romans 1:16). Something as important as this deserves our attention and is something we should be certain about.

Romans 1:1 says, "Paul, a servant of Christ Jesus, called to be an apostle and set apart for the gospel of God." That's our lifeword for today. Paul also writes in Galatians 1:1, "that the gospel that was preached by me is not man's gospel." Whatever this gospel is, it's from God and not from man. God initiated this message. It's His invention, and it's by His composition. So, we must never alter it. We don't improve it or make it more user-friendly. We must respond to it, but we don't mess with it.

The Galatians tried to mess with it, and Paul said they were "foolish" (Galatians 3:1). He said they had turned to a "different gospel" (Galatians 1:6) and were trying to "pervert the gospel" (Galatians 1:7). If anyone preaches a different gospel, Paul says, "Let them be under God's curse!" (Galatians 1:8). Then he repeats that in Galatians 1:9.

What is this gospel? **G**od's **O**nly **S**on **P**rovides **E**verlasting **L**ife. The gospel is about what has been done for you, not what you do. God gave. We believe. Then we become (John 1:12). "For the wages of sin is death, but the gift of God is eternal life through Jesus Christ, our Lord" (Romans 3:23). You may describe it differently, but you can't change it. It's God's gospel.

"For God so loved the world that He gave His one and only Son, that whoever believes in Him should not perish but have everlasting life" (John 3:16). Those are our lifewords for today. Any discussion of the gospel would not be complete without looking at this verse.

Why do we even have a gospel? John 3:16 tells us. "For God so loved the world…" The motivation behind God's gospel is His love for us. Every man, woman, boy, and girl is the recipient of God's love. No matter how sinful you may be… no matter what sin you have committed… God loves you. Love is not only something God does; it's who He is. 1 John 4:16 says, "God is love." God's love is unconditional, and it has no end. This love is hard to comprehend. The Apostle Paul prays that we "may have power, together with all the Lord's holy people, to grasp how wide and long and high and deep is the love of Christ." (Ephesians 3:18).

The love of God motivated Him to act. And our lifeword defines that act as the giving of "His one and only Son."

This giving literally demonstrated God's love. We learned in 1 Corinthians 13 that love is not just a feeling. Love is a verb. Love is an action. God gave His Son. "God demonstrates His own love toward us, in that while we were still sinners, Christ died for us" (Romans 5:8).

Because of this, it's important to know that God's gospel is centered in the person of Jesus Christ. Any gospel that does not have Jesus at the heart is a perversion. (Galatians 1:7). "There is one God and one mediator between God and mankind, the man Christ Jesus." (1 Timothy 2:5). Without Jesus, there is no gospel. Let me be more biblical. Without Jesus and His work on the cross, there is no gospel. Wait a minute; I must go farther. Without Jesus and His death, burial, and resurrection, there is no gospel. That's why the gospel is not only the gospel of God (Romans 1:1); it's the gospel of Christ (2 Corinthians 2:12).

We started breaking down John 3:16 yesterday, so let's complete that today. So far, we've seen that God's love motivated Him to give. Now, let's add the "If." There's always an *if*, right? Some call it a catch. The good news of the gospel has to come with a catch, doesn't it? It's too good to be true. Everything in life has an *if*. The gospel does too... it's our belief. "Whoever believes in Him." There is a human element of the gospel. We must accept, receive, or believe the gospel, whatever terminology you choose to use.

Salvation can't be earned by living a good life. If that was the case, why did Jesus have to die (Galatians 2:21)? Many have said that salvation is spelled "d-o-n-e," not "d-o." Still, some believe there are things they do or don't do that will earn them eternal life. Jesus, on the cross, said our salvation is done. "It is finished" (John 19:30). We simply respond to God's gracious gift. We put our trust in ourselves aside and trust Jesus' work on the cross.

Now listen closely. Believing in a biblical way is more than giving mental assent to the truths of the gospel. Let's say you were out hiking in the country and came across an old wooden bridge. I mean really old. You look at it and believe it would hold you. You see others walking across it, so you know it would hold you. But so far, your "belief" is not biblical belief because it's only in your head. Not until you step on the bridge do you believe in a biblical way. Biblical belief has to do with trust and commitment.

Finally, our verse says, "should not perish but have everlasting life." God's love motivated Him to give, so, there's an *if* and a *then*. If we believe, we THEN have a promise. And it's an eternal promise of everlasting life. God will keep His promise IF we respond with biblical belief. Have you done that? Have you ceased trusting in yourself and now trust in what God has done through His Son Jesus Christ? IF you have, THEN you can claim the promise!

Three days ago, I asked you, "What is the gospel?" We've used Romans 1:1 and said it is "the gospel of God." We don't mess with it or change it. It's His. We can't monkey with it. Also, two days ago, we said it was the "gospel of Christ" (2 Corinthians 2:12). Any presentation or explanation of the gospel must be centered in the death, burial, and resurrection of Jesus Christ.

The Apostle Paul also refers to the gospel as "my gospel." "Remember Jesus Christ, raised from the dead, descended from David. This is my gospel." (2 Timothy 2:8). There must be a time in all of our lives that God's gospel, this gospel of Christ, becomes ours. Understanding that this gospel comes from God and is lock, stock, and barrel about the person of Jesus Christ is crucial, but it's not enough. For the gospel to do its work in my life, it has to become personal. It has to be applied to my heart.

It's 100% correct that Jesus died for the world (John 3:16). That means everyone. But it must go deeper than that. There must be a day when I take it out of the context of the world and bring it home to my own sinful heart. He died for me. I am the sinner. He died for my sins. "For God so loved me…"

There was a day when Jesus asked the disciples, "'Who do people say the Son of Man is?' 'Some say John the Baptist; others say Elijah; and still others, Jeremiah or one of the prophets.' 'But what about you? Who do you say I am?' Simon Peter answered, 'You are the Christ, the Son of the living God'" (Mark 8:27-29).

It's great that it's your mother's gospel or your father's. I'm glad you were raised in a Christian home. I hope you attend a gospel-preaching church and can say "This is the gospel my church preaches." But until you make it "your gospel," the gospel has not done its work in your life.

June 3rd

A while back , I spoke to a friend of mine who is ill. He knows he's ill. He's not sure what the disease is, but he knows something's wrong. He refuses to go to the doctor. He doesn't want to know the bad news. No one enjoys hearing bad news, yet most of us know of its importance.

The word for "gospel" in the New Testament comes from a word that means good or pleasant, plus another word that refers to angels delivering a message. So, gospel means "good message" or "good news." While the gospel is the best news of all time, there is corresponding bad news. We are sinners, separated from God because of our sin, and we can't do anything that will merit heaven. That's bad news. Until we know we have a disease called sin, we won't recognize our need for a Savior. The bad news awakens in us the need for good news.

But it's important that the bad news ends there. The gospel is not loaded with do's and don'ts. It's not filled with you better go here and don't ever go there again. It's not loaded with condemnation. All of that is bad news. Our lifeword today is from John 3:17: "For God did not send his Son into the world to condemn the world, but to save the world through him." The gospel of God, centered in Jesus, offers forgiveness, a fresh start, and a new perspective on all things.

"The wages of sin is death..." (Romans 6:23) must be understood for a vibrant Christian experience. After all, the good news is "good" for a reason... because there's bad news. If I never know what I've been saved from, I certainly won't understand "Amazing grace, how sweet the sound, that saved a wretch like me."

A good diagnosis starts with bad news; the doctor of our souls has a remedy. The cure rate is 100% and will work every time if you believe the good news. "...but the gift of God is eternal life through Christ Jesus our Lord" (Romans 6:23).

Some of you will remember the story of the 33 Chilean miners who were trapped for 69 days one-half mile underground. Finally, on October 13, 2010, the men were brought to the surface. All were alive. One billion people watched worldwide. It is arguably the greatest rescue of all time.

All the miners were brought to the surface in a specially designed capsule. NASA engineers were responsible for the design, called Fenix. The interior, large enough for only one miner, was equipped with a microphone, oxygen, and wheels to make the 15-minute trip to the top as smooth as possible. Without this capsule, all the men would have died.

None of the miners complained that this method of rescue was chosen. They knew they were at the mercy of the rescuer. There was only one way to safety, and all the men were thankful for that way. Our lifeword today is from John 14:6, where Jesus said, "I am the way, the truth and the life. No one comes to the Father except by Me". Many resent the gospel because of the exclusivity of "one way."

By definition, truth is narrow. 2 + 2 = 4. That's a very narrow statement. How intolerant of mathematicians to say there's only one answer! My answer of 5 should be as good as your answer of 3. This is the way the world thinks. But, truth be known, if 2 + 2 does not equal four, our world can no longer function. It would be chaos without this intolerant statement.

If God had other options to save us, don't you think He would have utilized them? Why would God have sent His Son to die a brutal death? If there were other ways, other gospels, why did God offer His own Son to die?

Remember, this is not about which religion is right. We don't need a religion; we need to be rescued! The miners needed good news. Their rescue came by one means. There are many religions but only one gospel, and that gospel has only one Rescuer.

There are many verses one can use to explain the gospel. Our lifeword today is one of those. It comes from Ephesians 2:8-9: "For by grace you have been saved through faith, not of yourselves; it is the gift of God, not of works, so no one will boast." These verses say that our salvation is a gift of God's grace. If this is true, why are there people trying to be good enough? Hey, here's a news flash... you're not good enough, and you never will be. Stop trying. Don't stop trying to be good; just stop trying to be good enough.

Trying to be good enough is antithetical to the gospel. The gospel is there because you're not good enough. There is only one who was good enough, and His name is Jesus. He died for you. Trust in Him and His work on the cross and stop trying to be good enough.

We all know we don't get anything for free in this life. After all, if it's going to be, it's up to me. Maybe that's why people try to be good enough. That's certainly the way of the world, but it's not the way of the gospel. The gospel says you can't be good enough.

If good people go to Heaven, how good do you have to be? Where is the list of good things I have to do? How do you know if you've done enough good? The "good people go to Heaven" system makes no sense. Galatians chapter 2 says if you can be good enough, why did Jesus have to die? Don't stop trying to be good; stop trying to be good enough.

This Sunday at church, you'll have some who are there trying to be good enough. They are there paying off a debt, doing what they have to do. They hope God sees they are being good. Then you have people who believe the gospel, which says they aren't good enough and never will be. They have a smile on their face. They aren't there because they have to be but because they want to be. And they sing... man, do they sing. "Amazing love, how can it be, that Thou my God would die for me."

Today, let's start looking at the Ten Commandments. I would guess that most Americans believe that the Ten Commandments are a guide to a good life. That is encouraging until you find out that most people can't name more than four of them. Most people have heard of the Ten Commandments, but most people don't know them well enough to try to consciously live them out.

Before we go any farther, allow me to anticipate a question you may have. "Why study the Ten Commandments?" A person who knows their Bible may say, "We're not under the Law, we're under grace!" That is true, of course, but there are many reasons why this study is worth our time. Let me list just one here.

Humans have always needed a standard of right and wrong. Even Pontius Pilate said, "What is truth?" (John 18:38). If we don't have a standard by which we live, the world would be in chaos. We need law. Law is not bad though grace is better.

Where does law come from? It could be left up to the individual. But then what is right for this person would not be right for that person. We could be good Americans and say the majority rules. But the majority will change its mind from time to time. The majority can be fickle. The majority can be wrong. Both of these options, the individual and the majority, are problematic. Don't we need an absolute standard—one that is universal and will never change? Read the words of ABC's Ted Koppel in a commencement address at Duke University: "What Moses brought down from Mount Sinai were not ten suggestions; they are commandments. 'Are', not 'were'. The sheer beauty of the ten commandments is that they codify in a handful of words acceptable human behavior, not just for then or now, but for all time."

The Commandments are God's words-not man's. They have never been repealed. You can take them out of our schools and out of our courthouses, but not out of our hearts. We KNOW they are true. We need them.

Ron Mehl wrote a book that has greatly helped me in the way I look at the Ten Commandments. The book is titled, *The Tender Commandments*. Mehl pastored a church in Oregon for many years until his death in 2003. He's helped me see these as more than eternal standards of truth. To me, they have become words from the heart of a loving Father. I have taken much of this devotion from Pastor Mehl's writings.

I bet you don't describe the Ten Commandments as a love letter from the very hand of God. But think about it. What loving parent does not set boundaries for their children simply because they love them? The same is true of our Heavenly Parent.

Some people see these commandments as just the opposite. They don't hear love in these statements. They hear the balls and chains. If that's true, they may have missed the context of the commandments. Read these words from Exodus 19, the chapter preceding the first giving of the commandments. "And Moses went up to God, and the LORD called to him from the mountain saying, Thus you shall say to the house of Jacob, and tell the children of Israel: 'You have seen what I did to the Egyptians, and how I bore you on eagles' wings and brought you to Myself. Now therefore if you will indeed obey My voice and keep My covenant, then you shall be a special treasure to Me above all people; for all the earth is Mine. And you shall be to Me a kingdom of priests and a holy nation.' These are the words which you shall speak to the children of Israel" (Exodus 19:3-6). Those are our lifewords for today.

Are there any more precious and tender words in all of Scripture? God has spoken to His people. He has provided a way for them to walk with Him. He has provided a way of blessing for them. They come from the heart of a loving Father to His children. And He wrote them in stone... a Valentine's Day card written in stone. The Tender Commandments.

We have the Ten Commandments given to us in Exodus 20:3-17. Verse 2 of chapter 20 is very important. Don't skip over it. God said, "I am the LORD your God, who brought you out of the land of Egypt, out of the house of slavery." God gave these commandments after He had freed them from Egyptian bondage. Remember, never in the Old Testament do we learn that keeping the Law will result in our salvation. The notion that we can merit God's approval by keeping the Law is not found in the Bible.

The Bible is not made up of the Old Testament (a book of law) and the New Testament (a book of grace). In Genesis 15:6, we read that Abraham "believed in the LORD; and He reckoned it to him as righteousness." We see faith in the 15th chapter of the book... faith that the LORD counted as righteousness. That sounds like New Testament theology to me.

The most important truth we can learn from the Ten Commandments is they are rooted deeply in the grace of God. The Israelites were not freed from Egypt because they were good but because God was gracious. And now, in response to His grace, the Israelites are called to walk in His ways. We, who are Christians, were dead in our sins, but God made us alive through Christ (Ephesians 2:5). We now are eager to do His will because of His grace in our lives (Titus 2:11-14).

We are saved by grace through our faith (Ephesians 2:8). Our obedience is in response to God's saving work. We obey not as slaves but as children of God (Galatians 4:7). In the Old Testament and New, grace comes before works of the law. God starts the work; we respond to Him. God is the initiator, and we are the responders.

God saves people before He changes them. We don't have to clean ourselves up before we come to Jesus. Come, just as you are, with full faith and trust in Jesus and watch the change start to happen.

When one thinks about moral obligations, our minds usually go to our obligations to each other. So, you would expect to find that in the Ten Commandments. Of course, you do, just not at the top. The Ten Commandments start with our moral obligation toward God. The Bible has no concept of morality in our relationships that's not first grounded in a right relationship with God.

The first commandment is our lifeword for today, and it reminds us to keep first things first. "You shall have no other gods before Me" (Exodus 20:3). This commandment speaks to the totality of our lives. It says God must have the supreme place. He must have no competitor.

One day, the Pharisees tested Jesus with this question: "What is the greatest commandment?" He responded by saying, "You shall love the Lord your God with all your heart, with all your soul, and with all your mind. This is the first and great commandment" (Matthew 22:37–38). Jesus refers to this as the first and the great commandment. He's telling us how to obey Exodus 20:3. This means we focus on Him. He is true north on the compass of our hearts. We have no other gods by loving God!

In 1952, the Encyclopedia Britannica published a 54-volume set of books titled *The Great Books of the Western World*. This set is filled with the writings of the greatest contributors to science, medicine, law, and so forth. More pages are given to God, than any other topic. When asked why, the publishing chairman, Mortimer J. Adler, responded, "It's because more consequences for life follow from this one issue than any other issue."

The first Commandment reorients the focus of our lives from ourselves to God. That's foundational for living a life of faith. This commandment sets our bearings. It points us in the right direction. If we get first things first, it's more likely that all other things will fall in place (Matthew 6:33).

While the first commandment is about *who* we worship, the second commandment is about *how* we worship. God says there is a correct way to worship, and it has nothing to do with contemporary or traditional. Both are irrelevant if we don't worship God's way, which is in spirit and in truth (John 4:24).

God is spirit, and we must worship Him in spirit. We are not to make any images to facilitate worship. That's what the second commandment says, and it's our lifeword for today. "You shall not make for yourself an image in the form of anything in heaven above or on the earth beneath or in the waters below. You shall not bow down to them or worship them" (Exodus 20:4-5). We must worship Him in all His unseen splendor.

Worship must also be in truth. Our services can be vibrant, hands lifted, tears flowing, but if there is not truth, it's not biblical worship. If we are not singing and preaching truth from God's Word, then we fall short of God's way to worship. God knows if we don't worship in truth, we will redefine Him or reduce Him.

We humans can choose who we worship. We have the ability to redefine Him and make Him in our image. We don't carve an image out of stone, but we redefine Him when we worship less than the biblical God.

God plays many roles in Scripture. He's the Father, Shepherd, Creator, King, and so forth. All of us have our preferred roles. But if we see Him only in that role, we reduce Him. Yes, He's a Father, but He's also a Priest. Yes, He's a King, but He is also a Friend. There is no one image that can truly capture who He is.

God is serious about how He's worshipped. Don't break the second commandment by coming up with an image. I guarantee you it will redefine or reduce Him. He is more than any image can convey.

In my opinion, the third commandment is the most misunderstood of God's Ten Commandments. It's also a lot more serious that most think. Our lifeword today is from Exodus 20:7: "You shall not take the name of the Lord your God in vain, for the Lord will not hold him guiltless who takes His name in vain." My dad used to tell me, "Remember you are an Atherton." Basically, he was telling me not to disgrace the family name. That gets to the core of the third commandment.

"Vain" means empty or meaningless. Don't use God's name in an empty or meaningless way. Of course, we can do this in our speech. Swearing or cursing like "GD" or "JC" is the common way this commandment has been understood. But I think it just skims the surface of the true meaning here. The Hebrew word translated as "take" literally means "to carry or to bear." So, you have, "Do not carry the name of the Lord your God in an empty or meaningless way."

To carry God's name honorably means that if we profess to be Christians, then our lives should show that. If we carry His name by calling ourselves the people of God, then we should act like it. We should not attach the name Christian to our lives in an empty or meaningless way.

Jesus said, "You are the light of the world...Let your light so shine before men, that they may see your good works and glorify your Father in heaven" (Matthew 5:14-16). He also said, "'These people draw near to Me with their mouth, but their heart is far from Me. In vain they worship Me..." (Matthew 15:8-9).

God is our Father, and like most fathers, He's concerned about the family name. He commands His children to carry His name respectfully and not in vain. God includes a warning for those who don't : "For the Lord will not hold him guiltless that takes His name in vain." That's very serious and sobering. Such is the third commandment.

"Remember the Sabbath day by keeping it holy. Six days you shall labor and do all your work, but the seventh day is a sabbath to the Lord your God" (Exodus 20:8-10). The world tells us that more work equals more success. But God, who made our bodies, said we need rest and worship.

The Sabbath command is given so that we can learn to trust God. Do I trust God enough to take a day off? Do I trust Him enough to believe Him when He says six days of work is enough? Do I trust Him to take the time out of the work week to worship?

Jesus got in a lot of trouble over the Sabbath. He did not interpret it the way the religious people of the day did. On the Sabbath, Jesus did what was RIGHT. "…He went to the synagogue, as was His custom" (Luke 4:16). With all Jesus had on His plate, He considered it important to worship and rest.

Jesus did what was NECESSARY and GOOD. His disciples picked grain and ate it on the Sabbath. They had to eat, and Jesus saw no problem with that. Jesus healed on the Sabbath, much to the dismay of the Pharisees.

Jesus said the Sabbath was "made for man and not man for the Sabbath" (Mark 2:27). So, He understood the Sabbath as a day to do what is BENEFICIAL FOR YOU. The day is a gift God has given you. Maybe you need to exercise. Maybe you need to take a nap. Maybe you need to work in the flower garden. It's your day. What do you do that benefits your rest and worship the most?

We don't often see New Testament Christians observing a seventh-day Sabbath. Instead, the first day of the week is set aside for Christian worship. Whatever your feeling is about the Sabbath, Paul said that we should BE CONVINCED in our own mind about this day. He said not to let other people judge you (Romans 14:5). He also wrote that the Sabbath was a "shadow of things to come." The real thing is found in Christ (Colossians 2:16-17).

Commandment 5 says to "Honor your father and your mother, so that you may live long in the land the Lord your God is giving you" (Exodus 20:12). Commandments 1-4 speak to our moral obligations to God. Commandments 5-10 deal with our moral obligations to each other.

The first of our human relationships is with our parents. God is amazingly realistic in this commandment. He does not ask us to have greeting card sentiments for our parents. The commandment does not say to love your mother and father. God knew how difficult those relationships could be. He says to respect them and give them weight. The literal definition of the Hebrew word translated "honor" is to "make heavy." Give weight to the place God has given parents.

Honor changes according to our age. For children, honor means to obey. Parents need to teach willing obedience. Sometimes, it's enough to say, "Because I said so," but it will not cut it over the long haul. Children need to be taught why it's beneficial to obey. As kids become teens, this obedience continues, but it must turn into respect. The teen years are very difficult. Kids are getting more freedom and are making more of their own decisions. They may think Mom and Dad are hopelessly out of touch with the real world. During this tough time when kids are struggling, respect must prevail. During the adult years, obedience is not the issue; respect and care take over.

Honor goes both ways. Parents should be honor-worthy. Parents make it a lot easier to be honored if they fulfill their responsibility as parents. What do I do when a parent has not been honor-worthy? Forgiveness is the key. God has forgiven me; shouldn't I forgive my mother or father?

This authority given to moms and dads is the hope of our civilization. God ends the fifth commandment this way: "So that you may live long in the land the Lord your God is giving you" (Exodus 20:12).

There must be more to the sixth commandment than what is obvious. Why would God waste one of His Ten Commandments on a law that seems to be written on our hearts? Doesn't everyone know that it is not right to take someone's life? "You shall not murder" (Exodus 20:13). Even the people that do it know it's not right. There must be something beneath the surface of this command that God is trying to teach us. Of course, He doesn't want us to commit homicide, suicide, or abortion. That's a no-brainer. What is the deeper principle?

God wants us to revere life! We are created in His image, and so, there is a sacredness in our humanness. The Bible says that as Christians, our bodies are the temples of the Holy Spirit (1 Corinthians 6:19). We talk about Jesus living in our hearts. Paul says we can be filled with all the fullness of God (Ephesians 3:19). Because of the sacredness of life, we should take care of our bodies and not mistreat them with habits or practices that can bring damage.

We revere life because life is precious. When I think of life's preciousness, I think of its shortness. I've been around a lot of death beds in my time as a pastor. None of them could believe how fast the time had passed. James says life is but a mist, here today and gone tomorrow (James 4:14).

The Bible says we are made a "little lower than the angels" (Hebrews 2:7). Each life is precious to God. Even those lives that seem to have little worth in this world are precious to God. Especially the ones who don't look like us, talk like us, smell like us, and are not as educated as us. Christians are to have compassion on the needy, drunken, homeless, drug-addicted people of the world. They have worth in God's eyes, and His image is still there.

We should not murder because life is holy. We are created in His image. The song says, "Red, yellow, black, and white, all are precious in His sight." Pro-life is so much more than an anti-abortion slogan. If abortion did not exist, we would still be pro-life because the sixth commandment requires it.

Since the sixth commandment is so loaded with meaning, let's stay there one more day. It's this command that convicts me the most. Now, before you get the wrong impression, I don't want to murder people. Well, maybe a few board members at my church. And there were a few times I could have killed my little brother. But this commandment nails me when Jesus teaches it. He explodes it with meaning. He says if I have murder in my heart, it's just like I did the real thing (Matthew 5:21-22).

Wow, isn't that just like Jesus? He makes Christianity so hard. Jesus says I commit murder by having hateful thoughts or even calling someone an idiot! Perhaps the easiest way to murder is with a dirty look. "If looks could kill, we'd probably all be dead." I wish I could say I've never murdered anyone this way, but I have, and you have too. Actually, if the truth be known, I'm a serial killer.

According to Jesus, harboring anger is to be guilty of what the sixth commandment prohibits. Murder may be carried out with the gun, knife, hand, or heart. God is not pleased by people who manage to control their outward behavior only. What He's looking for is obedience that comes from a heart that's been changed.

Jesus gave us a new command, and it's our lifeword for today from John 13:34: "A new command I give you: Love one another." John later writes that anyone who "hates his brother is a murderer" (1 John 3:15). Sometimes, I wish we were Old Testament people with a "thou shalt" and a "thou shalt not" command. That seems easier to keep and a whole lot less convicting to me. The sixth commandment teaches me I need grace... and lots of it.

I want God to do deeper work in me so that the condition of my heart won't prompt murderous words or looks. How can I keep murder out of my heart? There's only one way, and it's not by trying harder. It's a life filled with the Holy Spirit and allowing Him to work on my murderous heart.

As we look at the seventh commandment, we see that Jesus is up to His same old tricks. Not only do we have the Old Testament command, "You shall not commit adultery" (Exodus 20:14), but we have Jesus raising it to a higher level. He says, "You have heard that it was said, 'You shall not commit adultery.' But I tell you that anyone who looks at a woman lustfully has already committed adultery with her in his heart" (Matthew 5:27-28).

Jesus said that adultery is not in the act. Jesus says it is in the heart. It is in the desire. If I have desired another woman, Jesus says that I have committed adultery in my heart. I've had impure thoughts, and Jesus says that is unfaithfulness. Jesus knows that the thought is the father of the deed. The deed is not the issue. Jesus says the issue is the thought. If we can take care of the thought, the deed won't happen.

Philippians 4:8 says, "Whatever is true, whatever is noble, whatever is right, whatever is pure, whatever is lovely, whatever is admirable—if anything is excellent or praiseworthy—think about such things." Now, let's not harbor false guilt. We can't help thoughts coming into our minds. We can't feel guilty about those stray thoughts, BUT, we don't have to linger on them. We don't have to fondle, wonder, and fantasize about that thought. In Jesus' interpretation of this command, it's here that we cross the line, and it's here that we need God's grace.

One aspect about faithfulness in marriage that doesn't get talked about enough is found in both the Old Testament and New. God's people should marry God's people. Christians should marry Christians. Don't marry outside the faith. If we do, we're making faithfulness and purity more difficult. "Do not be yoked together with unbelievers" (2 Corinthians 6:14). Hear me, single people... hold out! Wait for the right person. In my experience, it's the women who usually compromise here. Gals, don't marry outside of the faith. Trust God for the right man. If you do, staying faithful in marriage is easier.

Since adultery is so prevalent, inside and outside the church, let's linger with the seventh commandment one more day. The magazine *Christianity Today* took a poll of subscribers, asking if they had committed adultery. 23% responded yes. That's 23% of subscribers to a Christian magazine. What would that statistic be outside the Church? The Book of Proverbs speaks plainly. "Do not let your heart turn aside to her ways, do not stray into her paths; for she has cast down many wounded, and all who were slain by her were strong men. Her house is the way to Hell" (Proverbs 7:25-27). Those are our lifewords today.

Is it possible in the 21st century to refrain from sex before marriage and stay sexually faithful during marriage? It all starts with commitment. Until you're willing to jump into the Christian life with both feet, you can give up on being sexually pure. It's my experience it won't happen without you being "all in." Without that kind of commitment, purity and faithfulness in your sexual life is not possible. If you will live by God's ways, your chances of avoiding impurity and unfaithfulness greatly increase. It all starts with a commitment.

In the Old Testament, Job understood this. He said, "I made a covenant with my eyes not to look lustfully at a woman" (Job 31:1). That sounds like commitment to me. Wandering eyes are the real problem. King David allowed his heart to be led by his eyes when he saw a woman bathing (2 Samuel 11). David first committed adultery with his eyes and then with his body.

There's no question that God has made us to be sexual beings. He created man and woman and brought them together. Sex was God's idea. The Christian view of sex is often mischaracterized, but the truth is that God has given sex to us as a gift. You can't read the Bible without coming to that conclusion. God wants to be involved in our sexual lives. He wants to bless our sexuality. But there's a catch. He only blesses it inside the marriage relationship. That's one man and one woman.

The eighth commandment, "You shall not steal", not only shows up in Exodus 20:15 but is repeated in Ephesians 4:28. "Let him who stole steal no longer, but rather let him labor, working with his hands what is good, that he may have something to give him who has need." Those are our lifewords for today.

We all have the need for "stuff." God has ordained work as the means for getting the "stuff" we need. Acquiring by stealing is the opposite of working. Work is not a result of the Fall of Man. Before sin entered the world, "The Lord God took the man and put him in the Garden of Eden to tend and keep it" (Genesis 2:15). Through work we acquire the necessities of life. Paul wrote, "...If anyone will not work, neither shall he eat" (2 Thessalonians 3:10).

Our lifeword says we are to work so that we can give to those who are in need. Needy people are a fact of life. Jesus said, "The poor you will always have with you..." (Matthew 26:11). The needy are not to steal but are to receive from the hands of those who work. The essence of being Christian is giving. We are to be giving people. If I am a "getting" person, it denies my true identity as a Christian.

God's people are to trust Him. When I steal, I'm taking matters into my own hands. I'm being lord of my own life. It's the very epitome of not trusting God and leaning on my own understanding (Proverbs 3:5). God has promised to meet our needs. "And my God will meet all your needs according to the riches of His glory in Christ Jesus" (Philippians 4:19).

The eighth and ninth commandments are about honesty. Without honest people, it's impossible to have a fully functioning society. If dishonesty is not condemned and punished, it becomes one of the chief contributors to the collapse of any nation. It's fundamental to our existence and survival. Any nation that does not value it will crumble under the weight of deception.

Paul Harvey tells the story of four men in search of their golf balls in the high grass, close to the green. One slipped a ball from his pocket and dropped it on the fringe and said, "I found mine." Later, as they were about to putt, the flag was removed from the cup. There was the man's original golf ball. He had made a hole-in-one, but his lie had ruined the accomplishment. "You shall not lie" is a loose, but valid paraphrase of the ninth commandment.

God hates a lying tongue (Proverbs 6:17) because it goes against His nature. He does not lie. He cannot lie. "God is not human, that He should lie..." (Numbers 23:19). When we hear lies, we know they are not of God. Lies have their origination somewhere else, or maybe I should say with someone else.

Satan is the father of lies (John 8:44). Satan told the first lie recorded in the Bible. "The serpent said to the woman, 'You surely will not die!'" (Genesis 3:4). When we lie, we behave like children of the devil instead of children of God. Lying is contrary to who we are as new creations in Christ. "Do not lie to one another, since you have put off the old man with his deeds" (Colossians 3:9).

As we speak the truth, it should be spoken in love (Ephesians 4:15). Sometimes, the truth is hurtful. When this is the case, we should be truthful, but gentle. Our tone of voice and body language are crucial. We should not be happy about telling a hurtful truth, even though it's necessary.

This commandment is written in the language of the courtroom. "You shall not give false testimony against your neighbor" (Exodus 20:16). No nation can have a system of justice without the truth. Life and property cannot be protected without the truth. If lies are allowed to happen during testimony, lives will be destroyed and nations will be in chaos. Perjury must be punished. We see once again that the Ten Commandments are not for religious purposes only. These laws are very practical as well. They are the basis of a functioning society.

We often say the last six commandments are about our relationships with others. That's not wrong, but it's not 100% accurate either. This last commandment is deeply personal. It's internal. It's about our desires. While what's on the inside will have outward manifestations, this last commandment is about my heart. It's more about me than my relationships with others.

Our lifeword today is, "You shall not covet" (Exodus 20:17). I don't use that word covet, and I bet you don't either. It means to have an inordinate desire for what belongs to another and to set my heart on it. Desire alone is not an evil thing. God made this world good, and it's filled with good things to be desired. It's the object of our desire that's the issue.

Coveting happened in the Garden. The Bible tells us, "So when the woman saw that the tree was good for food, that it was pleasant to the eyes, and a tree desirable to make one wise, she took of its fruit and ate" (Genesis 3:6). Did you see the pattern? She saw... she desired... she took. It's the ancient pattern of sin. Coveting is a matter of seeing what I *don't* have instead of what I *do* have.

When I covet, I am discontent. I focus on what I don't have. Discontentment can even make me angry with God over my earthly circumstances. I am not satisfied with Him. I don't see Him as a good Father but One who is holding out on me. When I'm discontent, I see others not as ones to love and encourage but ones who have something I don't have. That leads to jealousy, bitterness, and envy.

Contentment means wanting what God wants for us. Someone has said, "God is most pleased with us when we are most pleased with Him." Contentment is not having all we desire but rejoicing in what we already have. God tells the Hebrews not to covet their neighbors' oxen. There will always be a bigger ox, better job, or nicer car. The secret to contentment is enjoying what you already have. God is good... all the time!

Today, let's wrap up our look at the Ten Commandments. As we look back on them, we see they are a compass. This compass shows us the way we should go. In Isaiah 30:21, God says, "This is the way, walk in it." These commandments show us how we walk with God. In the New Testament, we receive a new command. Jesus said, "A new command I give you: love one another" (John 13:34). It's impossible not to fulfill the new command if we are following the compass of the Ten Commandments.

This compass leads to blessings as well. Psalm 19, which is devoted entirely to God's Word, says, "They are more precious than gold, than much pure gold; they are sweeter than honey, than honey from the honeycomb. By them your servant is warned; in keeping them there is great reward" (19:10-11). We all want to have the blessing of God on our lives. He's told us right here how to do that: "In keeping them there is great reward."

This compass also points us away from danger. Referring to God's Word, our text says, "By them your servant is warned" (Isaiah 19:11). Loving fathers say no. They set boundaries. Our Heavenly Father does as well. He, who sees the beginning from the end, knows what's on the other side of that boundary. He understands the consequences of our behavior. Because God loves us, He warns us. "Thou shalt not" are tender words from the heart of a loving God.

Finally, the most important thing this compass does is point us to Jesus Christ. Our lifeword today is from Romans 3:20. It says, "No man will be made righteous in His sight by observing the law. Rather through the law we become conscious of sin." The Apostle Paul also wrote, "I would not have known sin except through the law" (Romans 7:7). The main purpose of the commandments is not a code of behavior. That is a purpose... just not the main purpose. The commandments are there to point us to Christ. They make us aware of our sin. If we know we are sinners, maybe we'll see our need for a Savior. Hopefully, as we've looked at the Ten Commandments the past two weeks, they have been like a compass that has guided you to Jesus Christ.

Have you ever felt like you just don't fit in? Everyone gets the joke except you? Everyone dressed according to the dress code except you? We all feel that way from time to time… even the Apostle Paul. That's why he wrote our lifeword for today: "…by the grace of God I am what I am…" (1 Corinthians 15:10).

Paul didn't feel like he was in the "in" group. After all, he was not one of the disciples. They had spent three years with Jesus and were firsthand witnesses to all His healings and other miracles. "For I am the least of the apostles and do not even deserve to be called an apostle, because I persecuted the church of God" (1 Corinthians 15:9). Paul may have never felt "worthy" because of his past.

I say, "It is what it is," a lot. When I don't know why something worked out the way it did, "Well, it is what it is." In a similar way, Paul says, "I am what I am." This was Paul's recognition that what was in the past, is in the past. There are some things he regretted, but he believed God would use them all to further the gospel.

God had prepared Paul for the ministry laid out for him. So, instead of moaning and groaning about what he lacked and how different he was from others, Paul basically just said, "It is what it is." "…by the grace of God I am what I am…" (1 Corinthians 15:10).

Paul surrendered his past to the grace of God. He believed that God's grace was enough to overcome the inadequacies he felt. He evidently did this or he would not have had such a powerful ministry. He certainly wouldn't have written 2 Corinthians 12:10: "…when I am weak, then I am strong." Paul felt strong, even amidst his difficulties, because of God's grace.

We all have weird quirks about us. We have things we wish were different. We have traits that make us feel out of place. We regret things in our past. Give them to God and see what His grace will do. It is what it is.

The writer of the Book of Hebrews tells us, "See to it that no one falls short of the grace of God..." (Hebrews 12:15). Those are our lifewords for today. Other translations tell us not to "miss the grace of God." Why would anyone do that? How could I miss God's grace?

I could be too hard on myself. No one is perfect. Only God's Word is perfect (Psalm 119:96). We all fall short of the glory of God (Romans 3:23). Accept the fact that you are human. You won't live up to your own standards. You certainly won't live up to God's. That's why there is grace. Here are some ways we miss the grace of God:

I don't understand that I'm loved by God. "See how very much our Father loves us, for he calls us his children, and that is what we are!" (1 John 3:1). When you become a Christian, you are adopted into the family of God (Romans 8:15). You're not a servant. You are a child of God, accepted because of who you are, not what you do. Because He loves you, He extends His favor... His grace to you.

I worry too much. There are so many things in life you have zero control over. You can fret and worry all you want, and it won't change the situation at all. People who are anxious about everything have control issues. People who are consumed by worry have trust issues. Psalm 37:1 says, "Fret not." "Cast all your burdens on Him because He cares for you" (1 Peter 5:7). Part of God's grace to you is that He wants to take the worry off your shoulders.

I can hold a grudge. Some allow bitterness to take hold of their spirit. Some sit around and somehow try to make themselves feel better with thoughts of revenge. "Do not take revenge, my dear friends, but leave room for God's wrath..." (Romans 12:19). Grace and peace are often used together in Scripture. No one who harbors unforgiveness in their heart has peace or grace. They miss them both.

Yesterday, we talked of ways to miss the grace of God. Today, our lifeword comes from Galatians 2:21: "I do not set aside the grace of God for if righteousness could be gained through the law, then Christ died for nothing!" The word translated here as "set aside" also gets translated as "rejected" or "refused." Why in the world would anyone have no use for, turn down, or refuse something as great as the grace of God?

Some of it stems from confusion about who God is. Some see God as a traffic cop who is just looking to give you a ticket. He does have a quota He has to meet, you know. Others see Him as a record keeper who has a long list of your sins. When we stand before Him, He will read these off one by one. Some see Him as a domineering parent who wags His finger at you. His hands are on His hips frustrated that you can't behave better than you do. It's hard to fathom grace flowing from these types of gods.

Others are confused about God's expectations. God understands our limitations and frailties better than even we do. He created us. He's not surprised when we fall short. Someone has said God is more concerned with your direction than He is your perfection. God desires your heart. He wants a heart that's bent toward Him. "Blessed are the pure in heart" (Matthew 5:8). David, even amidst all his failures, was a man after God's own heart (Acts 13:22)

Over 200 times in the New Testament, God is referred to as Father. That may be hard for some of us who did not have a good dad. But those people, especially those people, know what a good father should be. That's who God is.

Isaiah 30:18 says, "Yet the Lord longs to be gracious to you; therefore He will rise up to show you compassion." He is gracious to us continually. It is His character to be gracious, and He "does not change" (James 1:17). His grace is offered to us until our final breath. Those who reject His grace—set it aside, refuse it—miss the very heart of who He is.

Those who "set aside" the grace of God do it naturally. We don't learn to rely on grace from living in this world. "The early bird gets the worm" tells us if we outwork the others, we will get the reward. "No pain, no gain" is an expression from the athletic world. "If it's to be, it's up to me" basically says that no one will give you anything in this life. While those quotes have a purpose in the secular world, they do not echo biblical teaching for our spiritual life.

When we were young, we were promised a trip to McDonald's if we behaved during the shopping trip. If I was a "big boy" at the doctor's office, I could get a sucker. Elementary school teachers reward good conduct with stickers. My son didn't get to go on a skating trip with his classmates because he wasn't "detention free" at school. The best students go to the best colleges. If you perform well in your career, you will get promotions and raises. Everything in our lives teaches us that good performance is rewarded.

It's no wonder that the grace of God is a hard concept for some to grasp. All the way back to biblical times, it was a struggle. Our lifeword today is from Galatians 2:21: "I do not set aside the grace of God, for if righteousness could be gained through the law, Christ died for nothing!" The Christians in Galatia were reverting back to their old way. They believed they still had to follow all the Jewish traditions in the Old Testament. Believing in Jesus was okay, just not enough. The Apostle Paul would have none of it. "I do not set aside the grace of God..." This is what the Galatians were doing, and this is what we do if we think we can earn or add to our salvation. We reject God's grace. We set it aside.

I remember my dad pushing back his dinner plate, which signaled he was finished. He no longer needed the plate, so he pushed it aside. There is never a place in the Christian life when you aren't dependent on God's grace. Without His mercy and grace, we are lost. We are 100% relying on it. Don't push it aside.

Grace and peace. The Apostle Paul loved these words. He loved them so much, he used them together 13 times in the New Testament. Grace was a Greek word, and peace (shalom) was the Hebrew greeting. Paul didn't say, "Gentiles, grace to you, and to you Hebrews, peace." Paul said, "Grace and peace to you." He combined a Greek and a Hebrew greeting to create something brand new... a Christian greeting. We are reminded of his words in Galatians 3:28: "There is neither Jew nor Gentile, neither slave nor free, nor is there male and female, for you are all one in Christ Jesus." A new people required a new greeting.

Peter changes it a bit. He begins both his letters, "Grace and peace be yours in abundance" (1 Peter 1:2). Those are our lifewords for today. One translation has it, "May God give you more and more grace and peace." Still another, "May grace and peace be multiplied to you."

These words tell us that God's grace and peace is a never ending well that we can drink from. Your present understanding and experience of both can increase. They are not one and done. You don't get saved, get a measure of grace and peace, and it has to last you the rest of your life. "May God give you more and more grace and peace."

When Peter greets us this way, he assumes we need more grace and peace. Of course, he knew this from his own experience. Throughout life's good times and bad, its ups and downs, our need for grace varies. Not that we don't ever need it, but there are times we sense our need more than others. At those times, and others, we are wise to drink deeply from the well of grace and peace.

There is never a time in the Christian life when we can say that we are okay with our present supply. Even though things are going really well for you now, there is difficulty around the corner. Life is full of tough times that rock our boat and require grace and peace. God is ready to make them both abound to you... if you will simply ask.

The Apostle Paul wrote the book of Philippians around AD 60. He wrote it, or most likely dictated it, in a Roman jail. Philippians is something of a "thank you note." In it, Paul thanks the church at Philippi for a gift. He says, "Not one church shared with me in the matter of giving and receiving, except you only; for even when I was in Thessalonica, you sent me aid more than once when I was in need" (Philippians 4:15-16). In this "thank you note," he includes truths that can transform our lives. Let's take a look at some of them today.

Early in his letter, Paul encourages the Philippians by writing, "...He who began a good work in you will carry it on to completion until the day of Christ Jesus" (Philippians 1:6). God is an initiator. He starts things. The work of God that has started in the Philippians and in us is a work that He started. God does not wait for us to come to Him. He goes before us and plows the ground so that we can respond to Him. If I am seeking God today, it's because He first sought me.

The work that God will do is a "good" work. He won't turn you into a religious nut. Some people fret that they will go off the deep end and become like some evangelical stereotype that is portrayed on TV. He's a good God, and you can trust Him with the kind of person He will make of you.

What kind of work will God do in us? "Love is patient, love is kind. It does not envy, it does not boast, it is not proud. It does not dishonor others, it is not self-seeking, it is not easily angered, it keeps no record of wrongs" (1 Corinthians 13:4-5). Also, in Galatians 5:22-23, Paul lists the fruit that God wants to produce in our lives: "love, joy, peace, forbearance, kindness, goodness, faithfulness, gentleness, and self-control."

You can give yourself fully to God knowing that the work He has begun is a good work. He has come to make you fully human. He will turn you into the mother, father, husband, wife, employee, and friend that you've always wanted to be. Trust Him and His work in your life.

Paul has an eternal perspective on life that's seen in Philippians 1:21. It's our lifeword for today. "For to me, to live is Christ and to die is gain." Remember, he was sitting in a Roman jail as he wrote these words. How can Paul keep this perspective? How did he not get bogged down in the muck and mire of his daily life? How did he keep his mind not on the temporal but the eternal? Can we have this attitude?

Paul saw God's hand in his problems. Paul is in jail, but he sees the opportunity to share Christ with the guards. He also discovers that people speak boldly on the outside because of his situation (Philippians 1:12-13). Paul has all kinds of problems with people who view him as a competitor. But he rejoices that Christ is preached even with false motives or vain conceit! (Philippians 1:15-18). Paul saw Jesus as Lord of all... even the tough spots of his life.

Paul makes a decision in verse 18 to rejoice. We see a resolve in Paul's mind to rejoice, no matter the problem. Rejoicing is not only an emotion; it's a decision. It does not mean that I must jump up and down and wave my hands in the air. It means that I will decide my reaction to this problem, and I decide to rejoice. We have control of our attitudes. Paul made a decision to rejoice.

Paul writes, "Whatever happens, conduct yourselves in a manner worthy of the gospel of Christ" (Philippians 1:27). Paul sees past his problems to how God wants him to react to them. Our problems have purpose when we understand that others are observing us. God's grace will allow us to show how Christians react, especially in adverse times. That's when people are watching to see if Jesus makes a real difference in our lives.

Paul demonstrates here that the transformation of our lives is dependent on the mind (Romans 12:2). It's in how we think, our attitudes. Paul's attitude, his perspective, comes from an understanding that God is at work in every part of his life. So, he can say, "For to me, to live is Christ and to die is gain" (Philippians 1:21).

In the second chapter of Philippians, Paul continues to talk about our attitudes. He says Christians think differently than unbelievers. That thinking prompts the behavior that he encourages. It all starts in the mind.

Paul instructs us to live by a different value system than the world. "...be like-minded, having the same love, being one in spirit and of one mind. Do nothing out of selfish ambition or vain conceit. Rather, in humility value others above yourselves, not looking to your own interests but each of you to the interests of the others" (Philippians 2:2-4). In the world's system, there is a pecking order. But in the kingdom, we value others above ourselves. Because of God's grace, we play at a higher level.

Because of sin, we live in a narcissistic society. Sin focuses us inward. We become self-absorbed. It's all about us. That's the way of the world. God speaks to us in Philippians about what we value. God wants us to look outward. John writes that all men will know we are Christians by our love (John 13:34). The character trait God desires is love. How can I show love when it's all about me?

1 Corinthians 6:7 says that it is better to be cheated or wronged than fight for my own way and destroy my Christian reputation. I don't need to have my own way all the time. Christianity is loving one another, forgiving one another, serving one another, and accepting one another. I could go on and on. If my faith in Christ is just about Jesus and me, I don't have biblical Christianity. Jesus will always talk to us about our attitude toward others.

The way to succeed in God's kingdom, the way to the top of God's ladder, seems to be the way of servanthood. The way up is down... at least, down in the eyes of the world. This is total value inversion from the world's way of thinking. Our mindset, our attitude, should be like Jesus. His is described in Philippians 2:5-11. Take a minute to read it, and then ask God for the grace to live it.

For the last three days, we've been looking at truths from the book of Philippians that transform us. Here's another one: *Salvation is both an event and a process*. Paul says to "…continue to work out your salvation with fear and trembling…" (Philippians 2:12). A correct understanding of this teaching will transform your life.

Paul tells the church at Philippi to "work out your salvation." Not work *for* it! Work it out. There's a huge difference. We must be determined to get all that we can out of this free gift that God has given us. We must persevere in our efforts to make the most of our relationship with Jesus.

Paul writes in chapter 3, "…I press on to take hold of that for which Christ Jesus took hold of me…I do not consider myself yet to have taken hold of it. But one thing I do: Forgetting what is behind and straining toward what is ahead, I press on toward the goal to win the prize for which God has called me heavenward in Christ Jesus" (Philippians 3:12-14). Here and elsewhere, Paul encourages us to be determined, as we are empowered by the grace of God.

There is little that is more important to the Christian life than "hanging in there." Just keep putting one foot in front of the other and keep on walking with Jesus. Have you failed Him lately? Don't throw in the towel. Confess it and get on with your Christian life. If your car has a flat tire, you don't junk the car. You simply fix the flat and go on. It's the same way in our walk with God.

"Do you not know that in a race all the runners run, but only one gets the prize? Run in such a way as to get the prize" (1 Corinthians 9:24). Paul describes the Christian life as a race. In fact, it's a marathon. We have good days and bad. We have times of encouragement and discouragement. Persevere. Don't give up. It's a long race. Be determined to finish. "Let us not become weary in doing good, for at the proper time we will reap a harvest if we do not give up" (Galatians 6:9).

Paul says in Philippians 2:12 to "work out your <u>own</u> salvation." Don't try to be anyone else. God has a person in mind that only you can become. He needs you being you. God does not want cookie-cutter Christians. We are all different, with different likes and dislikes. God loves diversity. We Christians are compared to a body. "Just as a body, though one, has many parts, but all its many parts form one body, so it is with Christ...Now you are the body of Christ, and each one of you is a part of it" (1 Corinthians 12:12, 27). All the parts are different but important. They are different because He needs them as such. Don't imitate anyone but Christ. We must walk our own road with God.

We are to "work out our salvation with fear and trembling" (Philippians 2:12). This has nothing to do with living in a state of nervousness and anxiety. The word translated "fear" means "reverence" or "respect." "The fear of the Lord is the beginning of knowledge..." (Proverbs 1:7). Paul says he came to Corinth in "weakness and fear, and with much trembling" (1 Corinthians 2:3). He was aware of the awesome responsibility he had.

This "trembling" is the attitude Christians are to have: a healthy fear of offending God. He is a loving, merciful, and patient God, but He is a God of justice, judgment, and wrath as well. We do not want to come under His hand of discipline. As a father disciplines his son, so God disciplines His children (Hebrews 12:6).

"Trembling" may also indicate a shaking due to weakness. This weakness illustrates our dependency on God and His grace to become the Christian He desires. We know our limitations and temptations. Paul compares us to "clay pots," which are very fragile things, dependent on the power of God (2 Corinthians 4:7).

We have an awesome responsibility as Christians. We are "Christ's ambassadors, as though God were making his appeal through us" (2 Corinthians 5:20). To achieve this end requires God's grace, our determination, and a certain "fear and trembling" in our standing before God.

I was a high school and college basketball coach for 14 years. I had one desire for my players. I wanted them to play to their potential. Everyone did not have the same ability. Some had more potential than others. As a basketball player, to play to your potential is a very good thing.

Paul says pretty close to the same thing in Philippians 3:16. He tells us to "live up to what we have already attained." That's our lifeword for today. This is the obligation of every believer. The old-timers said it this way: "Walk in the light that you have." Light refers to knowledge or understanding. Whatever you know of Christ and whatever you know of the Christian life, walk in that light. Play to your potential.

"What I don't understand about the Bible does not worry me; what I do understand does!" Mark Twain said that, and it cuts to the core of what we're talking about. To play up to your potential, you can't worry about what you don't understand. Paul says that if you differ with him on something, God will make it clear to you (Philippians 3:15). Paul is not bent out of shape that these people don't see eye to eye with him about everything. He simply asks them to "live up to what they've already attained."

So, you don't understand much about all this Holy Spirit stuff? That's okay; just walk in the light that you have. Don't understand much about all this second coming stuff? Don't understand much about tithing? Are you confused about the Sabbath and what that means? Just walk in the light that you have. For every one thing in the Bible you don't understand, there must be 10 that you do. Play to your potential. "...live up to what you have already attained."

Just like we said yesterday, work out your own salvation. Play your own game. We all have different abilities. God brings us along as He knows we need to be brought along. Rest in that. He's at work. After all, the context of our lifeword today says that God will give understanding (Philippians 3:15).

We hear a lot of talk about citizenship today. With the immigration struggles we have, we talk about people who are citizens and some who are not. I've been in Papua New Guinea twice. I did not feel at home. Though I was treated well, I felt like a foreigner. I knew I wasn't a citizen. I've been to Puerto Rico twice. I don't read Spanish and trying to drive a car around was not the easiest thing. I felt like I didn't belong.

The Apostle Paul says we have a citizenship, and it's not in the USA or any other country, for that manner. If we are a Christian, this world is not our home. "Our citizenship is in Heaven" (Philippians 3:20). Paul says our homeland is in Heaven. This world is not our home. The transforming truth from this passage is that "We're not home yet!"

Since this world is not my home, my mind is not on earthly things (Philippians 3:19). Some say that you can be so heavenly minded that you're no earthly good. I suppose that's true. A bigger problem is that we're too earthly minded that we are no heavenly good. "Set your minds on things above, not on earthly things" (Colossians 3:2).

Philippians 3:17 says not to follow earthly models of behavior, "...you have us as a model, keep your eyes on those who live as we do." Paul follows Christ, and he expects us to as well (1 Corinthians 11:1). Don't imitate earthly values or attitudes. "Their destiny is destruction, their god is their stomach, and their glory is in their shame" (Philippians 3:19).

God will one day bring "all things under his control" (Philippians 3:21). We live in a fallen world cursed by sin. This place is not the end-all. Things will not be right or fair in this world. There is a time coming when God will set all things right. This world is a place where I reside until I reach my real home. I'm not home yet. There is a day coming when God will make all things right. A day when He will even the score. A day when we will understand even as we wish we understood now. Then, and only then, will I be home, where I'm a citizen.

Police officers are trained to aim their weapon at the largest part of the body if they have to discharge their weapon in the line of duty. But because of the seriousness of the situation, snipers and SWAT team members go for "head shots" for obvious reasons. In the Christian life, our enemy wants to go for "head shots" as well. If Satan can get inside our heads and control our thoughts, we will be at his mercy.

That's why the Apostle Paul spends so much time on how we as Christians think. Paul is concerned throughout his writing about our thought life. It's a special concern for him in the book of Philippians. "I plead with Euodia and I plead with Syntyche to be of the same mind in the Lord" (Philippians 4:2). Paul begged these two women to agree with each other. Literally, he was saying to "think the same things." As Christians, we don't have to agree on everything. But we must focus on our areas of agreement. Focusing on our areas of disagreement will lead to division in the church. For every one thing we disagree on, there are 20 we agree on. Why not allow that to be our focus?

In the same context, Paul says, "Do not be anxious" (Philippians 4:6). To be anxious, to worry, means to be troubled in my thoughts. My thoughts are divided. The same word is used in Matthew 13:22. A sower has sown the gospel seed, but the cares of the world and the deceitfulness of wealth choke out the seed. That's divided thinking. Paul says don't be divided in your thoughts. God is either in charge or He's not. He's either asked us to lay our burdens before Him or He hasn't. He either promised to supply our needs or He hasn't. Anxiety comes from being divided in our thinking.

Philippians 4:8 says to be careful what you think about. "Think on these things." Paul knows, as we do, that our thoughts control our behavior. As we've said before, the thought is the father of the deed. What goes on between your ears is crucial to your Christian life. Don't allow Satan to take a "head shot."

The most important principle of understanding the Bible is to read it in context. Context means the verses before and the verses after. All of those must be taken into account when trying to understand the meaning of a verse or passage. Nowhere is this more crucial than in our lifeword for today: "I can do all things through Christ who strengthens me" (Philippians 4:13). I can do all things? Because of Christ, I can run a 4-minute mile? Since I'm a Christian, I can lose 100 pounds? I have Christ, so I can get the most popular girl to date me? I think we all know this is not the proper interpretation. Let's look at the context.

Philippians 4:11 says, "I am not saying this because I am in need, for I have learned to be content whatever the circumstances." Paul went through some hard times in his Christian life. But he says here, no matter the circumstance, he's learned to deal with it... to be content. Basically, he says what happens to me doesn't matter. I have Christ.

Paul continues in Philippians 4:12: "I know what it is to be in need, and I know what it is to have plenty. I have learned the secret of being content in any and every situation, whether well fed or hungry, whether living in plenty or in want." He says, "I've had a little and a lot." Paul's been stuffed and been starving. He has found a secret that allows him to be content in any situation. He also says this is something he's learned. It did not come naturally.

The passage is about contentment. Paul says no matter his circumstance, no matter what he has or has not, he can do all things through Christ. All things in this context is obviously enduring all situations and still being content.

Jesus said in John 16:33, "In this world you will have trouble, but behold I have overcome the world." The secret is that what we have in Christ matters. By the way, Paul writes all this chained to a Roman guard. We can be chained as well. Chained to greener pastures. Paul has learned a secret. He wants us to learn it as well.

God has promises for us throughout His Word. Depending on who's counting, there are over 3,000. Did you sing this in Sunday school? "Every promise in the book is mine, every chapter, every verse, and every line." As I matured in my understanding of the Bible, I knew this wasn't true. Some promises were made to specific people and not to me. So, just like we learned yesterday, the promises must be read in their context.

Our last transforming truth in Philippians is "My God will meet all your needs according to the riches of his glory in Christ Jesus" (Philippians 4:19). In the preceding verses, Paul again thanks the Philippians for their generosity toward him. "Yet it was good of you to share in my troubles…you sent me aid more than once when I was in need" (Philippians 4:14-16). So, the promise of 4:19 comes with a premise. If you meet the premise of 4:14-16, you can claim the promise of 4:19. This promise is not for all people. It's for those who are meeting the premise. God wants us to be generous people. If we are meeting that premise, we can stand on the promise.

Philippians 4:17 says this promise comes with a reward. "Not that I desire your gifts; what I desire is that more be credited to your account." In some way that no one understands, there is an account in Heaven that keeps tabs on our generosity. "Do not lay up for yourselves treasures on earth where moth and rust destroy and thieves break in and steal. But lay up for yourselves treasures in heaven where moth and rust do not destroy, and where thieves do not break in and steal" (Matthew 6:19-20). "Give and it will be given to you" (Luke 6:38). In the context of secret giving, Matthew says, "Then your Father, who sees what is done in secret, will reward you" (Matthew 6:4).

The principle here is obvious. God supplies the needs of those who have been generous. Those who have their mind not only on their own needs, but on the needs of others.

With all the smart people in the world, someone should figure out a system where no one is lonely. They tackled that problem in the United Kingdom when Prime Minister Teresa May appointed a "minister for loneliness" in January of 2018. The former Surgeon General of the US wrote: "During my years caring for patients, the most common pathology I saw was... loneliness"

With all the smart people in the world, someone should figure this problem out... and somebody did. It's called the church. When some hear the word church, they think of a building, a place you go. Jesus didn't have that in mind. He had in mind a group of people who would care for one another.

Over 50 times in the New Testament, Jesus spoke of *one anothering*. "Forgive one another." "Submit to one another." "Comfort one another." "Be devoted to one another." "Pray for one another." This is the biblical understanding of church. Let's see how the church should function; how we should one another one another.

Our lifeword today is, "Carry each other's burdens, and in this way you will fulfill the law of Christ" (Galatians 6:2). What is the law of Christ? It's a new commandment. "A new command I give you: Love one another. As I have loved you, so you must love one another. By this everyone will know that you are my disciples, if you love one another" (John 13:34-35).

Carrying one another's burdens doesn't mean people are irresponsible, and you have to pick up all those responsibilities. The word for burden in the original language is like a boulder. You can't carry boulders by yourself. We must carry them together. They are meant to be carried by "one anothering."

Loneliness is a heavy burden. The church can help. The church is meant to bear each other's burdens. Together, we can carry what nobody can carry alone. You can do that. Anybody can do that. Remember, the church is you...me...all of us.

I'm a Protestant. I follow in the path of a group of people that over 400 years ago protested some abuses in the Roman Catholic church. There's at least one practice I wish we Protestants would somehow work into our church. The Catholic practice of confession is very biblical and needs to be worked out some way in all churches. The Bible says, "...confess your sins to each other..." (James 5:16). That's our lifeword for today.

As Protestants, we practice confessing our sins to God, but there's not much confessing to one another. This may go back to our problem with loneliness. Confessing our sins to one another demands a high level of trust and confidence. The church should be a place where one has a few close, meaningful relationships where confessing can happen. We need to be so connected to our church family that these types of friendships can develop. May I repeat: don't confess to just anyone. Choose a trusted friend or two when you confess. Since the nature of the relationship should be very close, I advise choosing someone of the same sex.

Confessing sins to a trusted friend is not easy. It means we have to humble ourselves and become vulnerable. It means admitting we need help. We're fearful of losing face or of the friend breaking confidence. Sometimes, this may be an excuse for not really forsaking our sin.

When we confess, accountability is the next step. The person we confessed to should be given permission to follow up and ask us how we are dealing with the issue. In 2 Corinthians 8:21, Paul says, "We are taking pains to do things right, not only in the sight of men, but also in the sight of God." He welcomes accountability, transparency, and vulnerability into his life.

Satan wants to keep us from sharing our faults and sins with others. That's why God inspired James to write our lifeword for today. God knows when we confess them to others, they lose their power over us. We can sense a cleansing and freedom when we confess.

Praying for one another is Christianity 101. Our lifeword today is from James 5:16: "…pray for each other so that you may be healed. The prayer of a righteous person is powerful and effective." Even if there was not a biblical command to do so, it would seem intuitive for us. Here are a few things that happen when we pray for one another.

As we pray for each other, God will answer. "Again, truly I tell you that if two of you on earth agree about anything they ask for, it will be done for them by my Father in heaven" (Matthew 18:19). I don't know how this works out. I know every prayer is not answerable. Nothing is impossible for God (Luke 1:37), and He acts in powerful ways when believers pray together and for each other.

As we pray for each other, God spreads His Word. "…pray for us that the message of the Lord may spread rapidly and be honored, just as it was with you" (2 Thessalonians 3:1). Paul believed that as people prayed, his ministry would enlarge. He continually asked people to pray that doors for the gospel would be opened (Colossians 4:3). God softens hearts to draw people to Himself. Any preacher, pastor, or missionary knows that God must go before us to plow the ground so the seed we plant can take root.

As we pray for one another, God helps us fight sin in our lives. "If you see any brother or sister commit a sin that does not lead to death, you should pray and God will give them life" (1 John 5:16). When someone struggles with sin, what should our response be? Judge them? Look down on them? God wants us to pray for each other. We should ask God to give deliverance from temptation and sin.

Things happen when God's people pray for each other. God hears the prayers, and His power to act is greater than our ability to ask. Paul reminds us that as we pray, God can do more than we could have imagined. "Now to Him who is able to do immeasurably more than all we ask or imagine…" (Ephesians 3:20-21).

Do you care enough about the people in your church to sing to them? I'm not talking about singing a solo. I'm speaking of corporate worship. Do you join in with the others? God desires that our voices minister to each other. Our lifeword today is, "Speak to one another with psalms, hymns, and songs from the Spirit. Sing and make music from your heart to the Lord" (Ephesians 5:19). With these words, Paul has just signed us all up for the choir.

In Ephesians 5:18, we are told "Be filled with the Spirit." But this verse ends not with a period, but a comma. The next verse describes the activity of people under the Spirit's control. They sing! Why? A fruit of God's Holy Spirit is love, and that is expressed through song. "And over all these virtues put on love...Let the message of Christ dwell among you richly as you teach and admonish one another with all wisdom through psalms, hymns, and songs from the Spirit, singing to God with gratitude in your hearts" (Colossians 3:14-16).

John Wesley, the founder of the Methodist movement, had rules for singing. This is rule number four: "Sing lustily and with a good courage. Beware of singing as if you were half dead, or half asleep...Be no more afraid of your voice now, nor more ashamed of its being heard, than when you sung the songs of Satan."

Our lifeword says, "Sing and make music from your heart to the Lord." That verse includes all of us who don't have a good voice. Anyone can sing from your heart. Everyone has a beautiful voice if they sing this way. You know what this means. It's the singing that comes from a saved sinner. It comes from a heart that knows their debt has been paid.

While our singing affects one another, we should not sing to others but to God. It's Him we are worshipping. As I aim to please Him, others will be blessed as well. Each of us has at least one ministry in the church. As we join in the singing, we minister to those around us.

We've been talking about God's cure for loneliness: the church. It's here we learn to *one another*. As we *love one another, forgive one another,* and *be devoted to one another,* we move past just going to church to being the church. We move beyond attending the church to belonging to the church.

Some will say they've been hurt by the church. I know that's true because I've seen it. The church, like any other organization made up of people, will be flawed. I don't understand why that bothers us. We keep all kinds of imperfect people, things, and organizations in our lives, so why does the church have to be perfect? If you are looking for perfect institutions, you will continue to be lonely. We all know if the organization has people in it, it won't be perfect. Why does it surprise us when the church is not the way it should be?

It never will be because it's made up of people like you and me. We're kind of like the Apostle Paul when he says, "The things I want to do, I don't and the things I don't want to do, I do." That's our lifeword today from Romans 7:19. Paul says we know what we ought to do, but many times, we don't do it. This gap in our thinking and behavior is called sin. It's what Jesus died for and is characteristic of every person sitting in a church pew this week.

The Christian life begins when one person encounters Jesus Christ. Though everyone must make this decision individually, it's been proven for years that the best environment for this new life is in the imperfect place called the church. The best place for the development of Christian maturity is among other people. The solitary Christian may enjoy not dealing with the imperfections of others, but the one who walks alone is not fully Christian. Hebrews 10:25 reminds us to "not neglect the gathering together." It's in that gathering, as we deal with the others who are imperfect, that we grow and mature and become fully Christian.

The Bible says God is the "giver of every good and perfect gift" (James 1:17). One of these gifts, the Bible says, specifically came from Jesus. "So Christ himself gave the apostles, the prophets, the evangelists, the pastors and teachers, for the building up of the body of Christ" (Ephesians 4:11-12). That's our lifeword for today.

Throughout the ages, God has gifted pastors and teachers to help His people. With this gift comes tremendous responsibility. James 3:1 says all who teach "will be held to a stricter judgement." Now, these pastors and teachers aren't perfect. I'm one of them, and I know lots of them. Some of them will preach too long or not long enough. Some allow music that is too loud or too traditional or too modern. They may talk about money too much. They won't live up to what they preach. In fact, they lead an organization that doesn't live up to what it believes.

Pastors are flawed, and they lead a flawed institution called the Church. It was designed to be a group of people gathered together to pool our imperfections to serve those around us. As far as I know, there's only one perfect thing about this imperfect church: Jesus loves her and gave His life for her (Ephesians 5:25).

This Sunday, somewhere near you, imperfect people will be listening to an imperfect pastor. Some of these people are called Methodists, Presbyterians, Lutherans, Pentecostals, Nazarenes, along with people who don't know who they are; they're called "non-denominationals." Jesus loves them no matter what name they meet under, and if Jesus loves them, maybe that's a good reason for you to love them as well.

Don't expect perfection out of these people, especially if it's my church you will attend. One thing I can promise you about my church; it's led by a pastor who won't always get it right. But he tries, with all the grace God will give him, to point you to the only perfect One.

Where should people go who are struggling? I mean, really struggling. A man struggles with same-sex attraction. I hope he would go to the church. Your wife has left you and the kids for her boss. I hope the husband would come to the church. Your business is about to go under because of your gambling debts. I hope you would come to the church. A wife caught her husband viewing pornography on the internet. I hope that couple would come to the church. Your teenager is pregnant. I hope your family would come to the church. Your husband is a drunk and you can't keep his secret anymore. I sure hope you would allow the church to help.

You and I both know the church is the last place some people go for help with these and other life situations. Unfortunately, we have a reputation of condemnation and judgmental attitudes. I'm sure some of that is undeserved, but not all of it.

I've shared this before in this book but it works well here. What if the church was more like this: "The neighborhood bar is the best counterfeit there is to the fellowship Christ wants to give His church. It's an imitation, dispensing liquor instead of grace, escape rather than reality—but it is a permissive, accepting, and inclusive fellowship. It is unshockable. It is democratic. You can tell people secrets, and they usually don't tell others or even want to. The bar flourishes not because most people are alcoholics, but because God has put into the human heart the desire to know and be known, to love and be loved, and so many seek a counterfeit at the price of a few beers. With all my heart, I believe that Christ wants His church to be unshockable. A fellowship where people can come and say, 'I'm sunk! I'm beat! I've had it!' Some AA groups have this quality. The church needs it."

I don't know who wrote that, but it's profound. If it offends you, that's okay. Get over it. The church should be more like a neighborhood bar, a place where *everyone knows your name*. Cheers!

Every Sunday, all over the world, Christians assemble together. What is the purpose of this gathering? Why do we as Christians get together in local congregations? Is it for evangelism? Does the church open its doors because of the unsaved people in the community? Maybe the church exists for discipleship. Those who hold this view believe the main objective is to serve and strengthen Christians. Others would say the church is there for the corporate worship of God. Let's see what the Bible says about the purpose(s) of the church.

Acts 2:42 lays out the activity of the early church. "They devoted themselves to the apostles' teaching and to fellowship, to the breaking of bread and to prayer." That's our lifeword for today. This verse encompasses all the activities we mentioned in the first paragraph. Each local congregation should focus on the worship of God, the maturing of the church, and reaching the lost, at home and abroad.

The local church exists to worship. In our lifeword today, prayer, breaking of bread (Communion), fellowship, and the Apostles teaching are all aspects of worship gatherings. Our worship services are a means of grace, one of the ways God gets His grace to us. The worship of God, through His Son Jesus Christ, is the focal point of any local congregation. Everything flows from this.

As the church gathers for worship, believers are strengthened and matured. The Biblical word for this is edification. "And he himself gave some to be apostles, some prophets, some evangelists, and some pastors and teachers...for the edification of the body of Christ" (Ephesians 4:11-12). Edification in the New Testament happens when we help one another along the road to Christlikeness.

If the worship of God and the edification of the Body of Christ are happening, reaching the lost will be the consequence. Any healthy church has an outward look. Churches that look inward only are not truly worshipping God and certainly aren't maturing in the faith. In the context of our lifeword today, the Bible says, "And the Lord added to their number daily those who were being saved." (Acts 2:47)

No doubt you've heard about the "genius of the 'and'." It happens when two different ideas or practices find their power when both are present. In the context of family, it's not about Mom or Dad; it's about Mom and Dad. Both are extremely different, but as they function together, they are invaluable to a family.

The church must practice the "genius of the 'and'" as well. In a book titled *AND* by Hugh Halter and Matt Smay, this quote is found: "The church exists as the people of God who are called out of the world as His children and sent back into it as His ambassadors. The church is the gathered worshipping community of God's missionary people scattered to our homes, our neighborhoods, to enemy territory, and the whole world." Did you see the "and?" It's in the words "called out and sent" and also "gather and scatter." The church is called to gather for worship, teaching, and community, but also to scatter as God's sent people.

Jesus confirms this in some of His last words to His followers. "Go...and make disciples..." (Matthew 28:19). "Making disciples" calls the body of Christ to gather together as believers who are maturing in the faith. This happens in a church building or small group, anywhere that "two or more are gathered in His name" (Matthew 18:20).

But it doesn't end with the gathering of the faithful. Jesus' charge to "Go" is a command to scatter. As we leave the gathering, we are called to go to our different places of residence, work, and recreation and "be the church." To be "salt and light" (Matthew 5:13-14) to a world that needs us. It's in the scattering that evangelism happens. Pastor Rick Rusaw says, "Good works lead to good will which gives us opportunity to tell the good news."

The church as an institution should give its congregants gathering and scattering opportunities. But more importantly, the church as a people should personally respond to the call for each of us to do the work of the church: gathering and scattering.

The older I get, the more I find myself repeating a phrase quite often. In response to many questions, I simply say, "I don't know." It's not because I forgot; it's because I don't know.

Now, this is disturbing to some people. After all, I'm the "man of God!" I have a Master's Degree in Divinity. I'm the paid religious guy at our church. I'm supposed to have an answer to all things religious. But the truth is there's a lot I don't know. I'm okay with that. The wiser I've become, the more self-assured I am in Christ, the more confidence I have to answer questions this way. After all, it's God I have to please, and He already knows I don't know a lot of the answers anyway. There's no sense faking it just to please people. Our lifeword today is "There are some things the Lord our God has kept secret, but there are some things he has let us know…" (Deuteronomy 29:29).

Those words teach us that the best Bible teachers in the world don't know all things. I hope that they only teach what they know- the things God has revealed in the Scriptures. These are for every Christian to know. But there are other things, unrevealed things, which we are not to know.

One thing I don't know is who the "real" Christians are. Jesus says, "I am the good shepherd. I know my sheep and my sheep know me" (John 10:14). The obvious question is… who are the sheep? Who are the real Christ followers and who is faking it? He goes on to say that, "My sheep listen to my voice; I know them, and they follow me" (John 10:27). The sheep are obviously the ones who follow, but I've known people who seem to follow and then they don't. I've known some who seem to listen and then they don't.

I'm glad I don't know who the real sheep are. I don't need that information. I'm just called to love people and tell them the truth. The secret things are left up to God. The older and hopefully wiser I've become, the more I trust Him with that information.

Okay, let me get something off my chest. One pet peeve I have concerning Christians is that some seem to think the return of Jesus is just around the corner. It wouldn't shock me if Jesus returned tomorrow. It also wouldn't shock me if it's another thousand years… or more! We just don't know.

No one can predict when Jesus will return. No one can know the day or the hour. If you read the Apostle Paul carefully, you'll see that he thought Christ's return was near. If Paul missed it, how would I know? He seemed to think in 1 Corinthians 7 that marrying was not necessary because "the time is short" (verse 29).

God's Word says even Jesus doesn't know! Here's our lifeword for today: "But concerning that day and hour no one knows, not even the angels of heaven, nor the Son, but the Father only" (Matthew 24:36). If Jesus doesn't know, how in the world would a mere mortal know?

Jesus' lack of knowledge regarding days or hours perplexes many believers, including me. In the mystery of the Trinity, Jesus is fully God (John 1:1). How could He be a member of the godhead and not be all knowing? The theological word for that is omniscience. I have no clue. You don't either. Let's leave the secret things to God (Deuteronomy 29:29).

The whole study of the End Times has never interested me. I don't see its relevance in my life. How would a study of the End Times make me a better husband or father? How would it make me love God or my neighbor more? How would it make me a more Christ-like disciple? These are the things that God desires of me, and I don't see how getting enamored with Jesus' return plays into that.

I have no clue when Jesus is returning, but I do know this: He will return when the time is right. How close are we to that moment? Perhaps very close, perhaps not. I really don't know. Just be ready. "So you also must be ready, because the Son of Man will come at an hour when you do not expect him" (Matthew 24:44).

More than once in this book, I have referred to the "one anothers" of Scripture. There are over 50 of them recorded in God's Word. We are called to look after one another. Because we are gracious and generous people, sometimes we go too far in this and promote irresponsibility. Nowhere in the Bible are we to be irresponsible. In fact, it's just the opposite. We are expected to take care of ourselves. Many times, "one anothering" happens for people who can't look after themselves or just need some assistance.

When a person or a group of people acts irresponsibly, someone else has to pick up the slack. So, when I act irresponsibly, I am expecting other people who aren't responsible for me to carry the burden of the mess or the chaos that I've created. This is not "one anothering"; this is irresponsibility.

In our families, someone has to move the bike out of the middle of the driveway. Someone has to close the box of cereal and put it away. Someone has to pick up the towels in the bathroom. Someone has to turn off the lights. Someone has to flush the toilet!!! Irresponsibility isn't just a personal thing because it affects everyone connected to the irresponsible act.

As Christians, we are to be responsible people. Personal responsibility is taught in the law of sowing and reaping (Galatians 6:7-8). People who are able should work for their food. "The one who does not work shall not eat" (2 Thessalonians 3:10). Men are to take responsibility for providing for their households (1 Timothy 5:8). Those who reject the truth of God "are without excuse" (Romans 1:20).

God has given all of us responsibilities for which we will be held accountable. Matthew 25, as well as many other places, teaches us this. Christians understand the connectedness of family, life, and culture. We should clean up after ourselves, because one day we will stand before God (Romans 14:12). We'll spend the next few days looking at this area of responsibility.

We come upon our irresponsible tendencies naturally. We've avoided our responsibilities since Genesis 1. Before there was sin in the world, there was responsibility. "God blessed them and said to them, 'Be fruitful and increase in number; fill the earth and subdue it. Rule over the fish in the sea and the birds in the sky and over every living creature that moves on the ground'" (Genesis 1:28). Those are our lifewords for today.

The Bible teaches us that we're created to be responsible. "The Lord God took the man and put him in the Garden of Eden to work it and take care of it" (Genesis 2:15). We know we are most happy when we are fulfilling those responsibilities. We all feel good when we are taking responsibility because we were designed that way. We have a desire that is bred into us to be responsible.

The story of the Fall of Man is basically a story of God holding man responsible. After being told not to eat of the fruit of one tree (Genesis 2:17), they do, and God holds them accountable. They point fingers at each other, at Satan, and even at God in an effort not to own up to their actions. "The man said, 'The woman you put here with me, she gave me some fruit from the tree, and I ate it.'

"Then the Lord God said to the woman, 'What is this you have done?' The woman said, 'The serpent deceived me, and I ate'" (Genesis 3:12-13).

What kind of world would we have today if Adam said, "Yes, I ate the forbidden fruit. It was my fault. Do with me what you will, but don't blame Eve." There would still have been consequences for their actions, but something tells me the outcome would have been much different.

I think the same is true today. God has created you to be responsible. But when you aren't, you can't blame others. God is pleased when I point the finger at myself. When I take responsibility for my own sins and failures, God is pleased. Scripture records that He'll make good out of the messes I've made. I simply must take responsibility for them.

We can't talk about human responsibility without addressing a law God has woven into the fabric of our humanity. It's from Galatians 6:7 and is our lifeword for today. "...what you sow, you will reap."

The law of sowing and reaping isn't good or bad. I like to say, "It is what it is." God is not for you or against you with this law. When you reap what you've sown, it's not because God is pleased or displeased. It is what it is. This law can work for you, or this law can work against you. It's up to you. It is what it is.

The Apostle Paul states, "For each of you should carry your own load" (Galatians 6:5). We've been saying for the last two days to "clean up your own mess." That's what Paul means here. We each have been given responsibilities that are specific to us. Don't compare your responsibilities to someone else's. You've got enough to worry about trying to keep up with your own.

Then, in verse 7, Paul says you can't outsmart God. "Do not be deceived: God cannot be mocked." You are not going to fool God. If you are irresponsible, you will pay the consequences. Paul calls it reaping what you have sown. Today depends on yesterday's decisions and tomorrow depends on today's decisions.

This works both positively and negatively. If I sow good things, I'll reap good things, and vice versa. If I'm struggling in my finances or in my relationships, it's not because of some cosmic plot out to get me. The devil hasn't jumped on my back. I'm simply reaping from past poor decisions.

The good news is I can reap good things. All I need to do is start sowing good seed. That means living my life according to the will of God. Paul writes, "Let us not become weary in doing good, for at the proper time we will reap a harvest if we do not give up" (Galatians 6:9). God has made us responsible creatures.

Let's talk today about taking responsibility for your marriage. If your marriage today is less than what you expected, it's because you or your spouse—probably both—have not sown enough good seed. The Scriptures are clear that we will reap what we have sown (Galatians 6:7). Those are our lifewords for today.

As we said yesterday, if you sow seeds of distrust and selfishness into your marriage, what do you think you will get? Sow seeds of love and kindness, and you'll reap great rewards later. Even the unbelieving world understands the law of sowing and reaping. "You get what you give." "What goes around comes around." These are the secular world's attempt to explain a biblical principle.

Here are a few good seeds that can be sown in any marriage. First, sow seeds of repentance. David writes in Psalm 51 that a broken and contrite heart will be honored by God (verse 17). Repentance simply means you desire change and will do what it takes to make that happen. If your heart is like that, watch God start to work in your marriage. If both hearts are like this, your marriage will be healed.

Second, we are humans, not robots. Sow seeds of patience. You cannot expect the wounded partner to respond magically to your changes. He or she has been hurt, and it will take time, God's grace, and fruit worthy of repentance for healing to occur. If you get frustrated because of a lack of change in your marriage, this reeks of you trying to manipulate your spouse.

Third, if you are the offender, it is your responsibility to sow seeds of trust. Your spouse has to want to trust again, but the offender must be the initiator. If he or she doesn't trust you anymore, you may feel like a little kid always checking in with Mommy or Daddy, but you're just reaping what you have sown.

Finally, if you both are ready, pray together. This may be too intimate early in the reconciliation, but when the time is right, just do it. It's amazing what God will do when couples pray together.

It must have been an evangelist's dream. A person of influence, with good standing in the community and who had connections to the Pharisees, approached the evangelist. He was seeking answers to the most important issues of life, such as, "What must I do to inherit eternal life?" (Mark 10:17). Those are our lifewords for today. Evangelists love opportunities to speak to seekers who ask these questions. A give and take ensued between the two. The evangelist answered the seeker's questions. This potential disciple of Christ then turned and walked away, thus rejecting Jesus. Then, an amazing thing happened. The evangelist allowed him to walk.

This is the story of the rich young ruler who is seeking spiritual answers. The evangelist, of course, is Jesus, who simply allowed this man to walk. Most of us would have chased after him and tried to help him understand what he was missing. There is no account of Jesus doing this. Also, there's no record of this potential new Christian ever coming back to Jesus.

Jesus always respected the choices of people He encountered. This is something we see as early in the Bible as Genesis 2. God respected Adam and Eve so much that He permitted them to make their own choices. Even though God knew what was at the end of their poor choice, He allowed it. In both the Old and New Testaments, we see this exhibited.

So often, as a parent, I want to save my sons from the consequences of their choices. I make them sit and do their homework. I make them do it again if they did a sloppy job. Am I teaching them to be responsible? If I let them suffer the consequences from their irresponsibility, would they learn the lesson of responsibility quicker? I guess I don't know for certain the answer, but I do know what is modeled for us in Scripture. God has made us responsible people and allows us the freedom to choose. He doesn't protect us from our irresponsibility and doesn't spare us from the consequences of bad choices.

There's a story in the book of Joshua that teaches us a lesson about irresponsibility. God is leading His nation of Israel as they fight the battle of Jericho. They win because they totally relied on God and did what He said. Their next battle is at Ai, and the results are devastating. The men of Ai "chased the Israelites from the town gate as far as the quarries, and they killed about thirty-six…The Israelites were paralyzed with fear at this turn of events, and their courage melted away" (Joshua 7:5).

Then Joshua prayed, "Oh, Sovereign Lord, why did you bring us across the Jordan River if you are going to let the Amorites kill us?" (Joshua 7:7). God tells Joshua that some of his men had taken idols from the people of Jericho. In this previous battle, God had told them specifically not to take these. God tells Joshua these things must be removed. "You will never defeat your enemies until you remove these things from among you" (Joshua 7:13). Joshua immediately dispatches a search party to find the stolen idols. He takes care of the issue, returns to Ai, and wins the second battle.

Here's the principle God was teaching this infant nation: When someone acts irresponsibly, the shrapnel of that bad decision affects many people. Israel was defeated at Ai because of one man's irresponsibility. Our lives are connected, and when one person is irresponsible, it affects the whole group.

We see this in athletics all the time. One player's actions affect the whole team. In families, a parent's irresponsibility will affect the kids. We see it in churches, as a pastor's irresponsibility will affect the ministries of the whole church. In marriage, when one spouse is irresponsible with money, the other spouse suffers.

Christians are to love and care for one another, and being responsible people is a way to do that. Also, confronting the irresponsibility of others is a very loving thing to do. We do it for the good of the irresponsible person and the good of the group.

Life isn't fair. As we look at who has this and who doesn't have that, we have to conclude that there are injustices in life. We all are not dealt the same hand. We can moan about that, complain about that, or we can deal with it. Good hand, bad hand is not the issue. The responsible person plays the hand you're dealt.

In Matthew 25, Jesus tells a story about unfairness, responsibility, and irresponsibility. It's the parable of the talents. In New Testament times, a talent was a unit of money. One servant was given five talents, another was given two, and the last one was given only one. They were all told to manage this money wisely until their master returned. No reason is given for the differing amounts.

The servants with the five and two talents went to work and doubled their money. When the master returned, he was pleased. "Well done, good and faithful servant! You have been faithful with a few things, so I will put you in charge of many things." That is from Matthew 25:21, and it's our lifeword for today. The servant who was given one talent buried it so he wouldn't lose it. When the master returned, he was not pleased. "...you should have put my money on deposit with the bankers, so that when I returned I would have received it back with interest" (Matthew 25:27).

The point Jesus is making is we are all one-talent, two-talent, or five-talent people. It's just the way it is. Life is not fair. Everyone is accountable for what they do with what they have. Our responsibility is to make the most of what we have. If the one-talent person came back with the money doubled, he would have received the same pat on the back as the servants who were given more.

Whatever you've been given—large, small, or something in the middle—God asks that you do something with it. The amount you're given is not the issue. Being responsible with that amount certainly is. Don't be irresponsible by burying your one talent in the ground.

Let's take a look at what the Bible calls the "fruit of the Spirit." These are nine qualities found in a Christian's life. They come not by trying hard but through a close relationship with Jesus. Fruit is the natural product of a healthy plant. An orange tree will produce oranges, provided the tree is healthy. That's what an orange tree does. These are not the "works of the Spirit," but the "fruit of the Spirit." But when Christ is allowed to live His life in us, this fruit will be produced naturally. "...the fruit of the Spirit is love, joy, peace, patience, kindness, goodness, faithfulness, gentleness, and self-control" (Galatians 5:22-23). Those are our lifewords for today.

These qualities produce a Christ-like individual. But the Christian life is not just about me and Jesus. These fruit are seen in our relationships as well. As we love God and love others, that love is exhibited by joy, peace, patience, kindness, goodness, faithfulness, gentleness, and self-control. The Apostle Paul is never concerned with just our private morality. He's always teaching about how we relate one to another. So, in the context of these fruit, it's not about *you* and the Spirit. It's about *us* and the Spirit.

These fruit illustrate the truth that Christianity is "being before doing." Our lives should not be about "doing," but about "being." As we "be," we will naturally "do." Maturing in Christ is not primarily about a list of spiritual activities. Reading the Bible, attending church, and praying are byproducts. They are not rules to obey but fruit born from a relationship with Jesus. Doing is about me; being is about God doing something in me. Doing is about my efforts; being is about faith. Doing can lead to spiritual pride; being should produce humility. Doing is religion; being is relationship.

As we begin our look at the "fruit of the Spirit," let's keep in mind these words of Jesus: "Abide in Me, and I in you. As the branch cannot bear fruit of itself, unless it abides in the vine, neither can you, unless you abide in Me" (John 15:4). The fruit we bear is evidence of our connection to the Vine.

The Apostle Paul starts his discussion of the "fruit of the Spirit" with the word love. It's the Greek word agape. This word is rarely found outside the New Testament. Agape appears in Homer's writing 10 times, three times in Euripides', but 320 times in the New Testament. It would have been unfamiliar to the Galatian readers. Agape describes a love that is not dependent on the other person. Agape is an act of the will. I may have no emotional feelings for the person, but I can still "agape" them. Agape is a decision to act in another person's best interest.

Agape is also sacrificial. It must cost you something. We commonly think of love as giving. Of course, that's true, but it's more than that. It's giving up for the sake of another. If I take a bullet for another person, I have loved them in an "agape" kind of way. Agape happens no matter who they are, no matter how you feel, and no matter what it costs.

Jesus demonstrates this kind of love when He washes the feet of His disciples. Foot washing was a lowly task. It was important in New Testament times as people sat on the floor with dusty and smelly feet. It had to be done, but no one wanted to do it. The one person in the room who shouldn't have done it was Jesus. But Scripture records, "So he got up from the table, took off his robe, wrapped a towel around his waist, and poured water into a basin. Then he began to wash the disciples' feet, drying them with the towel he had around him" (John 13:4-5). Those are our lifewords for today.

Peter was embarrassed and said, "No, you shall never wash my feet!" Jesus answered, "Unless I wash you, you have no part with me" (John 13:8) We now understand that Jesus was speaking of His death on the cross. But more than that, Jesus was teaching Peter what agape love was all about. It's a willful act, in the interest of another, that costs something. Wow, there better be some serious "abiding" (John 15) going on to accomplish this!

Let's begin with our lifeword for today: "The fruit of the Spirit is love, joy..." (Galatians 5:22). Joy is not an easy word to define. It's pleasure, but it's more. It's happiness, but it's more. Joy seems to be deeper than both words. The Greek word here describes a feeling of inner gladness. The word is used for a feeling of happiness based on inner realities. Joy is a deeply rooted pleasure. Joy is an inside job. Joy doesn't just happen; it flows from a connection to the Spirit. So, the source of joy is God Himself. As we live connected to Him, we sense joy.

In Luke 10, we're told of a time when Jesus experienced joy. Jesus sends out 72 of His followers to go minister. They return days later excited about healings and people coming to faith. The Bible then says in Luke 10:21, "At that time Jesus, full of joy through the Holy Spirit, said, 'I praise you, Father, Lord of heaven and earth...'" We're told specifically it was the Holy Spirit who produced that explosion of joy. Notice that Jesus was joyful because His followers were "getting it." He was excited they were starting to understand their identity as servants of God. He shouted praises to His Heavenly Father. Seeing His followers grow filled Jesus with joy.

Often, our greatest joys come from other people, don't they? It's not just a solo thing. It comes from being connected to others. In the spiritual realm, the joy of seeing friends and loved ones become the Christians God created them to be is like no other. Joy is a gift of God that we experience best in community.

Fathers, mothers, grandfathers, grandmothers, coaches, and teachers all know the joy of seeing someone "get it." This is the joy of seeing someone you love make a discovery, master a skill, overcome a fear, or even become more like Christ. This kind of joy happens when we allow God to lead us into real relationships with others. When God bubbles up joy in our soul, it's a function of our relationship with Him and our relationships with others. Joy is an inside job. God is the source of real joy.

When Paul lists peace as a fruit of the Spirit, he doesn't mean feeling calm or serene. He refers to a literal peace, not just peace of mind. "Make every effort to keep the unity of the Spirit through the bond of peace" (Ephesians 4:3). The Greek word translated peace is "eirene." It was used often to describe a village where things operated well and people got along with each other. It's interesting to know that our towns in the past had a "justice of the peace." Modern day police officers were once called "peace officers."

A good biblical example of this is James, an early leader in the New Testament church. Back then, the church was dealing with a major problem. The Gentiles who converted to Christianity didn't see a need for the Law of Moses. They did not see the sense in those old Hebrew laws. Acts 15 tells us of the debate. James settles the argument and makes peace. "It is my judgment, therefore, that we should not make it difficult for the Gentiles who are turning to God" (Acts 15:19). Except for a few things, the Gentiles were released from the bulk of the Old Testament laws. This was a tough issue, but James handled it in a way that honored God and made peace.

In the days after Jesus died, the disciples needed peace. Jesus had been executed. Some were saying His body had been stolen, and others thought He was alive. What should they do now? Who was in charge? Into this confusion, Jesus came and said, "Peace be with you" (John 20:19). Those are our lifewords today. Jesus, the Prince of Peace, was alive.

But He couldn't stay. He was returning to his Father. So He gave them the gift of His Holy Spirit to be with them and in them. In John's Gospel, we read that Jesus actually breathed on them and said, "Receive the Holy Spirit" (John 20:22). Jesus gave them peace, and then He gave them the Spirit to keep their peace. Like a "justice of the peace" or a "peace officer," the Holy Spirit brought order and harmony. He wants to do the same thing for us today.

One thing I love about being a Christian is that it's practical. It helps us in the day in and day out grind of life. The fourth fruit of the Spirit is about as practical as it gets. I need patience. Whether driving my car, raising my teenagers, leading my church, or trying to lose weight, I need patience every day.

The word "patience" is from a Greek word that literally mean "long anger." Older versions of the Bible translated it "longsuffering." That usually means you're putting up with a difficult situation for a long time. But the word used here in Galatians 5 is a relational word. So, in this context, patience means "long anger" with people. If I'm patient, I'm slow to get angry with other people.

In 1 Corinthians 13:4, Paul uses this word when he writes, "Love is patient." That's our lifeword for today. We read in Psalm 103:8 that "The Lord is compassionate and merciful, slow to get angry and filled with unfailing love." 2 Peter 3:9 tells us that God is "patient for your sake. He does not want anyone to be destroyed, but wants everyone to repent."

Jesus showed patience in His relationship with Peter. Peter was hard-headed, emotional, quick to fly off the handle, and prone to sticking his foot in his mouth. Also, when the game was on the line, Peter denied Jesus. But Jesus never gave up on him. After three long years of patience, Peter was the rock on whom Jesus would build His Church (Matthew 16:18).

That's biblical patience. That is a fruit of God's Holy Spirit in our lives. Being slow to anger, even when you're hurt and upset at how another person is acting. Patience is waiting until they mature. This is hard for me. I'm a fixer. I want to fix this problem and move to the next. But people aren't problems to be fixed. They're persons to be loved. And love is patient.

If you're old like me, you remember renting VHS movie tapes. This was way before the ease and convenience of DVDs and Netflix. These tapes had to be rewound before they were returned to the video store. You may remember the sticker that said, "Be kind. Rewind."

Our fifth "fruit of the Spirit" is kindness. It is simple courtesy, like "rewinding," but it's more significant than that. The word comes from a Greek word that often depicted rulers who were kind and benevolent to their subjects. This word refers to a person's inner disposition.

Paul says that God exhibits kindness. "But when the kindness and love of God our Savior appeared, He saved us, not because of righteous things we had done, but because of His mercy" (Titus 3:4-5). God recognized our neediness. He knew we were lost unless He did something. Kindness understands what is needed and then has the compassion to take action. In this context, that action was in the person of Jesus Christ.

The Old Testament story of David and Mephibosheth shows the Hebrew equivalent of kindness. As king, David reached out to a member of King Saul's family. This was unheard of. The outgoing regime was a threat. But because of David's friendship with Jonathan, Saul's son, he says in 2 Samuel 9:1, "Is there anyone still left of the house of Saul to whom I can show kindness for Jonathan's sake?" David found Mephibosheth and showed him kindness. The story ends with these words: "And Mephibosheth lived in Jerusalem, because he always ate at the king's table" (2 Samuel 9:13). Biblical kindness happens when one who doesn't have to do so reaches down and graciously helps an undeserving person.

This gives Ephesians 4:32 new meaning: "Be kind and compassionate to one another, forgiving each other, just as in Christ God forgave you." Those are our lifewords for today. Christ was gracious and did something He didn't have to do. Jesus did that for undeserving people. Paul calls us to do the same.

"The fruit of the Spirit is love, joy, peace, patience, kindness, goodness..." (Galatians 5:22-23). Those are our lifewords for today. Let's focus on "goodness" today. When someone does a good job, we usually refer to the quality of the work. He's a good tennis player. She's a good cook. They are a good company. But this is not the sense of our word today. The word "goodness" is the Greek word "agathusune." It means being good to someone. It's a relational word. It can mean generous or big-hearted.

Isn't this the same as yesterday's word, kindness? There is one key difference. Goodness has a spiritual component to it. It's when you help someone in a tangible way, but you also offer the person some form of spiritual guidance through the situation. That's goodness.

Kindness is helping someone move. Goodness is helping them move, and as we're loading the truck, we have a spiritual conversation, and I listen and offer counsel. This is an example of goodness—spiritual care and practical help.

It's harder to show goodness than it is to show kindness. A biblically good person takes the time to enter into someone's life and offer direction. Kindness is about the deed. Goodness is about the person. Getting involved with people can be messy and time-consuming.

In Acts 10:38, the Bible says, "God anointed Jesus of Nazareth with the Holy Spirit and power, and how he went around doing good and healing all who were under the power of the devil, because God was with him." We would expect Jesus not just to be kind, but to do good—to help in a spiritual way.

This is a challenge for all of us. As Christians, we are to be kind people, people of good deeds. There is a time and place for that and that only. But our heart's desire must be for goodness to shine through. We long to be good people who use the good deed as an open door for spiritual conversation. As we said before, good deeds create good which will open doors for good news.

Our seventh word in our look at the fruit of the Spirit is "faithfulness." It's a variation of the word "faith." Without faith, our Christian life would crumble. Faith in Christ, faith in God, and the exercising of our own faith are all core to Christianity. In Galatians 5:22, Paul uses this word to describe our relationships with each other. In essence, Paul says that just as God is faithful to us, we can be faithful to one another.

Paul wrote this letter to the Galatians and probably included "faithfulness" in his list because some people in Galatia had deserted him. After he left, the Galatians were not faithful to Paul's leadership and his message. "Those people are zealous to win you over, but for no good. What they want is to alienate you from us, so that you may have zeal for them" (Galatians 4:17).

Lewis Smedes, in his book *The Power of Promises*, writes, "Yes, somewhere people still make and keep promises. They choose not to quit when the going gets rough...they stick to lost causes. They hold on to a love grown cold. They make promises and care enough to keep the promises they make. If you have people you will not forsake, if you have causes you will not abandon, then you are like God." Smedes calls this place "somewhere." Maybe it should be the church.

"Somewhere," there's a church where people regularly attend worship even though the music is not always great, the kids aren't always cooperative, and the weather isn't always sunny. But people still come because others are counting on them. "Somewhere," there's a church where people support the ministry even when it's hard because people are counting on them.

This church named "somewhere" is not made of brick and mortar; it's made of people. People like you and me. If this "somewhere" church is to exist, it only does because of the faithful people in it. May the church you attend be that kind of church because of your faithfulness.

Gentleness is defined as being submissive to someone, voluntarily assuming equality with someone who is inferior. I don't know about you, but that doesn't sound very attractive to me. It sounds like you let someone step all over you. We often think of gentleness as weakness and spinelessness. Is that really a fruit of the Spirit? Let's see what the biblical word means.

The Greek word for gentleness can refer to tamed animals. Biblically, gentleness is power under control. You may picture a 2,000-pound horse that has been tamed. Gentleness describes an animal that has come under the control of a master. Gentleness is the natural outflow of that life that has been tamed. In this context, taming is done by God's Holy Spirit.

Let's apply this word to our relationship with God and others. As we walk in the Spirit, a taming has happened so that we can honor His will in our life. We are not to rebel and go against God. The Bible often refers to people with hearts like stone, or hearts that are cold or hardened. This is the opposite of a gentle person who has had their heart softened by God.

As we look at our relationship with others, it goes back to the idea of power under control. Jesus had "all authority in heaven and on earth" (Matthew 28:18), yet held little children in His lap. He was restrained, so as to be gentle and kind. On the night He was betrayed, Jesus speaks a powerful statement:" Don't you realize that I could ask my Father for thousands of angels to protect us, and he would send them instantly?" (Matthew 26:53). Jesus has strength under the control of His Father.

If you have the power to humiliate someone but do not, you have not shown weakness but gentleness. Not using the power you have is truly a fruit of the Spirit. People often say rude things and deserve what they have coming. But gentleness is "not returning evil for evil" (Romans 12:17).

Today, we come to the last fruit of the Spirit. We all have to admit that self-control is an elusive quality of the Christ-like life. "Just say no" is not easy. It's easier said than done. "Just say no" people are well meaning, but they underestimate the power of the sinful nature. The sinful nature wants to do opposite of what the Spirit wants. And the Spirit gives us desires that are the opposite of what the sinful nature desires. These two are fighting each other, so you are not free to carry out your good intentions (Galatians 5:17).

The Greek word translated self-control literally means "strength inside." It's the ability to govern your own behavior. Where can we find the strength to say "No" to ourselves? Before the fruit of the Spirit is listed, we have this verse: "So I say, live by the Spirit, and you will not gratify the desires of the sinful nature" (Galatians 5:16). This is our lifeword for today. We find strength by saying "yes" to God's Spirit. It's not "Just say no"; it's "Just say yes!"

Jesus said yes to the Spirit at His baptism (Matthew 3:16). Jesus said yes to the Spirit who led him to be tempted (Matthew 4:1). He said yes to the Spirit who anointed Him to preach good news to the poor (Luke 4:18). The night before the cross, He said no to His own will and yes to God's (Luke 22:42).

Saying "Yes" to the Spirit is an hour by hour and day by day decision. "...live by the Spirit" (Galatians 5:16). This is not a one-time decision. Old habits and ways of life tend to keep creeping into our lives. New temptations are just around the corner.

I wonder if there is any meaning to the order of the fruit of the Spirit? Allow me to speculate. Love may come first because all the rest describe how we love one another. Paul ends the list with self-control. Without saying "yes" to God's Holy Spirit, which allows you to say "no" to yourself, none of the others are possible.

Let's transition now to one of my favorite Old Testament stories. The story has fascinated me ever since I wore a needle through the Statler Brothers singing "The Fourth Man." For you young people, a needle was used to play an album. An album was this big disc... oh, never mind, just trust me.

It's the story of King Nebuchadnezzar and three Hebrew boys named Shadrach, Meshach, and Abednego. The king made a gold statue 90 feet tall and ordered everyone to bow to the ground to worship it. Anyone who refused would be thrown into a blazing furnace. The three Hebrews would not obey because they knew this was breaking God's first Commandment (Exodus 20:3).

King Nebuchadnezzar flew into a rage and ordered Shadrach, Meshach, and Abednego to be brought before him. The king gave them another chance, but the three refused to bow to the idol. Shadrach, Meshach, and Abednego said, "If we are thrown into the blazing furnace, the God whom we serve is able to save us. But even if He doesn't we will never serve your gods or worship the gold statue you have set up" (Daniel 3:17-18).

Did you catch it? Five amazing words..."But even if He doesn't..." Those are our lifewords for today. Shadrach, Meshach, and Abednego trusted in the will of God even if He chose NOT to deliver them. That's really important for us in our daily lives. In good times and bad, mountain tops and valleys, we trust the will of God... especially in the fire. We do what is right and leave the rest up to God.

If God says no to your hopes and dreams, will you still trust Him? If God says no to your plans for the future, will you still serve Him? Some of our prayers are answered; others are not. I have no clue why. It's not my business to know. It's my business to do what is right and then to trust in His will. The Bible says His will is good, acceptable, and perfect (Romans 12:2).

Someone has said there are three different types of people in the world: those who are getting ready to go through trouble, those who are in trouble now, and those who are coming out of trouble. I'm sure you can relate. It seems like there is always something just around the bend that we haven't planned for. The story of Shadrach, Meshach, and Abednego in the fiery furnace can help us deal with the difficult times of our lives.

Yesterday we saw where they chose to do the right thing and leave the results up to God. They trusted in His will no matter if the outcome for them was good or bad. "...But even if He doesn't..." (Daniel 3:17). "But even if He doesn't" illustrates a trust in God that doesn't lean on my own understanding (Proverbs 3:5). Today, we see that the three Hebrews made that decision *before* the hard time came. In the context of this story in Daniel 3, they decided *before* the fire that they belonged to God and would not deny Him. They made the decision *before* they stood before King Nebuchadnezzar and were faced with death. In the emotion of the moment, it's easier to compromise. That's why you need to decide before you're tested.

It's important to say one big *yes* to God now, and all the other *yeses* will be easier to say. You'll still have to say the little *yeses* but if you've already said the big *yes* to His way and His will in your life, your direction has already been set. That big *yes* is described for us in Colossians 3:17, and it's our lifeword for today: "And whatever you do, whether in word or deed, do it all in the name of the Lord Jesus, giving thanks to God the Father through him." Whatever we do, it's in the name of the Lord Jesus. Paul repeats this same thought in 1 Corinthians 10:31: "So, whether you eat or drink, or whatever you do, do all to the glory of God." If I say a big *yes* to God, the tough times of life can be dealt with.

We all face fires in our lives. Maybe not quite as hot as Shadrach, Meshach, and Abednego, but hot nonetheless. Today's devotional teaches an important lesson for everyone who's in a fire. Our story continues with King Nebuchadnezzar ordering the furnace heated seven times hotter than usual. He commanded his strongest soldiers to tie up Shadrach, Meshach, and Abednego and throw them into the furnace. The furnace was so hot that the flames of the fire killed the soldiers. Then, the King saw something in the fire that made him leap to his feet. He said, "Look! I see four men walking around in the fire, unbound and unharmed, and the fourth looks like a son of the gods." That's from Daniel 3:25 and is our lifeword for today.

God was in the fire with the three Hebrews! Even through your hottest fires, God will be there with you. God will join you in the fire. Few people went through the fires of difficulty more than Joseph in the Old Testament. Looking back on his life, Luke writes in Acts 7:9, "Because the patriarchs were jealous of Joseph, they sold him as a slave into Egypt. But God was with him." God was with Joseph when his brothers threw him in a pit and sold him into slavery. God was with Joseph when he was lied about, thrown into prison, and forgotten. "But God was with him."

God, through the prophet Isaiah, promised to be with His people during the hard times of life. "When you pass through the waters, I will be with you; and when you pass through the rivers, they will not sweep over you. When you walk through the fire, you will not be burned; the flames will not set you ablaze" (Isaiah 43:2). Jesus has promised His presence will be with us. "I am with you always, to the end of the age" (Matthew 28:20).

Shadrach, Meshach, and Abednego were walking by faith (2 Corinthians 5:7). Sometimes, faith leads to a hard place, but God has promised to be there with us. No matter where God leads, as you walk with Him, He will be with you. He'll join you in the fire.

Before we leave the story of Shadrach, Meshach, and Abednego, allow me to make three observations. First, Scripture records that three men went into the fire, four were seen in the fire, and three came out. The question must be, "Where is the fourth man?" As the Speer Family sang 30 years ago, "He's still in the fire." Praise God! He's there for the next battle you face. When the fires of life get hot, you can call His name, and He'll be there, because He's still in the fire.

Second, it's also interesting to see that Shadrach, Meshach, and Abednego were "walking around in the fire" (Daniel 3:25). Those are our lifewords for today. Have you ever been through a hard time that seemed to paralyze you? It was hard to put one foot in front of another. If you find yourself in one of those times, remember the three Hebrews. The Bible says they were walking around in the fire. They were in a literal fire, and they were walking around. They were functioning in the fire.

In the same way, Paul and Silas were "praying and singing hymns to God, and the other prisoners were listening to them" (Acts 16:25). They were singing and praising God in jail. Their fire did not defeat them. They were functioning in their fire, and you can too. You may feel weak, but that's when God's grace will be the strongest (2 Corinthians 12:10).

Finally, have you ever been through a difficult time and wondered the purpose behind it all? Of course, you have. I have, too. When that happens, remember Shadrach, Meshach, and Abednego. After God delivers them, King Nebuchadnezzar says, "No one will ever speak against the God of Shadrach, Meshach, and Abednego." That's our lifeword today from Daniel 3:29. You may never know it, but God will use your fire. Believers and unbelievers will watch you go through your fire. Your difficult times will give you a testimony of God's grace. As Paul and Silas were singing and praying in jail, "other prisoners were listening to them."

I wasn't much of a grammar student, but I do remember that the word "but" is a conjunction. Conjunctions are little words that connect sentences or phrases. "And" is a conjunction, but I don't like it as well as "but." When this word appears, things change. "I was going to mow the grass, but I took a nap instead."

Combine this conjunction with the word "God," and it's dynamite. Real change is about to happen. Throughout Scripture, we see over and over again the phrase, "But God." When you read that phrase, what came before it is immediately qualified, and many times, it's corrected, because God is on the move.

"But God" can be two life-changing words. After all, with God nothing is impossible (Luke 1:37). "For scarcely for a righteous man will one die...But God demonstrates His own love toward us, in that while we were still sinners, Christ died for us.(Romans 5:7-8). Those are our lifewords for today. You are a sinner, but God shows His love by sending Jesus.

We all understand the importance of making a good impression. We clean up the house before company comes over. We pick out just the right outfit when we go for a job interview. Our moms spit on their hands and tried to get our hair to lie down. Cleaning up is important. "But God" doesn't demand we clean ourselves up before we approach Him. "While we were still sinners, Christ died for us." He loves us when were not cleaned up. God doesn't love us because we "get presentable." He loves us in our sin and invites unclean people to accept Christ.

The fact that God loves in spite of man's sin is written on every page of the Bible. He loves you just as you are and has made a way for you. That way is the person of Jesus. Accept Christ today and stop trying to get presentable. Allow Him to do that for you through His grace. Then, you'll understand the power of "but God."

This week, we're taking about the phrase "But God." When those words are used, something is about to happen. Bad changes to good and worry changes to hope. For instance, Paul wrote of a friend of his who was seriously ill. "For indeed he was sick almost unto death; but God had mercy on him, and not only on him but on me also, lest I should have sorrow upon sorrow" (Philippians 2:27). Those two little words, "But God," changed death to life.

Our lifeword today is from Psalm 73:26, "My flesh and my heart may fail, but God is the strength of my heart and my portion forever." The psalmist is despondent. He's discouraged. But he speaks truth into his despondency and his discouragement. "But God is the strength of my heart and my portion forever." He battles unbelief with the truth of God.

The Hebrew word for strength literally means rock. "God is my rock" is a good translation. Further, the text says He is "my portion forever." In Old Testament times, portion referred to land given to families. God is our inheritance and legacy. But God is my rock and my inheritance forever!

The Bible is full of examples of God's people struggling with low spirits. Christians aren't immune from discouragement and depression. But we have the truth to counter our feelings. Psalm 19:7 says, "The law of the Lord is perfect, reviving the soul." If my soul needs to be revived, it was in some sense dead. It wasn't literally dead; it probably just felt that way.

The Bible is full of real people going through real problems. They struggled with the same things we struggle with. Their stories are there to help us fight unbelief and discouragement. We fight with the truth of God's promises like our lifeword today. "God is the strength of my heart and my portion forever." We repeat that. We put it on our refrigerator. We preach to ourselves. We memorize it. Most importantly, we believe it.

Have you ever felt inadequate to do what you knew God wanted you to do? Have you felt like He should have given someone else this task to complete? As a pastor, I've felt that way many times, more than you could imagine. Most pastors I know feel the same way.

There's a "But God" verse that has encouraged me during times of doubt. Paul writes in 1 Corinthians 1:26-27, "Brothers and sisters, think of what you were when you were called. Not many of you were wise by human standards; not many were influential; not many were of noble birth. But God chose the foolish things of the world to shame the wise; God chose the weak things of the world to shame the strong." These are our lifewords for today.

Throughout God's Word, He takes the "weak things" and uses them. God used Moses, but only after He humbled him in the desert. God used David, a shepherd boy, to confront and defeat Goliath. God called Gideon to save Israel, and Gideon couldn't believe it. " 'Pardon me, my lord,' Gideon replied, 'but how can I save Israel? My clan is the weakest in Manasseh, and I am the least in my family' " (Judges 6:15). In the face of Gideon's doubt and fears, God told him; "I will be with you, and you will strike down all the Midianites, leaving none alive" (Judges 6:16).

Why does God use nobodies? "That no flesh should glory in His presence" (1 Corinthians 1:29). In Heaven and on earth, no one should boast of their abilities. We should sing the praises of God only. We humans are prone to taking the credit if we can. There's a story of a woodpecker pecking on a tree. While pecking, a lightning bolt splits the tree. The woodpecker flew away and came back with three more woodpeckers. Proudly he said, "Just look at what I did." The lightning was a "but God." When we take credit for it, God will stop the lightning.

The last three days, we've been discussing the little phrase, "But God." These two words can help us climb any mountain. They will take us safely across any river and lead us through any dark valley. "But God" is full of the hope that there is ONE in this universe who can always come to my defense. There is ONE in this universe that is not limited. There is ONE in this universe who understands my heart.

"But God" is the very heartbeat of the gospel. It's the testimony of every Christian. What would have come of Adam and Eve if not for a "but God?" Without a "But God," what would have happened after the Tower of Babel? In the Old Testament, Joseph had more mountains, rivers, and valleys to go through than most of us will ever encounter. When the New Testament looks back on his life, it says, "but God was with him" (Acts 7:9). What would have happened to the whole nation of Israel without a "But God" at the Red Sea? Jesus would only have been another good teacher if it had not been for a "But God." The Apostle Paul would still be a Pharisee if not for "But God."

"But God" allows us to be honest about life. Sometimes, Christians, in an effort to express faith, ignore the reality of real problems in our lives. We shouldn't deny hardships but face them with a "But God." Placing those two words in a sentence can bring faith to every real-life battle you face. Here's an example. The doctor says I have lung cancer, but God has promised He will never leave me nor forsake me. How about this? My husband and I are still separated, but God is working on his heart. Those are our lifewords for today from Hebrews 13:5.

"But God" are powerful words that express faith in the midst of the difficult realities we all face. Those two words can testify to our trust in God. Those two words allow God to have the final say in every battle we face.

I played a video at church once titled, "How big is your but?" It's based on the premise that the bigger our "but," the less will happen in our lives. I need to lose weight **but** I lack the self-control. I need to go back to school **but** I have too much going on. I need to stop spending so much time on the internet **but** I'll start tomorrow. I need to start saving for retirement **but** my expenses are too high. What would change if I followed all of those statements with a "But God," instead of a "but I?" Here are some "But God" verses.

Genesis 50:20 – "You meant to harm me, **but God** intended it for good to accomplish what is now being done, the saving of many lives." Joseph saw God's hand in his life, and the turnaround could only be credited to a "But God" moment.

Acts 2:24 – "**But God** raised him from the dead, freeing him from the agony of death, because it was impossible for death to keep its hold on him." A "But God" turned a very bad Friday into Good Friday.

Romans 6:23 – "For the wages of sin is death, **but** the gift of **God** is eternal life in Christ Jesus our Lord." "But God" is the essence of the gospel of Jesus Christ.

Ephesians 2:4-5 – "***But God***...because of the great love with which he loved us, even when we were dead in our trespasses, made us alive together with Christ — by grace you have been saved." "But God" did something for us we could not do for ourselves.

Use these verses and others to lessen the size of your "but." Remember, the bigger your God, the smaller and smaller your "buts" are. Matthew 19:26 says, "Jesus looked at them and said, 'With man this is impossible, **but** all things are possible with **God.**'"

Many times, we have a "But God" experience in our life as a function of prayer. We pray, God answers, and things change. That's the very definition of "But God." But is there a right way to pray? In Luke 11, one of Jesus' followers asked Him to teach the whole group how to pray. If I'd been in Jesus' shoes, I would have said something like, "Just talk to God. Prayer is as easy as breathing. Just imagine Jesus sitting here right next to you. You can't mess it up." In fact, those very words have come out of my mouth before. But Jesus didn't answer that way. He taught them to pray. So, my question remains: Is there a right way to pray?

He proceeds to give them what we know as the "Lord's Prayer" (Luke 11:2-4). I don't think anyone believes these are the words we have to say all the time. He gave them a kind of synopsis. Then, He starts a discussion about prayer. To me, what comes after the "Lord's Prayer" is more important than the prayer itself. Jesus immediately started teaching about persistence in prayer. Check it out in Luke 11:5-12.

You don't need to be a Bible scholar to see the lesson Jesus is teaching. God desires that you just keep asking in prayer. Be persistent. If at first you don't succeed, try, try again. Never give up. Don't stop praying. Even if it seems to be taking a while, hang in there.

In Luke 11:8, Jesus says the man gets what he wants because of his boldness. Other translations say "shameless audacity." The word here could just as easily be translated persistence. Jesus basically says that because you have been shameless in your asking, shameless in your persistence, because you have boldly asked and asked, I will answer.

I don't like it when my son bugs me about something over and over again. That's earthly thinking. Heavenly thinking says we are to pray without being embarrassed about how often we ask God. God isn't annoyed by our persistent prayers. He loves for us to rely on Him.

In Luke 11:5-13, Jesus teaches about prayer. This is in response to one of His followers who asked Him, "Teach us to pray." Jesus could have gone any direction in answering this man's request. But He chose to talk about persistence. God is not irritated when you ask and ask and keep on asking. Don't quit asking, because your persistence may move the heart of God.

Our lifewords today are from Luke 11:9. Jesus says, "And so I tell you, keep on asking, and you will receive what you ask for. Keep on seeking, and you will find. Keep on knocking, and the door will be opened to you." Jesus uses three words to emphasize this persistence theme: ask, seek, and knock. Jesus says keep on coming on strong. Don't relent. Your Father is moved by persistent prayer.

The writer of Hebrews tells us, "So let us come boldly to the throne of our gracious God. There we will receive his mercy, and we will find grace to help us when we need it most" (Hebrews 4:16). The word "boldly," in the original language, means plain speech that hides nothing. It also has the idea of fearlessness. So, we speak to God plainly, not holding back, fearless of bothering or annoying Him.

Prayer is not a time when we try to make a good impression on God. Using flowery words or sounding pious carry no weight with Him. Prayer should not conceal what's going on in our heart of hearts. God wants to hear... warts and all. In our humanness, we may ask for the wrong thing. But God loves a passionate prayer.

Sometimes, God does not answer the way we want. Paul experienced that. Jesus experienced that! We're not talking about a divine vending machine that pays off if we pray long enough. I don't understand all the mysteries of prayer. But the Bible clearly teaches that God is moved by our persistent prayers.

I've been guilty of saying this: "You better be careful what you pray for, 'cause you just might get it." This was usually said in the context of God sending someone to the mission field... like that's a bad thing! While I said this jokingly, it gives the wrong impression of God. It denies His character as a good God. It assumes that God may give us something bad.

Into this unbiblical thinking comes our lifeword for today from Luke 11:11-13: "If a son asks for bread from any father among you, will he give him a stone? Or if he asks for a fish, will he give him a serpent instead of a fish? Or if he asks for an egg, will he offer him a scorpion? If you then, being evil, know how to give good gifts to your children, how much more will your heavenly Father give the Holy Spirit to those who ask Him!"

God's answers to your prayers will never be bad for you. If I, as an imperfect dad, want to give good gifts to my children, won't God, who is perfect, do the same? Trust your good Father to answer in a good way. Trust God's goodness that you will receive what is good, find what is a blessing, and have doors opened that will provide meaning and purpose in your life. God's Holy Spirit is the Father's best gift. It's the gift of Himself to live within us forever.

Here's what Jesus is saying in Luke 11: Every once in a while, maybe more than that, maybe more than we could ever imagine, God responds to persistent prayer. Jesus could have gone a hundred different directions when He was asked about prayer. But He chose to focus on persistence. So, when you ask, keep asking. And when you knock, keep knocking. And when you seek, keep seeking. God honors persistent prayer. That's what Jesus taught.

Many times, before smart phones and GPSs were common everyday things, my wife, Sue, and I would take drives in the country and invariably get lost. We'd have to stop and ask for directions. One guy told me to go to the first stop sign and hang a left. Then, go the next stop sign and hang a right. He said I'd come to a major intersection. I should turn right then but shouldn't go much farther before I stop and ask again. Stopping and asking again... that's a good spiritual principle. That's really what prayer is all about; stopping and asking God for directions. Again and again and again.

Our lifeword today comes from James 1:5: "If any of you lacks wisdom, you should ask God, who gives generously to all." This verse is an open invitation to stop and ask the Creator of the universe for directions. In a sense, we're tapping into infinite wisdom. Wow! With Him, we've got wisdom on tap, an endless well of guidance, direction, and insight. And the verse says He's not stingy with it. He's generous, and all we have to do is stop and ask.

Stopping and asking is a sign of wisdom. For one to do this, they must already possess some measure of it. Fools don't realize they need wisdom (Proverbs. 1:7). Continually stopping and asking is not a sign of ignorance. It takes wisdom to know what you don't know. Read that again; it's important. Psalm 25:9 says, "He leads the humble in what is right, teaching them his way." It takes humility to stop and ask, and it takes wisdom to be humble.

I always get a kick out of Psalm 32:8-9. It says, "I will instruct you and teach you in the way you should go; I will guide you with My eye. Do not be like the horse or mule..." So, the wisdom from God's Word today says, "Do not be like a horse or mule. Stop and ask of God."

Jesus made this promise: "If you abide in Me, and My words abide in you, you will ask what you desire, and it shall be done for you." That's from John 15:7, and it's our lifeword for today. We love the last part of that verse, "...ask what you desire, and it shall be done for you." But that is based on the first part of the verse, "If you abide in Me, and My words abide in you."

The word translated as "abide" means to remain or continue. Our relationship with Jesus isn't based on a one-time event but is the result of a day by day, week by week walk with Him. As we maintain vital communion with God, things start changing in our lives. As you abide with Him and His Word, you get in sync with His will. Your understanding of prayer will change. You won't see it as getting God to do for you, but getting you to conform to His desires.

First John 5:14–15 says, "Now this is the confidence we have in approaching God: that if we ask God for anything according to his will, He hears us." As we remain in Him, abide in Him, we know His words, and His words are in us. That gives us confidence and boldness that we won't ask anything contrary to His will.

When you know your prayers are aligned with God's will, you can pray with the confidence that John speaks of in 1 John 5:14. You don't demand of God, but you also don't have to sheepishly utter your petitions. You can boldly ask and expect God to answer. The more you abide, the more confident you are of your relationship with Him. This kind of walk with God leads to answered prayers because the person who walks closely knows what to ask for.

Let's spend several days gleaning from the book of Proverbs. In 1990, as his son was entering college, H. Jackson Brown wrote down important things he wanted his son to know. Eventually, the advice he gave his son would be published as *Life's Little Instruction Book*. It was a bestseller that sold millions of copies. In approximately 1,000 B.C., Solomon did the same thing. We know this as the book Proverbs. Solomon wrote to his son (Proverbs 1:8) tidbits of advice for living successfully.

We all need advice, and Proverbs teaches that it's essential for success in life. "Listen to advice and accept discipline, and at the end you will be counted among the wise" (Proverbs 19:20). Those are our lifewords for today. Taking the wrong advice can get you in deep trouble. "The way of fools seems right to them, but the wise listen to advice" (Proverbs 12:15).

Sometimes, I'll have an idea about something I want to do, and my wife will give me some reasons not to do it. I don't like that. I have my heart set on doing it, and I'm not receptive to any reasons why I shouldn't. That's not good. It's a prescription for failure. More than likely, pride is at the root of not wanting to hear an opposing opinion. I always need to be open for counsel. Proverbs 13:10 says, "Pride leads to conflict; those who take advice are wise."

Jesus said, "For which of you, desiring to build a tower, does not first sit down and count the cost, whether he has enough to complete it?" (Luke 14:28). Part of counting the cost is taking advice, especially opposing opinions. I always need to be open and receptive to advice that I may not want to hear. If I'm not, it's a prescription for disaster.

The book of Proverbs has much to say about choosing the right friends. Likewise, it wants you to be choosy when seeking advice. Lots of people may be willing to give advice, but be careful whose counsel you give weight in your life. Proverbs 14:7 says it very plainly: "Stay away from a fool, for you will not find knowledge on their lips." When you need advice, listen to the people you respect, who have the credibility to give advice. Look for a "been there, done that" kind of person. Listen to advice from people who've been there.

When you ask for counsel, you are putting yourself in a vulnerable position. You need to make sure this person has your interests at heart, that he or she isn't advising you with a hidden agenda. You can tell if a person is on your side if they don't tell you what you want to hear. "Wounds from a friend can be trusted..." (Proverbs 27:6).

Advice from the wrong people can lead you astray. "The thoughts of the righteous are just; the counsels of the wicked are deceitful" (Proverbs 12:5). A lot of advice may come your way. It's important to be very choosy about who you truly listen to because "Whoever walks with the wise becomes wise..." (Proverbs 13:20).

Also, among our wise counselors, we must understand that no one person has all the answers. Where in the world could we find one person qualified to advise on all subjects? It's best to have several people you rely on who can give you counsel. Solomon tells us that "Plans fail for lack of counsel, but with many advisors they succeed" (Proverbs 15:22).

If everyone agrees, your decision is easy. But that won't happen very often. Many times you have to sort through varying opinions. In the end, the decision will be yours. Solomon said, "Every prudent man acts with knowledge..." (Proverbs 13:16). Advice from several sources means you will have more knowledge. The more knowledge you have, the better your decision will be.

Here's a fact of life: Wherever you have people, you will have some level of conflict among them. Living a solitary life is the one way to avoid conflict with others. For 99.9% of us, that's not a realistic option. It's crucial for our sanity that we learn to deal with the conflict that comes up every day. Today, we'll see what the book of Proverbs says about handling conflict in our lives.

Solomon said, "It makes you look good when you avoid a fight - only fools love to quarrel" (Proverbs 20:3). These are our lifewords for today. Friction in our relationships is inevitable, but the verse says we can avoid fighting. If there's difficulty in a relationship, you can't stick your head in the sand. You must deal with it. Ignoring the conflict will probably make it worse. One way to avoid a quarrel is to deal with the friction before it gets to the level of an argument. Ignoring the issue will usually blow it up into a full-fledged quarrel.

Solomon said, "A fool shows his annoyance at once..." (Proverbs 12:16). The New Testament says, "Do not repay evil with evil or insult with insult" (1 Peter 3:9). When people irritate us, something inside of us wants to give it back to them. Somewhere, someone has told you not to hold it in. After all, sometimes you have to vent. This strategy doesn't work. You may feel better because you've vented, but more times than not, you've done damage to the relationship and to your reputation. Think before you speak. Consider your response. The Psalmist said, "Set a guard, O Lord, over my mouth; keep watch over the door of my lips!" (Psalm 141:3).

I'm not saying to hold it in forever. That would be sticking your head in the sand. I'm saying don't fly off the handle. "The heart of the righteous weighs its answers, but the mouth of the wicked gushes evil" (Proverbs 15:28). "Short-tempered people do foolish things..." (Proverbs 14:17). "People with understanding control their anger; a hot temper shows great foolishness" (Proverbs 14:29). Delaying your response helps you avoid conflict.

Let's remember our lifewords from yesterday: "It makes you look good when you avoid a fight...only fools love to quarrel" (Proverbs 20:3). Conflict in our relationships does not have to turn into a fight. It's a sign of Christian maturity when we can deal with conflict without it blowing up in our faces.

Several years back, a couple in my church came to me with some issues. Before we spoke about it, they led in prayer. I greatly respected that. That's usually the "pastor" thing to do. When a lay person did it, I was very encouraged. We had an adult conversation about the issues. I don't remember any of the issues we spoke of, but I do remember this: we all spoke in a calm way, without any anger or emotion. Solomon writes, "...a wise man keeps himself under control" (Proverbs 29:11). Those are our lifewords for today.

It's almost impossible to avoid quarreling if you don't take seriously what each other is saying. Say what you have to say, but do it gently. Don't do it apologetically. You won't be taken seriously. Say it firmly but gently. "A gentle answer turns away wrath, but a harsh word stirs up anger" (Proverbs 15:1).

While it's crucial for each side to air their own opinion, sooner or later, you have to turn the corner and seek a solution. This can't be about who is right and who is wrong. It can't be about blaming someone. We must seek resolution. Again, we go back to Romans 12:18: "If it is possible, as much as it depends on you, live at peace." Peace is the goal. Hopefully that can be a solution that is acceptable to both. If not, agreeing to disagree may be the only solution available.

Christian people should have no desire to keep the conflict going. We want to avoid it. Not by sticking your head in the sand but by dealing with it. Use words that are gentle and always strive for a solution. While friction in our relationships is inevitable, we can take steps to avoid it becoming a fight.

It's amazing to me that almost all of Proverbs 5, 6, and 7 is devoted to the dangers of the adulteress woman. Remember, Proverbs is a father writing to his son. It could just as easily be a mother writing to her daughter. If you're male or female, but especially male, you will have times in your life when you are tempted by sexual immorality. It may not be adultery, but it could be pornography or premarital sexual activity. You will be tempted to depart from God's ideal, which is one man and one woman, joined in marriage. Nearly one of 10 verses in the whole book of Proverbs is devoted to this temptation.

Allow me to paraphrase some of Proverbs 7:6-22. This is "wisdom" speaking: "While I was looking out my window, I saw a young man who lacked common sense. He was strolling down the path of an immoral woman's house. She approached him seductively. She threw her arms around him, kissed him, and said, 'You're the one I was looking for! My bed is spread with beautiful blankets and I've perfumed my bed. Come, let's drink our fill of love until morning. Let's enjoy each other's caresses.' So, she seduced him with her pretty speech and enticed him with her flattery. He followed her like an ox going to the slaughter. He was like a bird flying into a snare, not knowing it will cost him his life."

The message of the text is clear, isn't it? Sexual immorality will look good, feel good, and smell good. It will be tempting. But it will destroy you. You will not survive. God's wisdom says very plainly, "Don't go there." "Don't let your hearts stray away toward her. Don't wander down her wayward path" (Proverbs 7:25). Those are our lifewords for today.

The Bible teaches us that when it comes to sexual immorality, what looks good will ruin you. What starts out tasting sweet is going to turn sour. So it says of sexual immorality: "Her bedroom is the den of death" (Proverbs 7:27). The New Testament agrees. "Flee sexual immorality" (1 Corinthians 6:18).

Yesterday, our lifeword warned against sexual immorality. "Don't let your hearts stray away toward her. Don't wander down her wayward path" (Proverbs 7:25).

Pastor Kevin Miller says that when the Bible warns against sexual immorality, people assume God is a cosmic killjoy. Actually, God is a keepjoy. God desires to keep joy in your life. So, He says, "Don't go there." Let's look at a practical step on how to do that.

The first step appears obvious but is often overlooked: avoid situations you know are tempting for you. I know you think you can handle it. You can't. David, a man after God's own heart, couldn't handle it. How can you? Proverbs says, "While I was at the window of my house, looking through the curtain, I saw some naive young men, and one in particular who lacked common sense. He was crossing the street near the house of an immoral woman, strolling down the path by her house. It was at twilight, in the evening, as deep darkness fell" (Proverbs 7:6-9).

Did he have to be on that street? Did he have to cross right where she lived? Did he have to stroll past her house? Scripture is clear. He didn't have to do these things, but he "lacked common sense."

There is a line to be drawn. We all know where it is. It's that line we won't cross, or at least we say we won't. But sometimes, we will get real close. If we do, we are fools. "No temptation has overtaken you except what is common to mankind" (1 Corinthians 10:13). You will fall like all the rest. It won't take something special, just temptation that is common. Wherever that line is that you must not cross, draw it back about five steps. Avoid putting yourself in tempting situations.

You must take action and draw some lines in your life. Lines you will not cross. Places you will not go. Movies you will not see. DVDs you will not rent. People you will not go to lunch with alone. Make the battle easier by setting up some fences. God will honor you for it.

We cannot control who we have to associate with, but we can control who our friends are. Our lifeword today is from Proverbs 13:20, and it says, "He who walks with the wise grows wise, but a companion of fools suffers harm." Select your friends wisely. Your choice of friends determines whether you are counted among the wise or the foolish. Your choice of friends has everything to do with sexual purity.

Proverbs teaches us that those we hang out with will influence us. Call it peer pressure if you like. Don't allow work associations or neighbors to determine who your friends are. Just because you live next door to someone or work with them doesn't mean they have to be your friends. Choose your friends. Make intentional choices about who rubs off on you.

Proverbs teaches this over and over. "Do not make friends with a hot-tempered person, do not associate with one easily angered, or you may learn their ways and get yourself ensnared" (Proverbs 22:24-25). Proverbs 12:26 says, "The righteous choose their friends carefully." "A violent person entices their neighbor and leads them down a path that is not good" (Proverbs 16:29).

The Bible refers to fools as people who delight in not having understanding. "A fool takes no pleasure in understanding, but only in expressing his opinion" (Proverbs 18:2). Proverbs 1:7 says, "Fools despise wisdom and discipline." "Whoever trusts in his own mind is a fool..." (Proverbs 28:26). Our lifeword says a "companion of fools..." The Hebrew word for "companion" is most often translated in the context of sheep grazing together. So, companions spend time together, they think alike, go to the same places and follow each other. Don't "graze" with people who aren't serious about sexual purity.

Being picky about friendship doesn't mean I'm snobbish. Christians are to be polite and kind to all, but we are not friends with all. Not only will their foolish ways rub off on us, but it can harm our reputation as well. The old saying is right, "You're known by the company you keep." That's not a Bible verse, but it's wisdom based on biblical teaching.

Yesterday, we said that choosing our friends wisely is a good strategy in our battle for sexual purity. Today, our lifeword comes from Proverbs 27:17: "As iron sharpens iron, so a friend sharpens a friend." This most likely illustrates a pair of swords scrapping against one another. The end result is they're both sharpened.

In the same way, one friend will sharpen another. This is about a brother helping a brother, and a sister helping a sister, in an accountability relationship. Is there someone in your life who you can be honest with, who you can call when you're tempted? This should be a friend who will not condemn you but will be firm with you. This has to be a relationship of total honesty.

Immorality has power because it isolates you. It makes you hide from others. It makes you a loner. Just as a knife cannot sharpen itself, loners have no one to make them better. Loners never are sharpened and never sharpen anyone. You will not beat this by yourself. You need pastors and friends who will keep you accountable and give you support. "Two are better than one, because they have a good return for their labor. If either of them falls down, one can help the other up. But pity anyone who falls and has no one to help them up" (Ecclesiastes 4:9-10). The loner is to be pitied. He has no one to help him when he falls. The solitary life is foolish and will not lead to sexual purity.

As iron sharpens iron, sparks will fly. True friends will often correct you. Are you willing to accept their rebukes? "Let a righteous man strike me - that is a kindness; let him rebuke me - that is oil on my head. My head will not refuse it" (Psalm 141:5). Solomon said the "Wounds from a friend can be trusted..." (Proverbs 27:6).

Hebrews 10:25 says that we should "never give up meeting together" so that we can consistently encourage, support, and strengthen each other. Certainly, some sharpening can happen on Sunday morning. But we need more personal and intimate times where two, three, or four friends get together. This is iron sharpening iron.

As we battle for sexual purity in our lives, counting the high cost of immorality has been helpful for me. Speaking of the adulteress woman, "For she has been the ruin of many; many men have been her victims. Her house is the road to the grave. Her bedroom is the den of death" (Proverbs 7:26-27). Randy Alcorn is the author of an article titled "Consequences of a Moral Tumble." This list has been helpful to me.

- I will grieve the Lord who redeemed me.
- I will be a poor model for Christians and for unbelievers.
- I will be just another name on a long list of pastors who lost their ministries to immorality.
- I will cause hurt, embarrassment, and shame on Sue.
- I will lose Sue's respect and trust.
- I will let Christopher and Levi down by destroying my example and credibility with them.
- My sexual immorality will increase the chance of Christopher and Levi being sexually impure.
- I may lose my family forever.
- I will lose my self-respect.
- I will put things on my brain that can never be erased.
- I will make Satan smile.

The list could go on and on. The cost is astronomically high. Of course, God will forgive and He will redeem. But the consequences from prior choices will always remain.

God wants to save every one of us from the devastation that comes from sexual immorality. "So listen to me, my sons, and pay attention to my words. Don't let your hearts stray away toward her. Don't wander down her wayward path. For she has been the ruin of many; many men have been her victims. Her house is the road to the grave. Her bedroom is the den of death" (Proverbs 7:24-27).

You know, when I go visit someone important, someone I'd like to impress, I usually dress up. I try to look my best. I don't want them to see the real me, that person who wears jeans and a baseball cap most of the time. The Bible speaks of a time when we will all meet the most important person in the universe, God Himself. Romans 14:12 says "Each of us will give an account to God." That's our lifeword for today. As we close out our devotions on sexual immorality, let's remember that each of us will stand before God one day and "give an account."

On that day, looking good will count for nothing. It won't matter a bit what I wear. Clothes just cover up, and there is no covering up before God. On that day, He will judge my heart. All the outward appearances will fade away, and God will probe inward. And by the way, He'll be okay with my jeans and baseball cap as long as my heart is bent toward Him. So, it's crucial in this area of sexual purity to guard your heart. God says, it's "above all else" (Proverbs 4:23).

Our lifeword today encourages us to worry more about our own conduct than the conduct of others. "Each of us will give an account to God" Romans 14:12. Whenever my wife and I correct our youngest son, Levi, he's quick to point to his brother and say, "But what about Christopher?" By the way, Christopher does the same.

When we stand before the Lord, He won't quiz us about what Mr. Jones did or how Mrs. Smith lived. We'll answer for ourselves and no one else. I don't know about you, but I have more than enough to answer for myself!

God will judge our friends. After all, He knows them better than we do. He loves them more than we do, and He reads the thoughts and intents of their hearts, which we have no clue about. Let's be more concerned about our own conduct than the conduct of others.

In our lives, we have all kinds of appointments with doctors, dentists, lawyers, and accountants. If you're like me, it's easy to run late for these. But there are two appointments we won't be late for. Hebrews 9:27 is our lifeword for today, and it tells us that it is "appointed for us once to die and then the judgment." Two appointments: one is death and the other is judgment. You don't have to schedule these; they're already scheduled for you.

People talk about the "end of life." Remember, your life will not end. Death is not your last appointment. Our lifeword today tells us there is an appointment after our death, an appointment with God. In my 24 years as a pastor, I've found that people don't want to talk about either of these two appointments. But as sure as anything, they're coming for all of us. Are you ready for the two biggest appointments of your life, death and judgment? God sent his Son to us so that when those two times come, we can face them with confidence.

W. C. Fields was a famous comedian in the early part of the 1900s. He was known as an irreligious person, though when he faced his own death, he started reading the Bible. When asked about this sudden interest in religious things, he replied, "I'm looking for loopholes, my friend... looking for loopholes."

Who knows? Maybe Fields was reading our lifeword for today. Could he have been wondering what he would say when he stood before the Lord? At that time, there's only one statement that matters. It's something like, "I stand before you clothed in the righteousness of your Son, Jesus." I don't need a loophole if that's the testimony of my heart.

I want a lot of things in life, but there are only a few that I need. I need food, water, and air. A quick Google search told me I can't live without sunlight. There are a lot of really important things to me, but these are the absolute necessities of life. Obviously, only these wouldn't be much of a life. It would be a mere existence. No one wants to simply exist. People commit suicide when they feel as if they only exist. Let's look for the next few days at what we need to really "live." Living is not only physical but spiritual, emotional, and relational as well.

We all need power to live on. Tons of things rob us of our energy, strength, and vitality. We need to recharge, and we need to do it often. Where do we get the power to live on? Not merely to survive on… not only to exist on… not simply to keep us breathing… but power to really "live."

Though people will try many things, God is the source of all power. That power is available to you and me as we turn our eyes toward Him. Our lifeword today is from Isaiah 40:31: "But those who hope in the Lord will renew their strength. They will soar on wings like eagles; they will run and not grow weary, they will walk and not be faint."

Power comes from the hope we have in God. As we focus on Him, God has all the power we need. When I admit my neediness and weakness and turn to God for strength, He promises to supply. "'My grace is sufficient for you, for my power is made perfect in weakness.' Therefore I will boast all the more gladly about my weaknesses, so that Christ's power may rest on me" (2 Corinthians 12:9).

Worship is how we tap into God's power. Our hope is renewed as we focus on Him. Worship is not ritual or ceremony. Worship simply means focusing on God. Psalm 46:10 says, "Be still and know that I am God." Are you frustrated, overwhelmed, and stressed? God's power, that resurrected Jesus, is available to you (Romans 8:11).

What do we need to really "live?" What are the necessities of life... real life? Food, water, air, and sunlight are all needed to survive, but you won't have real life without other people. As we said yesterday, you need the power of God in your life, but you also need people. The Bible says Adam was in a perfect environment, and it still wasn't good enough. "God said, 'It is not good for man to be alone' " (Genesis 2:18). Those are our lifewords for today.

This doesn't mean you have to be married. You were made for other people. People who are alone are more likely to die an early death and more likely to be depressed. We're not meant to be lone rangers. You are supposed to have people that you depend on and that depend on you.

God's cure for "aloneness" is the Body of Christ, the Church. Church is not a building: it's not a place to go or an event you attend. Church is a group of people joined together because of their common faith and trust in God. You need the church because of what you'll hear and be taught. But you also need the relationships that happen among God's people.

We need a place where we can love one another, accept one another, forgive one another, rejoice with one another, and be hospitable with one another. We need those relationships for support. When the crisis comes, you'll have a support system in place to comfort you. In the church, you'll find people who have walked the road you're walking and will walk it with you.

Can you find these in your family? Of course, you can. Can you find them at work? You certainly can. Can you find them in your neighborhood? You bet. But in the church, you will find a togetherness that is tough to beat. At least, that's what God wants to happen in His cure for "aloneness."

My dad used to say, "If I don't stand for something, I'll fall for anything." What did he mean? He was teaching me that I need a code of behavior and conviction that I live by. He was saying that I need a moral foundation to base my life upon. There has to be a set of truths that govern my life. I need a set of non-negotiables that don't change with the times. What will be my value system? These are necessities of life.

God has given us His word for just this reason. "All scripture is given by inspiration of God, and is useful for doctrine, for rebuke, for correction, for instruction in righteousness" (2 Timothy 3:16). Doctrine is a body of truth. Rebuke means to show me the error of my ways. Correction means to point me to the right way. Instruction in righteousness trains us in the way God wants us to go.

In Psalm 119:19, the psalmist says, "I am only a foreigner in the land. Don't hide your commands from me! I am always overwhelmed with a desire for your regulations." The standard to live my life by is right in God's Word. But there's a problem. His truth for me is many times opposite of what the world will teach. So, these two standards that I'm taught are often in conflict with each other.

In modern day, we need truths to live by like never before. Things are changing rapidly, and culture is on a steady downgrade. We need to stand today, like never before, for the truths in God's Word. In a culture that tells us there's no such thing as truth, we must stand for truth as it has been revealed to us in the Scriptures.

When you do, you'll be called a hater, a bigot, and worse. When you say some things are always right and some things are always wrong, you'll be labeled as intolerant. Some will always consider the truth intolerant but the truth will set you free (John 8:32). Stand for God's truth or you will fall for anything.

September 1ˢᵗ

We all need to feel useful and purposeful. We need something to accomplish. Call it a goal, a purpose, or whatever you like, but it's a necessity of really living. It's not a necessity to exist or survive, but if we want to live, in all the fullness of that word, we need to contribute to this world in some way.

In God's economy, our purpose is to love Him and love other people (Matthew 22:37-39). Mostly, we love Him by showing His love to others. Some feel useless in this life with no purpose. God's antidote is a life spent in service and ministry to others.

Ephesians 2:10 is our lifeword for today. It says, "God has made us what we are. In Christ Jesus, God made us to do good works, which God planned in advance for us to live our lives doing." We were created to do something. Our lifeword says "to do good works." In the Bible, good works are almost always geared toward someone else. If I live my life for myself, I will be unhappy and unfulfilled. Count on it. I'm heading down the road to depression. God wants me to contribute. He wants me to give back. The Bible says in 1 Corinthians 12:7, "But to each one is given the manifestation of the Spirit for the common good." We have been given special talents and abilities to use for the "common good," not to keep to ourselves. We feel useful and productive as we use what God has given us.

Would you be open and available for God to use you where He chooses? Sometimes, it will be in big ways, but most of the time, it will be in small ways. Don't sit around waiting for that BIG thing God has for you. That may be nothing but your ego. As you serve, minister, and love other people, God will accomplish something in you that you need in life. You need to feel useful.

Storms just happen. I've lived in several states, and one thing was for certain in each of them; storms would pop up every now and then. Rainstorms, thunderstorms, and snowstorms. You can count on it. Storms just happen.

That's a spiritual principle as well. One day, Jesus and the disciples were in a boat, and a bad storm came up. The Bible says the waves were so bad, the boat nearly sank. The disciples went to Jesus and said, "Don't you care if we drown?" That's our lifeword today from Mark 4:38. Remember, most of the disciples were experienced fisherman. This was not their first time on the water. So, if they were scared, this was no small storm.

Can I tell you something about life with Jesus? Even if He's in the boat with you, storms will happen. You can't always explain them. There's not always a reason they pop up. They just happen - to the good and the bad - to believers and unbelievers - to saints and sinners. Jesus said God "causes His sun to rise on the evil and the good, and sends rain on the righteous and the unrighteous" (Matthew 5:45). If I'm going through a storm in my life, it doesn't mean I'm living in sin. It doesn't mean that God is displeased with me. Storms just happen. It's part of living in a fallen world. We don't need to moan and groan or cry and complain. It's a fact of life. Storms just happen.

The Christian life is not all wine and roses. In 2 Timothy 2:12, Paul writes, "Indeed, all who desire to live a godly life in Christ Jesus will be persecuted." Nowhere in the Bible is the Christian promised a smooth ride to Heaven. Jesus said, "If the world hates you, know that it has hated me before it hated you" (John 15:18).

The Bible and our own experience tell us that bad things happen to God's people. In the Old Testament, Joseph was thrown into the pit and then into jail through no fault of his own. Moses wandered around the desert as he put up with a bunch of grumblers for 40 years. David had to run for his life from King Saul. Jeremiah had a rough life. He preached and preached, and no one believed him. The people of God go through hard times just like everyone else.

Paul was left for dead, shipwrecked, beaten, and thrown in jail. He got so depressed that the Bible says he "despaired of life" (2 Corinthians 1:8). This was the man who opened up the whole Western world to Christianity. God did not spare him from hard times. Historians believe that all of Jesus' disciples died a martyr's death except John.

So, we should not be surprised when Jesus' disciples go through a hurricane. That's an accurate translation for the Greek word for storm in Mark 4:37. Storms happen! Our lifeword today comes from John 16:33 when Jesus said, "I have told you these things, so that in me you may have peace. In this world you will have trouble. But take heart! I have overcome the world."

Disciples of Jesus can expect big waves and strong winds. It's not the absence of storms that defines the one who follows Christ. It's the peace we have in the storm. Someone has said, "When the train goes through the tunnel, and your world turns dark, don't jump out. Sit still and trust the engineer to get you through."

During the storms of life, many times the age-old question is asked. "Why?" Sometimes, we wonder whether God cares for us when the difficult times come. Modern man is not the first to ask this question. Our lifeword today is from Mark 4:38. In the middle of a bad storm at sea, Jesus was asked by His disciples "Don't you care about us?"

During the storm, Jesus was sleeping. The disciples woke Him and were upset that He wasn't upset. "Don't you care about us?" It's amazing that Jesus doesn't answer this question. He simply gets up and quiets the storm. You remember that Job demanded an answer from God about the storm he was going through. God didn't answer him either.

God's silence doesn't mean our questions aren't important to Him. The Bible is full of questioning people. David wrote many of them in the Book of Psalms. "How long, Lord? Will you forget me forever? How long will you hide your face from me? How long must I wrestle with my thoughts and day after day have sorrow in my heart? How long will my enemy triumph over me?" (Psalm 13:1-2) Some of David's questions were answered, but many were not. Even through God's silence, David's faith was stronger than his need for an answer. "But I trust in your unfailing love; my heart rejoices in your salvation. I will sing the Lord's praise, for He has been good to me" (Psalm 13:5-6).

Jesus told his disciples, "You don't understand now what I am doing, but someday you will" (John 13:7). That "someday" may not be on this earth. God doesn't answer all of our questions. I'm sure some of these answers we could not comprehend anyway. The Psalmist writes, "I do not concern myself with great matters or things too wonderful for me" (Psalm 131:1). If we walk by faith and not by sight (2 Corinthians 5:7), we must learn to be at peace with the question. It's a mark of faith to live with the unanswered questions.

We have spoken of living with faith amidst the unanswered questions of life. We said our faith should be stronger than our need to know the answers to those questions. While the Bible doesn't give us all the answers, it does give us clues. For instance, a clue to why Christians go through hard times is found in James 1:2-4, and it's our lifeword for today. "Consider it pure joy, my brothers and sisters, whenever you face trials of many kinds, because you know that the testing of your faith produces perseverance. Let perseverance finish its work so that you may be mature and complete, not lacking anything." These verses say difficult times will test our faith and test it for a reason... so our faith will grow. It's through testing that our faith will mature.

God puts us through tests to build our faith. That's a fascinating concept. You could be going through a test right now. Maybe you just came out of a time of testing. One of the ways God tests our faith is through the trials of life - "Even though you must endure many trials for a little while. These trials will show that your faith is genuine" (1 Peter 1:6-7). The problems and difficulties in your life come to prove your faith.

I like what Pastor Rick Warren says. For the Christian, everything is "Father filtered." While God doesn't sit in Heaven and plan bad things to happen to you, He does allow them. Nothing happens to the child of God unless it has passed through the Father's filter. Nothing catches God off guard. He filtered Job's difficulty (Job 1:12), and He filters yours as well.

Isaiah 48:10 says, "I have refined you though not as silver. I have tested you in the furnace of affliction." When you're stressed, burned out, unfairly criticized, or in a hundred other "furnaces of affliction," you can know that God is using this to help your faith to grow. Maybe instead of WHY, I should ask HOW. "God, how will you use this to grow my faith?"

God tests our faith by asking us not to "lean on our own understanding" (Proverbs 3:5). I want to lean on me. You want to lean on you. It's part of our humanity. We want to walk by sight when God calls us to walk by faith (2 Corinthians 5:7). God gives us many opportunities in life to trust in Him or trust in ourselves. These are tests to see if we truly "believe God" or just "believe in Him." There is a difference, you know.

When I read or remember a command of God, and it seems like I can't follow it, who am I going to believe? Will I believe God, or will I believe my own feelings about the situation? My feelings may tell me I can't forgive that person. But I know what God's Word says. My faith is being tested. Will I believe God or lean on my own understanding? God's commands are not always reasonable. Will I live by my reason or will I have faith in God?

It wasn't reasonable for the people of Israel to only gather enough manna for the day. This food that God provided them would spoil if they took more than they needed for the day. It's not reasonable to leave a lot of good food out there. But God was testing their faith. Our lifeword today is from Exodus 16:4: "Then the Lord said to Moses, 'Look, I'm going to rain down food from heaven for you. Each day the people can go out and pick up as much food as they need for that day. I will test them in this to see whether or not they will follow my instructions.'"

Abraham was asked to do an unreasonable thing... have a child through his wife who was well past child-bearing years. This was a test. Noah was asked to build an ark when the sun was shining. This was a test. Moses was asked to cross the Red Sea. This was a test. Is God testing you? He sure is... in big ways and small. Believe Him; take Him at His Word. Don't lean on your own understanding.

For the last two days, we've been talking about ways God tests your faith. We can't discuss this area without talking about money. I know... no one likes to talk about it. You need to get over that because God speaks of our finances through His Word. The way we handle our money is one of the biggest tests of faith we will ever have. In Luke 16:11, Jesus says, "And if you are untrustworthy about worldly wealth, who will trust you with the true riches of heaven?" Those are our lifewords for today.

There is a direct correlation between how I handle my money and the spiritual depth in my life. Hear me, It's a direct connection. "For where your treasure is, there your heart will be also" (Matthew 6:21). "Moreover, it is required of stewards that they be found faithful" (1 Corinthians 4:2). Money is a test.

Paul wrote in 2 Corinthians 8:7-8, "...Excel in the grace of giving. I'm not commanding you but I want to test the sincerity of your love..." In 1 Chronicles 29, King David and the people of Israel were raising money to build the temple. In verse 14 and following, David says "For all things come from You, And of Your own we have given You...I know, my God, that You test the heart and have pleasure in uprightness."

You ignore these verses at the peril of your own spiritual growth. Every time I give God His tithe and my offering, it helps to break the grip materialism has in my life. Every time, it helps me trust in God and not on my own understanding.

I've got to be honest; my giving tests God as well. In Malachi 3:10, God says, "Test me and see if I won't come through for you if you are faithful in giving." Giving tests me, and it actually tests God. If you're not faithful with God's tithe (10%) and your offering, God cannot bless you as fully as He wants. God knows that our wallets are one of the last areas we will surrender to Him. If you haven't put God to the test, do it today, and watch your faith increase.

If our prayers were immediately answered, if all of our needs were instantly met, if every problem was solved as quickly as it arose, you wouldn't need faith. But you know as well as I that's not the way things work. We have to wait, and it's in the waiting that our faith is tested.

I don't know anyone who enjoys waiting on anything. Traffic, doctors, Santa Claus, or answered prayers. None of us, old or young, enjoy it. Yet, we have to do it. If we don't learn to wait on God, we'll take matters into our own hands and trust in our own ability to solve our problems.

It took the people of Israel 40 years to travel from Egypt to the Promised Land. A journey that should have taken three weeks took a generation or more. What looks like wasted time from our viewpoint was time well-spent from God's. He was more interested in developing their faith than giving them a quick trip. Our lifeword today comes from Deuteronomy 8:2: "And you shall remember that the Lord your God led you all the way these forty years in the wilderness, to humble you and test you, to know what was in your heart, whether you would keep His commandments or not." Times of waiting may be times of testing.

Isaiah 64:4 is a favorite verse of mine: "For since the beginning of the world men have not heard nor perceived by the ear, nor has the eye seen any God besides You, who acts for the one who waits for Him." God acts for those who are patient. Lamentations 3:25 says, "The LORD is good to those who wait for Him, to the soul who seeks Him." While you are waiting, God is working. In Scripture, waiting is synonymous with trusting.

There are things that God hasn't done for you yet. You've asked and asked. Maybe you're being tested. You've cried out, "God, when? God, how long?" Don't give up. "Blessed are all those who wait for him" (Isaiah 30:18). We are blessed as we trust. We are blessed as we wait. Our faith grows and matures as it's being testing through the waiting.

September 9th

As God increases my faith and as my faith grows and matures, it's natural for me to have a bigger impact on others. My faith is not this thing that's just between me and God. My faith should, in some way, help other people. As I walk by faith, my eyes are not on me; they are on God. God will always want to direct my attention to the needs of others. The more my eyes are on Him, the more He'll use me as His ambassador in other people's lives. Our lifeword today comes from Philippians 2:4: "Each of you should look not only to your own interests, but also to the interests of others."

Thinking about other people doesn't come naturally, does it? If I want to make an impact on others, I must learn that the world does not revolve around me. When I focus on myself, I won't make an impact on other people. Now, I know you want some of your needs met in life. I do, too. I get it; that's natural. But God's kingdom is upside down. God has promised that when you focus on meeting the needs of other people, He will meet your needs. Jesus said, "Give and it will be given to you" (Luke 6:38). As we look to the interests of others and not just to our own interests, we'll make an impact in people's lives. The key is faith in God. As we look to Him, He'll divert our attention to the needs of others.

Willie Davis played for Coach Vince Lombardi of the Green Bay Packers. When the coach was dying, Willie visited him. Reporters asked why he came all that way. Willie's response? "That man made me feel important."

Do you want people to say that about you? Here's an easy way. Get them talking about themselves. Ask them about their family, their background, their interests, or their weekend plans. Don't be so focused on yourself that you bore others with all of your issues. As you look to the interest of others, you'll impact others. If you do that, people may come to your death bed, like Willie came to Coach Lombardi's.

If I desire to live a life that makes an impact on others, I must choose to live differently than most. Most live looking out for #1 and doing whatever it takes to succeed. That's the way of the world, but that's not the way for the people of God, and it's not a prescription for making an impact.

Our lifeword today is from Philippians 2:1-2. The Message Bible puts it this way: "Don't push your way to the front; don't sweet-talk your way to the top. Put yourself aside, and help others get ahead. Don't be obsessed with getting your own advantage. Forget yourselves long enough to lend a helping hand." That sounds as if it's from another planet. Come to think of it, it is. It's from God's Kingdom, and that is not of this world (John 18:36). If you want to make an impact on others, you cannot be like everyone else. Titus 2:14 calls Christians a "peculiar people." Other translations say "people of His very own."

Here are some practical ways to impact others. In your work life, have you noticed a co-worker who doesn't seem like their normal self? Who knows? Maybe there's something going on that you can pray about. Why don't you ask them about that? Sometimes, someone will mention to you a problem in their personal life. Tell them you'll add that to your prayer list. Ask them if you can add it to your church's prayer list. What a marvelous way to witness to your faith in God. One thing I will promise you... you'll impact their life.

If you want to be a person who has an impact on others, you won't be like everyone else. But after all, God doesn't want you to be. You don't belong to this world (John 15:19). Peter describes Christians as "...a chosen race, a royal priesthood, a holy nation, a people for his own possession, that you may proclaim the excellencies of Him who called you out of darkness into his marvelous light" (1 Peter 2:9). I don't know about you, but Peter sounds like he's describing a person who impacts others.

September 11th

Everyone, Christian or not, wants their life to count. Mostly, that means making an impact on others. As usual, Jesus is our model. Our lifeword today comes from Matthew 9:35-38. Here, we learn that Jesus went through all the towns and villages, teaching, proclaiming, and healing. When He saw the crowds, He had compassion on them. He said to His disciples, "The harvest is plentiful but the workers are few. Ask the Lord of the harvest, therefore, to send out workers into his harvest field." These verses can guide us to ways we can make an impact on those around us.

The text says, "Jesus saw the crowds." It sounds so simple to say, but Jesus noticed people. I can get so busy that I miss people. I've been so focused for the last 10 weeks on writing this book that I'm sure I've missed opportunities to impact people. How many people have crossed my path, and I was too occupied to "see them"? Oh, I know, I saw them, but I really didn't. Jesus didn't just see crowds of people. He looked deeper and saw the needs of those around Him.

Our lifeword says, "He had compassion on them." He didn't merely notice them with His eyes. He saw them with His heart. People who make an impact on others allow their feelings to get involved. I know that's risky, but it's the way of the Christian. Jesus knew He couldn't meet all the needs Himself, so He knew His Father must get involved. We make an impact on others when we ask God to intervene in their lives.

Jesus went beyond compassion and prayer. He did what He could do. He preached, taught, and healed. Although the need was massive, it didn't stop Him from rolling up His sleeves and doing what He could. You may not be able to do much, but you can do something. Maybe you can't impact the world, but you can impact a small slice of it. As Christians do this north, south, east, and west, our impact for Christ will be great.

On December 21, 1968, Apollo 8 lifted off. It was the first time humans flew into the moon's orbit. I remember watching the launch, and the countdown words were impactful to me. "The engines are armed. Four, three, two, one, zero—we have commit." "We have commit." Those words should be included in every marriage ceremony right before, "I now pronounce you man and wife."

After all is said and done, a healthy marriage is about commitment. Without it, your marriage will not make it. With it, your marriage will survive even the toughest of times. Commitment is Marriage 101. Marriage has many important ingredients, but none is as vital as commitment. Even secular experts agree. Dr. Alfred Kinsey and others wrote that there is nothing more important than the determination that the marriage shall persist.

God agrees with Dr. Kinsey. I guess I should say, Dr. Kinsey agrees with God. Jesus said in Matthew 19:6, "What God has joined together, let no one separate." Those are our lifewords for today. Our lifeword says that marriages are made in Heaven. God came up with the institution of marriage. We didn't. The marriage is not only recorded at the county courthouse; it's written down in Heaven.

Our lifeword also says that God doesn't end marriages. Man does. Divorce was never in God's plan. God didn't create a back door for a husband or wife to sneak out. Jesus says, "Moses permitted you to divorce your wives because your hearts were hard" (Matthew 19:8). Divorce is not about irreconcilable differences. There are no friendly divorces, only hard hearts. If the couples were friendly, there would have been no divorce.

You all remember the words, "For better or for worse, for richer or for poorer, in sickness and in health." To keep those vows takes more than the feelings of love. It takes something more important than love. It takes old-fashioned commitment. I think I'll adjust my wedding ritual. "Three, two, one... I now pronounce you husband and wife. We have commit."

Malachi 2 describes dark days in Israel. Men of Israel were divorcing their wives and marrying non-Israelite women. In verse 14 God says, "...You have broken faith with...the wife of your marriage covenant." In discussing commitment in marriage, it's important to know that marriage is not a contract but a covenant. Contracts are based on the consent of two people. Both agree to do certain things thus fulfilling the contract. If they don't, the contract is broken.

Covenants are different. A covenant is a promise. It's not based on what the other person does. A covenant is based on trust, while a contract is based on distrust. When I agree to a covenant, I have unlimited responsibility. A contract states the limits of my liability. A contract has each person's interests in mind. A covenant has the other person's interest in mind (Philippians 2:4).

When a couple stands and makes a public commitment to each other, that's not a contract; it's a covenant. It's saying, "I love you no matter what." If one says "I love you if...," that's contract language. "'Til death do us part" doesn't sound like a contract. It's a promise, a covenant.

It's much easier to keep the promise you make in marriage if you follow the biblical prescriptions for marriage. One of the most important is found in 1 Corinthians 6:14, and it's our lifeword for today: "Do not be yoked together with unbelievers." Christians marry Christians. It's easier to stay committed if you're yoked together with someone that has the same morals and values that you do. So many times, couples will be concerned with finding common ground in other areas but will neglect the most important. You do that to the detriment of your marriage.

Committed love is covenant love. It will last for a lifetime. The covenant love that the wedding vows speak of doesn't depend on the other person. When both parties love in this way, you have something very special. You have a biblical marriage.

Today, let's discuss one very practical way to be committed in your marriage. Our lifeword today is "In your anger do not sin. Do not let the sun go down while you are still angry" (Ephesians 4:26). Emerson Eggerichs, author of the marriage book *Love and Respect*, believes anger is the most dangerous emotion to allow in a marriage. When anger takes control, the Devil is ready to move in and wreak havoc (Ephesians 4:27).

John Gottman, author of many books on marriage, identifies four predictors of divorce. One of them is contempt. It can be defined as deep, long-term anger. That's anger that the sun went down on. That's anger the Devil has taken hold of.

The Bible speaks to the dangers of anger. Proverbs 14:29 says, "People with understanding control their anger; a hot temper shows great foolishness." Also, in the book of James, "Your anger can never make things right in God's sight" (James 1:20). "Do not be quickly provoked in your spirit, for anger resides in the lap of fools (Ecclesiastes 7:9).

Our lifeword today says there should be a time limit on our anger. If I roll over and go to sleep angry, little things become bigger. Molehills become mountains, and slight irritations become sore spots. This can happen overnight.

Keep short accounts. Settle them quickly. Don't allow one irritation to become two, two to become four, and four to become eight. What was once easy to get over now becomes a real challenge. It all starts with one little thing that went unresolved. Ephesians 4:27 says the devil enters the picture when we refuse to resolve our differences. He'll lie to you and say you were right. He'll convince you that your spouse should apologize first.

Commitment in marriage means to commit to clear the decks often. It's a commitment to open and honest dialog. It's a commitment to say, "What you said tonight really bothered me." That open conversation may ruffle a few feathers, but it will save your marriage.

Commitment in marriage is possible when we believe that God is good. Our lifeword today comes from Psalm 107:1: "Give thanks to the Lord, for he is good."

When we doubt God's goodness, we may feel our marriages were a mistake. But, as a Christian, if I prayed for years for God to lead me to the right spouse, if my parents prayed for the same thing, we believe our good God has heard that prayer and led us to the right person. Parents, early on, allow your kids to hear you pray for their future spouse.

Often, when we are angry with our mates, our real issue is with God. We're angry with Him for allowing this marriage to happen. We're angry with Him for allowing me to make this dumb choice. We're angry with Him for getting me stuck with this person, while I doubt His power to change me or change my spouse.

Do you really believe Jeremiah 29:11? "For I know the plans I have for you," declares the Lord, "plans to prosper you and not to harm you, plans to give you hope and a future." Sure, my lousy choices and sin can frustrate that plan. But, as I get my life back on track with God, His promise is to lead me to a good life because He is a good God.

Believing God is a good God allows me to stay committed to my marriage. When I believe God is good, I will look for the blessing in all situations. When I believe God is good, I will expect that He will work on me and my spouse to improve our marriage. If I believe God is good, I will have a positive outlook on my marital issues instead of a negative one.

Single people, pray now for our good God to lead you to the right person. Make sure your heart is open to His leading. Don't enter marriage until you're sure He's done that. When you marry, thank God for His good and perfect gift for your life (James 1:17).

There are a lot of jokes about marriage. Here's one: "Marriage is a three-ring circus: engagement ring, wedding ring, and suffe-ring." And another: "Wife: Do you want dinner? Husband: Sure, what are my choices? Wife: Yes and no." One more: Every man wants a beautiful wife, a smart wife, a loving wife, a sexy wife, and a cooperative wife. Sadly, bigamy is against the law." We all like to laugh, but the book of Hebrews reminds us not to get too flippant about marriage. "Marriage should be honored by all" (Hebrews 13:4). Those are our lifewords for today.

What does it mean to honor something? The word connotes respect, preciousness, and value toward some person or something. 1 Peter 1:9 speaks of the "precious blood of Christ." The same word that's translated "precious" here is the word "honor" in our lifeword for today. We could translate the verse, "Marriage should be precious to all." It should be treasured like gold and silver. It should be respected, esteemed, and valued. Marriage should never be treated as common. My marriage is precious, and so is everyone else's. If the institution of marriage is precious so is your husband or wife.

Honoring marriage means we don't bail when it gets tough. Since we've "all sinned and fallen short of the glory of God" (Romans 3:23), all of our marriages will have rough spots. Honoring marriage means that we pay the cost to preserve what's valuable and precious.

Honoring marriage means that I'm careful how I speak of marriage. I don't hear this much anymore, but I used to cringe when a husband would call his wife "my old lady." As a pastor, I've officiated at countless weddings. There are always jokes about the groom losing his freedom. I try always to say that getting married was one of the two best things to ever happen to me.

Hold your marriage in high esteem. It is precious, and it's to be honored. Marriage is good. "He who finds a wife finds a good thing, and obtains favor from the Lord" (Proverbs 18:22). Our lifeword today has a second phrase. More on that tomorrow.

Hebrews 13:4 was our lifeword yesterday, and it will be today also: "Marriage should be honored by all, and the marriage bed kept pure, for God will judge the adulterer and all the sexually immoral." The writer states that marriage should be honored, and then his mind goes straight to the marriage bed. Sex is a great part of marriage and also a great problem in marriage. Sex between a husband and a wife is sacred ground and is not to be defiled.

The call to keep the marriage bed pure is a call to receive one of God's greatest gifts to us. Scripture speaks often of delighting in this gift. "May your fountain be blessed, and may you rejoice in the wife of your youth. A loving doe, a graceful deer—may her breasts satisfy you always, may you ever be intoxicated with her love" (Proverbs 5:18-19). "The husband should fulfill his wife's sexual needs, and the wife should fulfill her husband's needs...do not deprive each other of sexual relations..." (1 Corinthians 7:3-5). In the Old Testament, Song of Solomon is downright X-rated!

So, sexual relations is a good thing between a husband and a wife, but Hebrews 13:4 contains a warning as well: "God will judge the adulterer and all the sexually immoral." Sex is dynamite, but dynamite can be used for good or bad. God will judge. Make no mistake about that. His judgment may not be swift, but it will happen. God judges because He's good. If God does not hate racism, He's not good. If He doesn't judge child abuse, He's not good. If God doesn't judge adultery, He's not good. If He did not hate pornography, He's not good.

As you read this, some of you come under great condemnation. You have not kept the marriage bed pure. There is hope, but please understand how serious adultery and sexual immorality is. Forsake it now. Seek the forgiveness of God and get help now. Confess it to a trusted friend or your pastor. Make yourself accountable. You can start today with a clean slate. You can start today to honor your marriage.

A couple came to see me with marital problems. The wife was terribly depressed and unresponsive to her husband. During the course of our counseling, the wife was unresponsive to me as well. After an hour going nowhere, I jumped up and put a big kiss right on the woman's mouth. I turned to the husband and said, "That's all your wife needs once per day." The husband said, "I can only bring her in on Tuesdays."

Obviously, I made that up, but I did it to make a point. Some spouses are clueless about marriage. I'm sorry to be that direct, but it's true. For those clueless folks, there are counselors, seminars, books, DVDs, and sermons. There is nothing wrong with any of those, but you can't do any better than to open your Bible to 1 Corinthians 13. Here we get a biblical perspective on love and marriage.

It's hard to talk about love because I *love* baseball and apple pie. But I'm supposed to love my wife. The word "love" means lots of different things. Biblically, there are three Greek words for love: eros, phileo, and agape. Eros has to do with sexual attraction. Some clueless spouses think this is what love is about. Phileo is a friendship and companionship type of love. Some clueless spouses think love is about companionship. Agape love is concerned for the well-being of the other. In 1 Corinthians 13, Paul doesn't speak of eros or phileo. He speaks of agape.

1 Corinthians 13:4-8, Paul describes agape love. Biblical love behaves; that's the important thing to see. The feelings are great, but if I'm not feeling something, I can still behave in a loving way. That's agape.

If I'm having marital trouble, I'm not behaving in an agape kind of way. Marriages will get through all kinds of trouble if we will continually seek the best interest of the other person. Go to all the seminars you want, read all the books you want, but you'll never find better marriage counsel than that. Hey spouses, get a clue! Agape one another.

Let's spend several days with James, the brother of Jesus. His book is found in the back of the New Testament, and it's a favorite of mine because it's uniquely practical and direct in how it teaches us to live life. James is right where the rubber meets the road. The cookies come off the high theological shelf and get right down where we can touch them.

James begins his book with, "James, a servant of God and of the Lord Jesus Christ, to the twelve tribes scattered among the nations: Greetings" (James 1:1). James is writing to a scattered and dispersed bunch of believers. They are scattered because of persecution.

Things were not going well for these Christians. To them he writes these words: "Consider it pure joy, my brothers and sisters, whenever you face trials of many kinds..." (James 1:2). These are our lifewords for today.

James says when (not if) you go through hard times, consider it pure joy. The choice of the word "consider" is interesting. He basically says, "Just consider this. Just think about this. Here's a new way to think when you go through rough spots. I'm not talking about how you feel, but what you think about it. How you interpret these things."

What you believe or think about the adversities you encounter will determine your response to them. James is encouraging us to consider not just the negative of the trial, but to be open to a different way of thinking. There may be another way you can consider this, another way to think about it that will give you hope and encouragement.

Paul says that Jesus "...being in very nature God, did not consider equality with God something to be used to his own advantage" (Philippians 2:6). Jesus thought about Himself differently. That led Him to be a servant (Philippians 2:7). The thought is the father of the deed.

James invites us to see our trials and our struggles through a different lens. A lens that shows us God is at work, using this trial to build our character. More on that tomorrow.

As we said yesterday, James asks that we think about the trials of life in a different way. He says, "Consider it pure joy, my brothers and sisters, whenever you face trials of many kinds, because you know that the testing of your faith produces perseverance" (James 1:2-3). These are our lifewords for today.

James encourages us to open our minds to the fact that the struggles we go through reveal our true character. We know this is true. Our true selves come out when we are stressed. Our lifeword says the challenges we face in life test us and reveal us. Hard times almost always reveal what we're made of. It shows us what's in our heart. The trial you're facing is not about the problem out there, but the problem in here - your heart. James says open your mind to the fact that God is teaching you something through this challenge. He's allowing us to see something that we would not have seen if it wasn't for this trial. When we see it, we can start working on that and asking God to change what's deep inside.

"Consider it pure joy, my brothers and sisters, whenever you face trials of many kinds, because you know that the testing of your faith produces perseverance." Through the tough time, we will gain something we would not have gained if it wasn't for the difficulty. In this case, James says you gain perseverance. You gain the ability to get through what felt un-get-through-able. Perseverance is just hanging in there. Gaining that ability is a very good thing.

God is more concerned with your character than with your circumstances. Struggles in our lives are not a sign of God's absence or that He doesn't care. He allows them so that we can grow in our faith and become stronger. The events in your life that have matured you are not fond times to remember. You did not enjoy going through them. But now, you think about them differently. You are thankful for them. James wants you to do that as you go through the trial. "Consider them pure joy."

James has been encouraging us to take a different look at our struggles. "Consider it pure joy, my brothers and sisters, whenever you face trials of many kinds…" That's our lifeword from James 1:2. Trials aren't fun times. They aren't happy times, but we can think differently about these tough times. We can consider our God may take these and use them in a positive way in our lives.

One thing is sure about us going through challenges. You will either get closer to Jesus, or you will drift farther away. No one, I mean no one, stays in the same place spiritually. When James says to consider these rough spots as joy, he's asking us to draw closer to our source of strength during the pain. The old cliché is true… you can grow better not bitter.

During these trials, you can learn that His grace is sufficient (1 Corinthians 12:9). You can learn that you have a friend that sticks closer than a brother (Proverbs 18:24). You can learn that God will never leave you or forsake you (Deuteronomy 31:6). You'll learn this if you intentionally think differently about your difficulties.

One last word, and it's found in James 1:4: "Let perseverance finish its work so that you may be mature and complete…" Whatever your trial, there will be a finish line. James doesn't describe the finish line in terms of your circumstances. He describes the finished product as you. He says, "One day, you will be mature and complete…" At the end of the day, that's what this has been all about. The pain, the heartache, the suffering… all of that was heading toward a finish line: your sanctification, your maturity in Christ.

"Let us run with perseverance the race marked out for us, fixing our eyes on Jesus, who, for the joy set before him endured the cross, scorning its shame…Consider him who endured such opposition…so that you will not grow weary and lose heart" (Hebrews 12:1-3). The writer says consider Jesus…. think about Him… so you'll make it to the finish line.

The New Testament world was a place of favoritism. Treating people according to their status or rank was a way of life. It was accepted just the way it was. So, when James told these new believers in Jesus Christ that they were not to show favoritism, he really rocked the boat. This was a revolutionary thought. Nobody thought that. When the United States was formed, people were still struggling with this concept. The founders wrote, "We hold these truths to be self-evident: that all are created equal..."

Our lifeword today is from James 2:1: "My brothers and sisters, believers in our glorious Lord Jesus Christ must not show favoritism." This was such a crucial topic to the New Testament writers that it gets repeated. In Israel, they thought God favored Jews over Gentiles. Peter thought the same thing and had to have an attitude adjustment. He writes in Acts 10:34, "I now realize how true it is that God does not show favoritism." Paul addresses this topic in the books of Romans, Ephesians, and Colossians.

When James writes about no favoritism, he actually has to make up a word. That fascinates me. It's like it was so common to treat people according to rank that no one had ever thought of a word that prohibited it. James literally says Christians aren't to turn their faces up to people. Author Dallas Willard writes of "the great inversion." Jesus turns everything upside down. Christianity supersedes culture and politics. It gives us a new way to think and act about everything.

Right before our lifeword, James writes that "...religion that God accepts...is...to look after orphans and widows in their distress..." (James 1:27). Jesus said, "Blessed are the poor" (Matthew 5:3). Jesus Himself was part of the "great inversion." "Though He was rich, for our sakes He became poor..." (2 Corinthians 8:9). That's the Christmas story.

How about you? How are you doing with our lifeword today? In the Mark Atherton translation, it says, "Believers in the Lord Jesus Christ should never show favoritism."

September 23rd

Yesterday, we read how James stated that if your belief in Christ is legitimate, it will show up in a tangible way. In this case, it was not showing favoritism. He continues the same discussion as we move through James 2. This is the famous passage that teaches that faith without works is dead.

Our lifeword today comes from James 2:14-17: "What good is it, my brothers and sisters, if someone claims to have faith but has no deeds? Can such faith save them? Suppose a brother or a sister is without clothes and daily food. If one of you says to them, 'Go in peace; keep warm and well fed,' but does nothing about their physical needs, what good is it? In the same way, faith by itself, if it is not accompanied by action, is dead."

At the very heart of this passage is this question: What does it really mean to believe? James bears down hard on the understanding that belief is not just a mental activity. Our behavior shows what we really believe. Some say they have belief but really don't. They're hypocrites or liars. Politicians come to mind here. There are also beliefs I think I have. But when push comes to shove, I don't. Kind of like if I believe that rickety bridge will hold me up but I still refuse to cross it. Obviously, that's not belief at all.

Others live their life not contradicting what they believe. If they say they believe that rickety ole bridge will hold them up, they don't have an issue stepping out on it.

In chapter 1, James says, "Do not merely listen to the word, and so deceive yourselves. Do what it says" (James 1:19). He also says true religion is helping the needy. At the start of chapter 2, James writes that favoritism to the rich over the poor is sin. James insists in our lifeword today that faith is not merely an intellectual agreement. James doesn't claim that works earn salvation but that it is to faith like breath is to the body... a sign that life exists. Faith without works is like a body without breath. It's dead.

In James chapter 1, he focuses on when to speak and when to listen. Now, in chapter 3, James shifts his attention to that 2.5-ounce piece of flesh in your mouth that is more powerful than any other part of your body. James says our tongues control us in the same way a bit in the mouth of a horse or a rudder on a ship does (James 3:3-5). He wants us to know that our words are not insignificant. They matter.

What comes out of our mouths has tremendous power. Our words can determine the trajectory of our lives. Your words got you your first job. Your words landed you your first date. They, in large part, determined your academic career. With your words, you built intimacy and friendships. For you married folks, your words promised a lifetime of fidelity.

James has set the groundwork for his main point. "How great a forest is set ablaze by a small fire! And the tongue is a fire. The tongue is placed among our members as a world of iniquity; it stains the whole body, sets on fire the cycle of nature, and is itself set on fire by hell" (James 3:5,6). Those are our lifewords for today. James wants us to understand the destructive power of our words. Even though they are small, like a bit or rudder, they are powerful. James must feel this is an underestimated truth or he would not have taken time to write about it.

Don't doubt the power of your words. In large part, your reputation is determined by the words you choose to speak. You underestimate that truth to your own detriment. "Those who guard their mouths and their tongues keep themselves from calamity" (Proverbs 21:23).

James makes one more statement about the power of the tongue. He says it is so powerful, no man can tame it (James 3:8).

The inference is that only God can tame it. Don't try to do it yourself. You will fail. That's the power of the tongue. James tells us to "Submit to God" (James 4:7). That would especially include our tongues.

Yesterday, we read in James 3 of the power of our words. We've all heard the phrase "Sticks and stones may break my bones, but words can never hurt me." In reality, that couldn't be further from the truth. Words have power. It still makes me cringe to remember what was said to me in fifth grade. Also, that rumor that spread through the high school. It still hurts. That's the power of the tongue.

While words can be used to hurt, they can have the opposite power as well. It happened 49 years ago, but it's still fresh in my mind. Mr. McIntosh was my PE teacher at Garden Springs Elementary School in Lexington, Kentucky. One day, I was working hard to be a better basketball player. While all the other guys were goofing off, Mr. McIntosh came over to me and said, "I got into teaching because of guys like you."

Proverbs 18:21 says, "Death and life are in the power of the tongue." Those are our lifewords for today. Mr. McIntosh spoke life to me that day. Even though that was only 10 seconds of my life, I still remember it. That's the power of our words.

Proverbs 12:25 tells me that a "kind word cheers up an anxious heart." One of the best choices I can make with my words is to choose to encourage. In the language of the Bible, the word encourage means to come alongside. I'm sure there are people in your life that need you to come alongside of them. Encouragement isn't distant; it's close. It's the voice that says, "I relate, I understand, I've been there too."

Jesus said our words originate from the heart: "Out of the abundance of the heart the mouth speaks" (Matthew 12:34). So, when Mom washed out my mouth with soap, it really didn't help. That's why James says, "No man can tame the tongue" (James 3:8). Allow God to do deep work in your life that you can't do. Allow Him to harness the power of your tongue and use it for good.

I was a high school math teacher for several years. I like math because two plus two equals four. I don't have to worry about that changing. Some new mathematician won't come up with a new answer. All of math crumbles if two plus two doesn't equal four. It's truth.

You see, truth can't be played with. It's not dependent on my emotions or my feelings. The truth stands in good times and bad, in sunshine and in darkness. Christians must get a handle on this reality. You don't play around with truth. In fact, as John is introducing us to Jesus, he insists that we know that Jesus is "full of grace and truth." Those are our lifewords today from John 1:14.

People seem to easily grasp grace. We sing of how amazing and marvelous it is. Jesus actively demonstrated God's grace as He died on the cross. Jesus forgives our sins, transforms our lives, and showers us with blessings. We *get* grace.

When we come to truth, we don't seem to *get it.* Truth, for so many, is pliable. You've heard people say that you can have *your truth* and I can have *my truth.* In the eyes of the world, truth can be something that is truth for me and me only. So, for me, two plus two can equal four, but for you, it can equal five. And if I dare to say it only equals four, I'm intolerant.

Our lifeword today reminds us that Jesus came as the embodiment of God's grace, but also as absolute truth. In fact, He is the Truth (John 14:6). His truth is true whether I believe it or not. The old saying, "God said it, I believe it, and that settles it" is false. My belief doesn't have anything to do with the truth. It's the truth whether I believe it or not. My believing it doesn't make it true. Two plus two is four no matter if I believe it or not. The same is true of God's Word. "All your words are true; all your righteous laws are eternal" (Psalm 119:160).

September 27th

One of the best descriptions of Jesus' life is found in John 1:14. It's here the Bible says, "Jesus came full of grace and truth." Those are our lifewords for today. This is one of my favorite verses in all of God's Word. Not only do they describe Jesus, but they are meant to describe our lives as well. We are called to be "Christ-like disciples." There is no better way to describe "Christlikeness" than grace and truth.

This is one of the biggest challenges we have today, and it certainly requires the power of God's Holy Spirit in our lives. As Jesus' followers, it's common for us to have one more than the other. When we function with only truth, it comes across as egotistical and arrogant. When we respond with only grace, many times, we love people in their sin but never help them get out of it.

We emphasize one over the other because of the way we were raised. It's common for our parents to be "gracers" or "truthers." Sometimes, our DNA is bent more toward grace or truth. It's just more natural for us to be one or the other. Often, we were raised in a church that preached one at the expense of the other.

As we look through the New Testament, we see that Jesus sometimes seemed to emphasize grace and sometimes truth. In John 8, He deals with the woman caught in adultery and He strikes the perfect balance between them both. He acted graciously toward her and did not allow the men to stone her. When the men left and no one was left to accuse her, Jesus said, "Then neither do I condemn you," Jesus declared. "Go now and leave your life of sin" (John 8:11). There's grace and truth in this verse of the Bible.

Our lifeword says Jesus was "full of grace and truth." In our humanness, maybe the best we can hope for is to balance the two. But Jesus was full of both grace and truth. His truth was gracious, and His grace was truthful. By the power of God's Holy Spirit, let's emphasize both and apologize for neither. That's what Jesus did.

We continue today with yesterday's lifeword John 1:14, where the Bible says Jesus came "full of grace and truth." Not *just grace* and not *just truth*, but grace *and* truth. Truth without grace does us no good and is received as judgment. Grace without truth can be viewed as a license to sin. To this, Paul would say, "God forbid" (Romans 6:2).

The prevailing culture of the day seems to be high on grace and low on truth. In other words, almost anything goes. This is the "cheap grace" that Dietrich Bonhoeffer wrote of in his book, *The Cost of Discipleship*. He defined "cheap grace" as "the preaching of forgiveness without repentance. Communion without confession. Cheap grace is grace without discipleship, grace without the cross, grace without Jesus Christ."

These days, we are asked to accept and welcome all people, which we as Christians are called to do. High-grace and low-truth people demand we affirm them in their decisions or lifestyle choices. Acceptance and affirmation are no longer two different things. They have been joined at the hip. To not condemn means you must condone. If you don't condone, you are viewed as condemning.

Then you have the opposite viewpoint, which is low on grace and high on truth. This is legalism... rules and regulations, dos and don'ts, but no grace. When there is truth without grace, I'm left with a God who is always mad at me, demanding that I do it better than I did yesterday. Judgment and condemnation do not lead to a Christ-like life.

Jesus accepted the woman at the well (John 4). We have no clue how scandalous this was in Jesus' day. He followed that acceptance by confronting her directly about her promiscuity. We don't need a feel-good theology that avoids serious talk of sin. We also don't need harsh legalistic attitudes. We need the Jesus way... full of grace and truth.

We desperately need grace because we're all sinners who fall short of the glory of God (Romans 3:23). We long for truth because we all need life-transformation and direction. Jesus gives us both.

We continue today with our lifeword from John 1:14, where the Bible says Jesus came "full of grace and truth." Grace and truth is messy. The mixture between the two is muddy and confusing. As Christians and as churches, we must be okay with the confusion of trying to be full of both.

We shouldn't be surprised when we struggle with these two areas because even the Bible seems to. Grace says all can come to God. "Come, all you who are thirsty, come to the waters; and you who have no money, come, buy and eat! Come, buy wine and milk without money and without cost" (Isaiah 55:1). Truth says all must come through Jesus Christ. "For there is one God and one mediator between God and mankind, the man Christ Jesus" (1 Timothy 2:5).

Grace says God loves you just the way you are. "But God demonstrates his own love for us in this: While we were still sinners, Christ died for us" (Romans 5:8). The truth says His grace won't allow us to stay that way. "For the grace of God has appeared that offers salvation to all people. It teaches us to say 'No' to ungodliness and worldly passions, and to live self-controlled, upright and godly lives in this present age" (Titus 2:11,12).

Grace says there is a Heaven, and you can go there. Jesus said, "In my Father's house are many mansions: if it were not so, I would have told you. I go to prepare a place for you" (John 14:2). Truth says there's a Hell, and you can go there. "He will punish those who do not know God and do not obey the gospel of our Lord Jesus. They will be punished with everlasting destruction and shut out from the presence of the Lord" (2 Thessalonians 1:8-9).

Do you feel the tension? That's okay. Grace and truth is messy and muddy. Don't try to resolve that tension. Just live with it. It's the way of Jesus. His way is not on the extremes of grace or truth.

Some of the worst damage ever done to the gospel of Jesus Christ is done by professing Christians who do not hold together grace and truth. We have one book of the Bible written solely for this purpose. "I was very eager to write to you about our common salvation, I found it necessary to write appealing to you to contend for the faith that was once for all delivered to the saints...some ungodly people have wormed their way into your churches, saying that God's marvelous grace allows us to live immoral lives" (Jude 1:3-4). Here we have a threat to the faith from inside the church. It's a problem of grace and truth.

This is what was probably happening here. Evidently, some people were teaching grace minus truth, and Jude says they were perverting the grace of God. So, they used grace to nullify the truth of the teachings of Christ and deny His lordship. Jude 1:17-19 says the apostles predicted this would happen.

Teaching heresy from inside the Church is a major biblical topic. Paul criticizes the church at Corinth because they put up with false teaching. "You happily put up with whatever anyone tells you, even if they preach a different Jesus than the one we preach, or a different kind of Spirit than the one you received, or a different kind of gospel than the one you believed" (2 Corinthians 2:11). Paul predicts in Acts 20:30 that false teachers will "distort the truth."

Much false teaching arises from perverting God's grace or hiding His truth. In our churches, we must insist on the preaching and teaching of the fullness of God's grace and the fullness of His truth. This will cause conflict because our churches are full of "gracers" and "truthers." If you know which way you naturally lean, be sure you give an ear to the other. You will move yourself closer to Jesus, who was full of grace and truth.

Today, let's talk about a truth that takes a lot of grace to live out. Our lifeword today is from John 10:14-16. Jesus says, "I am the good shepherd...I have other sheep that are not of this sheep pen....and there shall be one flock and one shepherd." In Old Testament and New, God's people are called sheep. Jesus, speaking to Jewish people, shocks them when He says there are other sheep. It was hard for them to grasp that He came not only for the Jews but Gentiles as well. Jesus says there is one flock, which has one Shepherd.

No doubt today, the sheep are too many to count. No matter the number, Jesus sees us all as one flock. That's good for me to remember. With all the differences in the Body of Christ, it's important to know and internalize that we are one flock, led by one Shepherd. Sure, there are lots of differences in that one flock. But our differences shouldn't define us; who our Shepherd is should. Let's be gracious enough to live out this truth.

These sheep tend to cluster in groups, and these groups have weird names like Baptists, Presbyterians, Methodists, Lutherans, Episcopalians, Assembly of God, Church of God, Church of Christ, and there's even a really weird bunch called Nazarenes. Then there's a group that doesn't know what they are and they call themselves non-denominational.

I deeply appreciate my Nazarene heritage, but I've learned much about the grace of God from my Baptist friends. I've learned about the sovereignty of God from Presbyterians. Lutherans have taught me about the sufficiency of the cross. Pentecostals have taught me about worship. Brennan Manning, a Roman Catholic, has increased my understanding about the love of God. I'm so glad I didn't stay just within my little group. I'm thankful I've benefited from the whole Body of Christ. After all, according to Jesus, we're one flock, led by one Shepherd. God give us the grace to accept this truth.

We continue today with the truth found in John 10. Jesus says there is one flock, and He is the Shepherd. The sheep pen must be as big as the east is from the west. One thing is interesting about this pen: There is only one gate, and it is manned by the Good Shepherd. In John 10:7, Jesus says, "I tell you the truth, I am the gate for the sheep." That's our lifeword for today.

Many walk around the pen looking for other gates. There must be more than just this one. How intolerant and narrow-minded it would be if there is only one gate. But Jesus says in Matthew 7:14, "Narrow is the gate that leads to life and few will find it." Many are okay if Jesus is *a* gate to the pen. After all, all religions lead to God. Mohammad is a gate, and so is Buddha. But when you draw the line that Jesus drew and insist He is the *only* gate, you may be accused of being bigoted.

Entering through this gate named Jesus requires a personal encounter with the Shepherd. Though this is demanded of all the sheep, this experience goes by different names. Some call it receiving Christ, and others call it accepting Christ. Many call it getting saved or being born again. There are others who will refer to it as when they were baptized. No matter the terminology, it's the personal encounter with the Shepherd that defines the sheep. The sheep do not all look alike, and they certainly don't all think alike. But all can testify to a time when Jesus was no longer just the Shepherd of the sheep but He became "my shepherd."

It's great to believe that Jesus is the Savior of the world. But it's life-changing when He becomes your Savior. It's a true statement to say that Jesus is the Son of God. But it's life-changing when He becomes God the Son Who was sent for me. No one enters the pen unless they have this personal encounter.

My dad was probably like yours. He had these little sayings he would repeat all the time that I still remember to this day. To teach me the importance of emotional control, he would say, "Grin and bear it." He would say this when I hit my thumb with a hammer or stubbed my toe. He didn't see the sense in throwing a fit, so he'd just say, "Grin and bear it." To "bear it" meant to put up with it.

My dad also told me that "Life is the sum total of the choices you make." The country music legend George Jones would agree with my dad. George had a hit with a song titled "Choices". In that song, he sings "I'm living and dying by the choices I've made." Check that song out on the internet. It's great. Not only did George agree with Dad; more importantly, Dad agrees with the Bible.

Our lifeword today is from Deuteronomy 30:19. Moses encourages the Israelite people to "choose life." As the people of Israel are on the verge of the Promised Land, Moses sees fit to remind them that their choices matter.

He says in Deuteronomy 30:15, "See, I set before you today life and prosperity, death and destruction." Moses is telling his people about the primacy of choice. He counsels them to "choose life."

You only have to go 46 verses into the Bible until the text screams to you that our choices matter. God told Adam to eat of any tree he chose but not from the tree of the knowledge of good and evil. If they did that, they would die (Genesis 2:16-17). Forty-six verses into His Word, God tells me that my choices matter.

That theme runs continually through the Bible even to the end of the book. Four verses from the end, John writes that we are not to add anything to this book or take anything away from it. If we do, there will be consequences (Revelation 22:18-19). God has given us great dignity as human beings. Our choices matter.

Our lifeword today is from Deuteronomy 30:19. Moses is speaking to the people of Israel. "This day I call the heavens and the earth as witnesses against you that I have set before you life and death, blessings and curses. Now choose life…" Before the Israelites enter a great blessing, the Promised Land, a land flowing with milk and honey, Moses wants to remind them of something: Your life can be blessed or your life can be cursed. It all depends on your choices.

The New Testament says it this way: "A man reaps what he sows" (Galatians 6:7). We are responsible human beings. God made us persons of worth and dignity, so much so that our choices matter. We have great freedom to choose, but we must accept the consequences that come from those choices.

We try to avoid this truth. We say, "What will be, will be." Biblically, what will be in my life is directly related to the choices I make. Some may say, "Everything happens for a reason." Though they don't say it, they are blaming what happened on God. They are trying to excuse their bad choice and subsequent consequence on some "plan" that God has for their lives. God does have a plan, but it's for you to make good choices.

Some of you are reading this with doubt in your mind. Some are going through difficulty because of someone else's choice in your life. That is certainly a possibility, and I don't want to minimize that. But I do want to say to you that no matter what evil someone else may have done to you, you still have the choice of how you will respond. What will you do with the lemons you have been given? Will you let them make you sour, or will you turn them into lemonade?

Choice + choice + choice + choice + choice = my life. The best choice I can ever make is to make Jesus the Lord of my life. If He's Lord, then my choices will be better, and so will my life. All of our choices matter.

For the last two days, we've been talking about our choices and how much they matter. In fact, our lives are the sum total of the choices we make. As humans, we don't like this truth because we'd much rather blame it on someone or something else. Husbands blame wives, and wives blame husbands. Parents blame kids, and kids blame parents. Employers blame employees, and employees blame employers. Republicans blame Democrats, and Democrats blame Republicans.

This runs deep in us because we inherited it from our first mom and dad. When Adam and Eve took of the fruit they shouldn't have, we see the first blame game start. When God asks him what has happened, Adam says, "The woman you put here with me…she gave me some fruit from the tree, and I ate it" (Genesis 3:12).

This inability to take responsibility for our choices is part of our sinful nature. Adam blames it on the woman, and it's the "woman YOU put here with me." He blames it on God, too. Eve doesn't do any better. When God approaches her, she says, "The serpent deceived me, and I ate" (Genesis 3:13). The Devil made me do it! I can't find one passage of Scripture where the Devil makes us do anything. He lies to us, and then, we have a choice to believe that or not.

"Our choices matter" is usually heard as a negative thing. We've made a bad choice, and we are suffering consequences. But the truth is all choices matter. The law of sowing and reaping is actually given to us in a positive context: "Let us not become weary in doing good, for at the proper time we will reap a harvest if we do not give up" (Galatians 6:9). Those are our lifewords for today.

If you will sow good seed- if you will make good choices- you will reap good things. No matter what's gone on in your life before you read this, if you start making good choices, you will start reaping good things.

After reading the last three devotions, I hope some of you are asking, "Where is God in all of my choices? This is a humanistic teaching, Mark. Where's the grace of God?" Great question. The answer lies right in the passage we've been studying. Deuteronomy 30:19 says, "This day I call heaven and earth as witnesses against you that I've set before you life and death, blessings and curses. Now choose life." God is not some deity in the sky who has spun this world into existence and now is wondering what we're going to do. He says "Choose life." He's pulling for us. He cares about the choices we make.

Theologically, we call this prevenient grace. It is divine grace that precedes human decision. The word prevenient comes from a Latin root word that means to precede. Prevenient grace is simply the grace that goes before your choice. Jesus describes this in John 6:44: "No one can come to Me, unless the Father who sent Me draws him." This is speaking of salvation, but grace works in all of our choices.

God is helping you move toward the good choice. He will put friends in your life. He will put situations in your life. He will put churches in your life. He'll put preachers in your life. God has put the Bible in your life. He's saying, "Come on child, choose life." He will do all He can except pull you across the line of decision.

The God of the Universe that said, "Thus far shall the oceans come and no farther" (Job 38:11) is the same God who is pulling for you. This is our God. Here's what God is like: He says, "Choose life... Choose life." God is for you, not against you (Romans 8:31). In all the choices that you face this week and all the other weeks of your life, know this: You have a Father God who's pulling for you. Don't choose death; choose life. With whatever choice that is before you, God is saying, "Choose life."

For the last four days, we've been focusing on an Old Testament passage that makes very clear that our choices matter. Today, we'll go farther in that same passage. Deuteronomy 30:19-20 says, "This day I call the heavens and the earth as witnesses against you that I have set before you life and death, blessings and curses. Now choose life, so that you and your children may live and that you may love the LORD your God, listen to his voice, and hold fast to him."

The very first choice that's laid before us here is to love the Lord your God. This is before Moses tells us to obey God, before he tells us to serve God, before he tells us to give to Him. Moses says the choice that must be made, which is foundational to all those other choices, is choosing to enter into a heart-relationship with God.

Jesus was asked the same thing. In Matthew and Mark, He was asked what the greatest of all the 600+ commandments was. He responds, "Love the Lord your God with all your heart and with all your soul and with all your mind" (Matthew 22:37). Those are our lifewords for today.

This is not to say that obedience is not important. In fact, if we say we love God but hate other people, John calls us liars (1 John 4:20). Also, John says, if you say you know God and don't obey His commandments, you're lying as well (1 John 2:4). Obedience is important, but it's not the foundational issue. That obedience should flow out of a love relationship with God. I can obey Him but not love Him. Maybe that's why Jesus told His disciples, "I no longer call you servants...I call you friends..." (John 15:15).

St. Augustine said, "Love God and do as you please." When we love God first and foremost, then all we think, say, and do will be generated from that love. Obedience, faithfulness, and right thinking will flow inevitably from that love. Our choices matter, and the choice to love God is the first choice.

It's important not to get the cart before the horse. That old saying is applicable to our relationship with God. It's not about obedience first; it all starts with the heart. We must first choose to love God and enter into a heart-relationship with Him. Moses says as much in Deuteronomy 30:17-18: "But if your heart turns away and you are not obedient...You will not live long in the land you are crossing the Jordan to enter and possess." Those are our lifewords for today. We spoke a few days ago about how the Israelites had the choice to be blessed or cursed (Deuteronomy 30:19). Moses indicates here it's your heart condition that determines if you are blessed or cursed. "...if your heart turns away..." (verse 17).

The heart of the matter is the matter of the heart. Jesus taught this over and over again. Jesus' toughest words were for the Pharisees. Their hearts were not right toward God. "You outwardly appear righteous to men, but inside you are full of hypocrisy and lawlessness" (Matthew 23:28). Jesus was looking at their hearts. "Blind Pharisee! First clean the inside of the cup and dish, and then the outside also will be clean" (Matthew 23:26).

When the New Testament describes our relationship with God, it always speaks in words that indicate a relationship. Born again... new birth... God is our father. Those are relationship words. We have been adopted into the family, and now, we are children of God. We cry out to God, "Abba Father" (Romans 8:15). "Abba" means papa or daddy. It's a very tender word.

The Apostle Paul prays for all of us in Ephesians 3:17-18: "I pray...that Christ may dwell in your hearts through faith. And I pray that you, being rooted and established in love, may have power...to grasp how wide and long and high and deep is the love of Christ..."

This relationship we have with God, through His Son Jesus Christ, is to be a love relationship. The more we grasp His love for us, the more we can respond to that love with love of our own. That way, we won't get the cart before the horse.

As we said yesterday, the choice to love God is made easier when we can grasp God's love for us. Our lifeword today is from 1 John 4:10: "This is love: not that we loved God, but that he loved us and sent his Son as an atoning sacrifice for our sins." The more we know of His love for us, the more we can return that love.

Erma Bombeck, in her book, *Motherhood, the Second Oldest Profession*, writes about the unending love of a mother. She wrote this to each of her three children. To the first born, "I've always loved you best because you were our first miracle. You were the genesis of a marriage, the fulfillment of young love, the promise of our infinity. You sustained us through the hamburger years. The first apartment furnished in Early Poverty...the 7-inch TV set we paid on for 36 months. You were the 'original model' for unsure parents trying to work the bugs out."

To the middle child, "I've always loved you the best because you drew the dumb spot in the family and it made you stronger for it. You cried less, had more patience, wore everything faded and never in your life did anything 'first,' but it only made you more special. You are the one we relaxed with and realized a dog could kiss you and you wouldn't get sick. The world wouldn't come to an end if you went to bed with dirty feet."

To the baby, "I've always loved you the best because endings generally are sad and you are such a joy. You readily accepted milk stained bibs. The lower bunk. The cracked baseball bat. You are the one we held onto so tightly. For, you see, you are the link with the past that gives a reason for tomorrow. You darken our hair, quicken our steps, square our shoulders, restore our vision, and give us humor that security and maturity can't give us."

To each of you reading this, "God loves you best." He loves no one more than He loves you. Would you not only believe that, but would you choose to love Him best too?

Every now and then, one of the pages in my Bible will fall out. Those pages can only be turned so many times. I try to Scotch tape them or paper clip them back in, but it doesn't work very well. I need to break down and buy a new Bible because sooner or later, I will lose a page.

If there's one page in my Bible that I don't want to lose, it's the page that Genesis 15:6 is on. Leading up to this verse, you have God and Abram having a conversation: "'Do not be afraid, Abram. I am your shield, your very great reward. But Abram asked, 'Sovereign LORD, what can you give me since I remain childless and the one who will inherit my estate is Eliezer of Damascus? You have given me no children...' Then the word of the LORD came to him: '...a son who is your own flesh and blood will be your heir.' He took him outside and said, 'Look up at the sky and count the stars...' Then he said to him, 'So shall your offspring be'" (Genesis 15:1-5).

Now here comes the verse you can't lose. It's our lifeword for today. "Abram believed the LORD, and He credited it to him as righteousness" (Genesis 15:6). As we continue to discuss our choices, I don't think I do any damage to that verse by saying, "Abraham chose to believe the Lord." He chose to believe the promise God gave him in verses 4 and 5. Abraham chose to believe, and the Lord counted his belief as righteousness. We can be righteous before God because of our belief, not our works. You take that verse out of the Bible, and we have to erase much of Paul's theology in the New Testament.

Abraham believed the Lord, not believed *in* the Lord. A lot of people believe in God, but fewer believe Him. Our Christian lives change when we go from believing in Him to believing Him, taking Him at His word and believing His promises.

As we said yesterday, the issue for us is choosing to "Believe God." Most people believe there is a God that somehow spun this world into existence. But simple belief is not the issue. Do you take Him at His word? The issue is not do you believe in Him but do you believe Him? "Abram believed the LORD, and He credited it to him as righteousness" (Genesis 15:6). Those are our lifewords for today, and some of the most important words in the Bible.

We wouldn't have a Romans 4 if it wasn't for our lifeword today. "Against all hope, Abraham...believed and so became the father of many nations, just as it had been said to him, 'So shall your offspring be' " (Romans 4:18). Abram choose to believe God and His promise despite "the fact that his body was as good as dead [and] that Sarah's womb was also dead" (Romans 4:19). Though he and Sarah were past childbearing years, he chose to believe he would be the father of many nations.

This is some of the deepest theology we have in the Bible. Paul is arguing for justification by faith and not by works. He's using Genesis 15 as the basis for his argument. "...being fully persuaded that God had power to do what he had promised. This is why 'it was credited to him as righteousness'. The words 'it was credited to him' were written...also for us, to whom God will credit righteousness—for us who believe in Him who raised Jesus our Lord from the dead" (Romans 4:21-24). Our right standing before God because of our belief about Christ is tied to Abram's belief. That's why I don't want to lose Genesis 15:6. It's crucial to our faith.

Somewhere along the line, a Sunday school teacher told you to believe. Maybe it was your mother or father. It could have been a preacher or an evangelist. They told you the story of Jesus and asked you to believe. You did, and it's made all the difference in the world. It all goes back to Genesis 15:6.

You cannot, with mathematical certainty, prove the existence of God. You cannot prove that Jesus turned water into wine. Even though there are marvelous intellectual reasons to believe, when push comes to shove, there comes a time when you must take a step of faith and say, "I choose to believe." That belief must be deeper than a generic belief "in God." James says, "Even the demons believe…" (James 2:19).

Do you believe that God sent His only Son for you? (John 3:16). Do you believe that Jesus was the payment for your sins? "He himself bore our sins in His body on the tree, that we might die to sin and live to righteousness. By His wounds you have been healed" (1 Peter 2:24). Do you take him at His word? Are you a believer?

The Bible says you are "salt of the earth" and the "light of the world" (Matthew 5:13-14). If you believe that, your life will change. God says because of my faith in Christ, I'm His adopted child (Romans 8:14-15). I know I'm the son of Clarence and Ann Atherton. But if I know I'm an adopted son of God and an heir of Christ, think what security and confidence that gives me. This is what I mean by choosing to "believe God," not just "believing in Him."

Dr. Allan Coppedge was one of my professors at Asbury Seminary. He wrote a note to me one day. I don't remember what the note said, but I do remember how he ended it. As Christians, we sometimes write "In Christ" or some other kind of spiritual salutation. At the end of Al's note, he wrote, "Living as a son." That was impactful on a young Christian. How would my life change if I'm a believer and I'm truly walking in belief that I am a son of Almighty God?

Are you a believer? Are you choosing to believe God no matter what? Do you believe that God will supply all your needs? Do you stand on His Word? I encourage you today to go beyond "belief in God" to "believing Him."

Are you a believer who deals with unbelief? Could you be an unbelieving believer? A father brings his son to Jesus and asks for Him to heal the boy. Jesus replies, " 'Everything is possible for one who believes.' Immediately the boy's father exclaimed, 'I do believe; help me overcome my unbelief!' " (Mark 9:23-24). Most believers have some unbelief in them. These questions might help you discern areas where you have unbelief.

Are you a believer who is characterized by worry? Are you a believer who is unwilling to forgive someone? Are you a believer who holds anger or resentment toward someone? Are you a believer who lives in regret or guilt about decisions in your past? If you answer yes to any of these questions, you are struggling with unbelief.

What would your answer be to this question? "I would be more successful if _____. How would you complete that sentence? Here's how the Bible does. God tells Joshua, "Be strong and very courageous. Be careful to obey all the law my servant Moses gave you; do not turn from it to the right or to the left, that you may be successful wherever you go." That's from Joshua 1:7, our lifeword for today. Does what you believe about being successful agree with what God says about it? If it does, you're a believer.

How would you answer this question? "I would be more satisfied if _____." How would complete that sentence? The Bible says in Psalm 63:4-5, "I will praise you as long as I live, and in your name I will lift up my hands. I will be fully satisfied as with the richest of foods; with singing lips my mouth will praise you." God says our satisfaction is in Him. Do you believe that? If you do, you are a believer.

As we mature in Christ, we realize that believing is greater than just believing in Jesus. He wants us to believe God- to take Him at His word- to stand on His promises. We can live our lives choosing to believe Him. When we do, He makes us a believing believer.

Do you believe? Many people will respond positively and tell me about when they "asked Jesus into their heart." I'm thankful for that, but as I've grown in the Lord, I realize there is so much more to being a believer than that. The writer to the Hebrews tells us to "...move beyond the elementary teachings about Christ and be taken forward to maturity, not laying again the foundation of repentance from acts that lead to death and of faith in God...the resurrection of the dead, and eternal judgment" (Hebrews 6:1-2).

As we grow up in Christ, we learn that believers must believe. We leave our elementary school beliefs about Jesus behind in favor of deeper, more mature truths from God's Word. Here's what I mean: Believers who believe have confidence in God and not in themselves, not just for salvation but for everyday needs of life. Believers who believe don't lean on their own understanding. Believers who believe don't neglect the gathering with other believers. We do these things and more because God has clearly spoken of them in His Word, and we choose to believe Him.

What we're talking about here is sanctification. That's a theological word that means the act or process of God that makes one holy. God sanctifies us by His grace. But also, in a real sense, we sanctify ourselves by our daily choice to believe Him. As we lean hard on Him in our daily life, we live out our beliefs and become a believer (salvation) who believes (sanctification). The more we trust, the more we lean on Him and not on ourselves, the further we travel on the journey of sanctification.

Our belief must shape our behavior. It is not simply a mental exercise. The fact that I believe must show up in my daily life, not just in my decision to "give my heart to Jesus." This is what I mean by a believer who believes. This is what James means by a faith that is accompanied by works (James 2:14-26).

October 15ᵗʰ

Joshua was the successor to Moses as the leader of the people of Israel. At the end of his life, Joshua made a farewell address to the leaders of Israel. Joshua, in his parting words says, "Now fear the Lord and serve Him with all faithfulness. Throw away the gods your ancestors worshiped beyond the Euphrates River and in Egypt, and serve the Lord. But if serving the Lord seems undesirable to you, then choose for yourselves this day whom you will serve…But as for me and my household, we will serve the Lord" (Joshua 24:14-15).

Our lifeword today comes from Proverbs 22:6: "Train up a child in the way he should go, and when he is old he will not depart from it." Don't ever underestimate the influence and impact of moms and dads. There will be many people who will make an impression and contributions to your children's lives. None are more impactful than moms and dads. That impression can be positive or negative.

What is taught in the home stays with you. Our lifeword today is not a promise that your child will become a Christian. But it does promise that if you raise them in a godly way, they won't be able to shake that influence.

I didn't make my choice for Christ until I was 34. I was haunted by the upbringing I had. Though I was choosing sin, I knew I wasn't making the right choice. I was haunted by it until I bent my knee to the truth that Mom and Dad taught me.

Parents, your choice to choose family will never be regretted. The seeds you sow into your sons and daughters will take root. Now, it will be up to them if they act upon your example and influence. Your job is simply to raise them up in the right way and trust God with the result.

The first words I can remember my son Christopher saying to me was "Bye-bye, Daddy." I was busy doing the Lord's work planting a church and was gone a lot. So, Christopher learned to say "Bye-bye, Daddy."

That reminded me of the song "Cat's In the Cradle." It was popular when I was a sophomore in high school. "When you coming home dad, I don't know when, but we'll get together then, I know we'll have a good time then." That song is about priorities. It's about choices, family choices. One of the godliest choices I can make is to choose family. "Anyone who does not provide for their relatives, and especially for their own household, has denied the faith and is worse than an unbeliever" (1 Timothy 5:8). The Apostle Paul, mentoring young Timothy, tells him you are "worse than an unbeliever" if you're not mindful of your family.

We don't live in a family-friendly world. The cost of living forces many families to have two income-earners. You don't have to be too much of a student of the culture to look at all forms of advertising and conclude that the corporate world doesn't help us to keep family a priority. I see ads that do the opposite. I see advertisers that use sex and sexual content to sell everything from car wax to baseball tickets.

How do we choose family in this culture? Joshua 24 gives us a clue, and it's our lifeword for today. "As for me and my household, we will serve the Lord" (Joshua 24:15). Do you hear the responsibility that Joshua is taking? Joshua is stepping up to the plate. One way to choose family is to step up and shoulder the responsibility that has been given to you. When a man and a woman choose to bring a child into this world, they bring into this world an eternal being that will spend eternity somewhere.

The world will do as it chooses, but as for me and my family, we will choose the Lord. And choosing the Lord means to make my family the priority in my life, only behind my personal relationship with Him.

For the next few days, let's investigate a word that will transform our lives. It's not a word we hear often. It's often misunderstood and certainly is politically incorrect. If you say this word, people will talk behind your back, they will ostracize you, and maybe even unfriend you on Facebook. It's thought to be a harsh word but is actually one of the most loving words you can say.

Are you ready for it? You may want to make sure the children aren't looking over your shoulder right now because some don't think kids should be exposed to this word. Okay, here it comes. Brace yourself. It's the word "NO." Or as my mom used to say, "N-O spells NO!" Sorry to offend you like that. I know it's a tough word to hear, but we need to say it often as Christians.

I say *yes* a lot out of a sense of obligation or a desire to please people. Sometimes, I say *yes* even though I know I should say *no*. My schedule is already crowded. I'm not sure I have time to do this. It's probably not the best use of my time, but I don't want to let people down. I want them to think well of me.

Our lifeword today is from John 12:42-43. Speaking of some of the Jewish leaders in Jesus' time, it says, "Yet at the same time many even among the leaders believed in Jesus. But because of the Pharisees they would not openly acknowledge their faith for fear they would be put out of the synagogue; *for they loved the praise of men more than the praise of God.*" Unfortunately, that sounds like me sometimes, and it's the reason I say *yes* when I should say *no*.

Jesus said *no* over and over again, and if Jesus said it, I think we can. Now, be sure you say it with humility and love, but also with the confidence that saying *no* may mean saying *yes* to something better.

Yesterday, we looked at one of most important words in the English language. It's the word "No." God's people in Old Testament times said *no* to work on the Sabbath. God even considered this important enough to make it the fourth commandment: "Remember the Sabbath day by keeping it holy. Six days you shall labor and do all your work, but the seventh day is a sabbath to the Lord your God. On it you shall not do any work, neither you, nor your son or daughter, nor your male or female servant, nor your animals, nor any foreigner residing in your towns" (Exodus 20:8-11). Obviously, God was very serious about saying *no* on the Sabbath.

In Jesus' time, even the innocent act of plucking grain and eating it as one walked was regarded by the Pharisees as work, thus a violation of this commandment. Jesus strongly disagreed and said that man was NOT made for the Sabbath but Sabbath was made for man. That's our lifeword today from Mark 2:27.

Jesus interpreted this commandment as a gift to God's people. Look at the verse again. It was "made for man." So, man should not feel burdened by this command or struggle to keep it in the most absurd ways. It should be seen as a gracious gift from God.

We all need down time in our lives. That means we must say "NO." It's not about a certain day of the week that is legalistically adhered to, but it's a principle of taking time to say *no* to the normal routine. Americans go at a frantic pace, one that can't be good for family life. There is much activity we can crowd into our kids' lives. That's why God gave them parents. Our children need our help. They need us to teach them to say *no*. They need the gift of the Sabbath.

All family members need to rest, recharge, and refocus. Remember to say this godly *no*. Your body, mind, and spirit will thank you.

When you were a kid, did you ever say, "Cross my heart and hope to die?" Did you ever swear on your life? I did, and you probably did as well. There were times when I said, "I swear to God!" That usually got me a good spanking if my folks heard it.

Our lifeword today comes from James 5:12: "...do not swear--not by heaven or by earth or by anything else. All you need to say is a simple 'Yes' or 'No.' Otherwise you will be condemned." Here James repeats Jesus' command as recorded in Matthew 5:34–37, "...Simply let your 'yes' be 'yes' and your 'no' be 'no.'" My parents would get on me when I said, "I swear on a stack of Bibles." I've heard people say, "I swear on my mother's grave." Jesus and James say this is not Christian behavior.

In scripture we see Jesus wasn't concerned about whether we should take an oath or not. He was talking about truthfulness. We aren't truthful people because we take an oath. We tell the truth because it's who we are. It's who God has called us to be. An oath should have nothing to do with it. The issue is about integrity and honesty. A simple *yes* or *no* is enough because people should know they can trust the word of a Christian.

That's a word for all of us, but especially for those of us who are parents. "Let your *no* be *no*." Kids don't need parents whose *no* might mean *yes*. Children need boundaries. They need to know where the limits are. There's safety for the child when the parent is consistent with their *yes* and *no*. Now, children will test us, but the parent whose *no* means *no* doesn't have to keep repeating it. Children will learn that you mean what you say. That is an extremely important lesson for them to learn in life. It's a vital trait for them to pick up from their parents.

Jesus taught about saying *no* without using the word. For instance, when He spoke of fasting, He was teaching about saying *no* to food. Fasting is voluntarily abstaining from food or some other regularly enjoyed gift from God, for a spiritual purpose. Jesus assumes we will choose to fast. He doesn't say *if*, but *when you fast* (Matthew 6:16). And He says His followers *will fast* (Matthew 9:15). Those are our lifewords for today.

Biblically, fasting is used to prepare for ministry, to seek God's wisdom, to show grief, to seek deliverance or protection, to repent, to gain victory in war, and to worship God. As you can see, fasting is not about depriving ourselves. God wants me to say "No" so that I can carve out room for better things. Fasting is always accompanied with prayer and seeking God.

In Matthew 6:16-18, Jesus said not to make a public spectacle of yourself when you fast. It's between God and you. Don't be obvious about it. Now, there are Biblical examples of people fasting together. Jesus wasn't putting that down. He was condemning fasting *so that* people will know you're doing it. Who knows about it is not the issue. It's all about your motive, your heart. Why did you fast, for people or for God?

Another benefit of fasting is that it allows us to refuse to indulge the desires of the flesh. Though the bodily desire for food is not forbidden, saying "No" may help us practice the discipline of saying *no* to other bodily desires that are forbidden. Paul says in 1 Corinthians 9:27, "I beat my body and make it my slave." Controlling my body, rather than my body controlling me, has positive spiritual benefit.

When we say *no* to some of the stuff of life, when we do that for the right reasons and with the right motive, it can help to mature us spiritually. *No* is a wonderful gift of God.

October 21st

Temptation is part of life- even a part of Jesus' life. Resisting is a challenge, a real challenge, even for Jesus. While there are strategies to help us deal with Satan's attempt to sidetrack us, a lot of resisting simply comes down to saying *no*. This "No" to temptation is always a "Yes" to something better.

As Jesus was about to start His public ministry, the Bible says, "Jesus was led up by the Spirit into the wilderness to be tempted by the devil" (Matthew 4:1). Those are our lifewords for today.

Look at the words, "Jesus was led..." This was not a spontaneous or accidental event. The Holy Spirit was leading Jesus to the temptation to prepare Him for the ministry God had for Him. The *no's* Jesus would need to say would be preparation for the three years Jesus would spend in active ministry on this earth. No doubt this is not the only time Satan came against the Savior. I'm quite confident the devil returned time and time again in an attempt to detour Christ from the road God had for Him. These were the first of many *no's* Jesus would have to say to finish His work on earth.

Jesus said "No" to the lies of the devil by quoting the truth of God's Word. It's tough to say *no* to a lie if you don't know the truth. To respond correctly, we need to know the Word. When our minds are filled with truth, we can recognize the enemy's schemes and say No to them.

We never walk through these temptations alone because the Lord lives inside us. Through His Holy Spirit and because of His grace, we are empowered to say "...no to ungodliness and worldly passions..." (Titus 2:12). Though the enemy left Jesus until a more "opportune time" (Luke 4:13), each *no* strengthened Him for the task of saving the world. Each *no* we say will prepare us for the tasks God has for you and me down the road.

Our lifeword for today comes from Luke 12:13-14. A man said to Jesus "Tell my brother to share the inheritance with me." Jesus replied, "Who appointed me a judge between you?" We've been looking at appropriate times to say "No." Here's an example of Jesus turning down a request. What can we learn from Jesus?

It's clear He didn't feel the need to solve everyone's problems- and if He didn't, we shouldn't. Sometimes people try to draw us into what does not involve us. They may ask us to take sides in a family dispute or some community issue, and we don't feel we should. We can't be afraid to say no.

A no response may be the best when we are asked to settle a dispute that involves two adults who can work out their own differences. Leaders often experience this. While there are times when leaders may need to intervene, there also are times when the leader should let the adults be adults and work it out themselves. Accountability is important, and a follow-up meeting to see that the issue is resolved is mandatory.

In Luke chapter 4, Jesus cured a demon-possessed man, and word spread. Many people came to Him for help. The next morning, Jesus left, and the people went looking for Him. When they found Him, they wanted Him to stay but He said He must go to other towns to preach because "for this purpose I have been sent" (Luke 4:44).

Jesus says no to their request. He had not come to save only Capernaum. There are others who need His time. Saying no may allow us to stick to our purpose and not get distracted from the mission God has given us. Sometimes requested help deserves a no, and we can follow Jesus' example in doing so without feeling guilty.

Paul says in Galatians 5 that self-control is a fruit of God's Spirit in your life. Self-control implies a struggle within us to say no. Paul compares believers to athletes: "Every athlete exercises self-control in all things" (1 Corinthians 9:25). In the Greek language, we have a word here from which we get our English word agonize. Exercising self-control won't be an easy thing. Paul says he disciplines his body and keeps it under control (1 Corinthians 9:27). But it's not a struggle we fight in our own power. The Holy Spirit in our lives gives us the desire and the power to say "No."

Essential to Paul's concept of self-control is that it is a gift, a fruit of the Holy Spirit. How do we say "No?" Paul answers in Colossians 1:29, and it's our lifeword for today: "To this end I strenuously contend with all the energy Christ so powerfully works in me." He "strenuously contends" by the power of Christ through God's Holy Spirit living in him. In Romans 8:13, Paul writes that it's by the Spirit we put to death the deeds of the body.

Titus 2:11-12 is one of my favorite passages: "For the grace of God has appeared that offers salvation to all people. It teaches us to say "No" to ungodliness and worldly passions, and to live self-controlled, upright and godly lives in this present age."

There is a divine impartation of grace that teaches us, empowers us, and gives us the desire to say "No" to what we ought to. It teaches us to live a self-controlled life. Will it take our discipline? Yes. Will it take our determination? Yes. But God has empowered us in this fight. We don't have to "Just say no." We can say a Holy Spirit-led and grace-empowered "No."

Although it's not Easter, the good news of the resurrection of Jesus Christ is too good to limit it to only one week per year. So, let's take a few days in the fall to talk about Easter.

How would you answer if I asked you, "What happened at Easter?" Certainly, you could go to 1 Corinthians 15:3-8 and give me the factual answer: "For I delivered to you as of first importance what I also received: that Christ died for our sins in accordance with the Scriptures, that He was buried, that He was raised on the third day in accordance with the Scriptures, and that He appeared to Cephas, then to the twelve. Then He appeared to more than five hundred brothers at one time, most of whom are still alive, though some have fallen asleep. Then he appeared to James, then to all the apostles. Last of all, as to one untimely born, He appeared also to me."

There's another way to answer the question, "What happened at Easter?" This answer focuses on the meaning of this event. 2 Timothy 1:9-10 says, "…Who saved us and called us to a holy calling, not because of our works but because of His own purpose and grace, which He gave us in Christ Jesus before the ages began, and which now has been manifested through the appearing of our Savior Christ Jesus, who abolished death and brought life and immortality to light through the gospel…" These verses speak to the meaning of Easter, and it's our lifeword for today.

In these verses, we learn that Easter did not begin when the stone was rolled away. The resurrection of Christ began in the mind of God "before the ages began." Revelation 13:8 echoes the same theme. It speaks of Jesus as the "the Lamb slain from the foundation of the world." So, Good Friday and Easter Sunday were in the mind of God eons ago. That means that when God created the heavens and the earth, He had already planned to give us His "purpose and grace." Easter didn't start 2,000 years ago. It started in the mind of the Father, Son, and Holy Spirit before He spoke this world into existence.

Humanity occupies a small place in an infinite universe. If we traveled at the speed of light, it would take us 100,000 years to cross our galaxy. But the Milky Way, the galaxy where Earth is located, is just one of 2 trillion galaxies. And those are only the ones we can see. Imagine that the Earth is shrunk down to the size of a grain of sand. Now compare that single grain to the entirety of the largest desert in the world, the Sahara. We're still nowhere near understanding how tiny a position we occupy in space.

When I think about all this, I get a sense of the smallness of man. Can we humans really matter to the God of the universe? When I look at our lifeword for today from 2 Timothy 1:9-10 and see that God, "...saved us...because of His own purpose and grace, which He gave us in Christ Jesus before the ages began," I realize we're part of something big. Before anything existed, God had already planned to give us—to give me—His purpose and grace. This makes me very grateful. We are humbled to know that, simply by His grace, God has chosen to save us and call us to Himself.

As I'm humbled, I also get a feel for how important a place humanity has in the mind of God. Psalm 8:3-6 says, "When I look at your heavens, the work of your fingers, the moon and the stars...what is man that you are mindful of him...Yet you have made him a little lower than the angels and crowned him with glory and honor. You have given him dominion over the works of your hands; you have put all things under his feet..."

The true meaning of Easter gives me a sense of the importance of man in the plans of God. Though God has a whole universe to govern, He still thought man important enough to sacrifice His own Son. Though God is making sure 2 trillion galaxies don't collide, He still is mindful of you and me.

For the last two days, we've dug into 2 Timothy 1:9-10. These verses don't merely describe the facts of Easter; they explore the meaning of this event. These verses describe God who"...saved us and called us to a holy calling, not because of our works but because of His own purpose and grace, which He gave us in Christ Jesus before the ages began, and which now has been manifested through the appearing of our Savior Christ Jesus, who abolished death and brought life and immortality to light through the gospel..." Did you notice the end of verse 10? "...who abolished death and brought life and immortality to light through the gospel..." Those are our lifewords for today.

As a pastor, I hear a lot of weird ideas about death. Some talk of death like it's no big deal. This was famously spoken by Simba's father. You remember *The Lion King* movie, don't you? Mufasa said, "You see, it's all part of the circle of life. There's nothing unusual about death. It's just the next step of growth. It's just the next stage of life." Hogwash! Death is a big deal. It's a problem for us. It's not the way it's supposed to be. Death is not natural to us. It only came as a result of sin.

Enter Jesus and the good news about Him. Our lifeword today says He "abolished death." On Good Friday, around 2,000 years ago, Jesus faced death. When He rose from the dead, He showed that He had defeated death. Because Jesus rose from the dead, we no longer have to fear death.

The Greek word translated "abolish" means to render inoperative. Obviously, death still exists, but it holds no power over us. "O death, where is your sting?" (1 Corinthians 15:55). Jesus said of the believer, he shall never die (John 11:25-26). 1 Corinthians 6:14 says, "And God raised the Lord and will also raise us up by his power."

Because of the resurrection of Christ, death has died for the believer. It has been abolished, rendered inoperative. That's the meaning of Easter.

Our lifewords for today are from Paul's words in 1 Corinthians 15:55: "O death, where is your sting?" What follows was written by Pastor John Piper upon the death of Victor Watters. This was read at Victor's funeral:

"Hello, Death." Victor said. "Have you come to talk to me again? I'm not the person you think I am. I'm not the one you used to talk to. Let me ask you a question, Death. 'Where is your sting?'

"My sting is your sin, Victor," Death answered. "You're a sinner. And that is my sting." Victor said, "I know that, Death. But that's not what I asked you. I didn't ask, 'O Death, what is your sting?' I asked, 'O Death, where is your sting?'"

Death said, "Perhaps, Victor, you have forgotten the power of this sting. This is no ordinary bee sting." Victor replied, "You still won't answer me. I'll ask you again, where is your sting, O Death?" Death said, "My sting is your sin and it's in the courtroom of your heart and the courtroom of heaven. In your heart you know you are guilty and condemned."

Then Victor said, "No, Death, my sin is not in my heart or in heaven. You are dead wrong. Listen, Death, Jesus came to me and said 'Victor, you are a sinner. But because of your belief, I've cancelled the record of your debt of sin. I stripped out of Satan's hand his only weapon: the record of your debt.' Then Jesus said, 'So, Victor, when death comes, you know how to deal with him.'

"So, where is your sting, O Death? Where is my sin? It's nailed to the cross. And here is something else that you know. It won't be long till my body will be raised from the ground and, Death, you will be no more. Death, here's something you didn't know. My story will be told at my funeral. And many will hear and believe." Victor closed his eyes, put his head on his pillow and died a death that had no sting.

We return to 2 Timothy 1:9-10 as our lifeword for today: God "...who saved us and called us to a holy calling, not because of our works but because of His own purpose and grace, which He gave us in Christ Jesus before the ages began, and which now has been manifested through the appearing of our Savior Christ Jesus, who abolished death and brought life and immortality to light through the gospel..."

Let's focus today on those last nine words: "brought life and immortality to light through the gospel." Here's what happened on that first Easter morning: Jesus shone a floodlight on life and immortality. We now can see a little bit of what life and immortality are all about.

Because of the resurrection of Christ, we can be born again. We can have new life in Christ. "And if the Spirit of Him who raised Jesus from the dead is living in you, He who raised Christ from the dead will also give life to your mortal bodies because of His Spirit who lives in you" (Romans 8:11). Whereas we once lived for temporal things, we now live for eternal things. Whereas we once lived a life that had no purpose or meaning, we now live a significant, fulfilling life. I am not random. There is a specific reason that I am here. I am created in His image.

Not only do we experience a new life now, but our lifeword says we have the hope of life immortal. The Bible tells us of a new heaven and a new earth. Here we will never grow old. Here we will never become weak or ill. Here there will be no more tears (Revelation 21:1-4). We can expect all things to be restored to their original state in which God said they were "very good."

For five days now, we've explored the *meaning* of Easter, not just the fact of Easter. When God raised Jesus from the dead, He revealed an eternal plan. He abolished death and shone a floodlight on life and immortality. Now, that's good news!

Christianity lives and dies with the resurrection of Jesus Christ. If the resurrection is true, then the implications are staggering. If the resurrection is a hoax, then the Christian faith has no validity at all and we should renounce it. If the resurrection is not true, I would cease being a pastor. I would encourage everyone to leave my church. The Bible agrees with me. Paul writes, "If the dead are not raised, let us eat and drink, for tomorrow we die" (1 Corinthians 15:32). Paul also says, "If in Christ we have hope in this life only, we are of all people most to be pitied" (1 Corinthians 15:19). When I preach, I am either promoting a cruel lie, or I am speaking the most profound truth anyone could ever speak. There is no middle ground.

The resurrection of Jesus was as hard to accept in biblical times as it is today. Everyone struggled with it until they were compelled by the evidence to accept it. What evidence, you ask? Let's take a look at that for the next two days.

The evidence that Jesus died is irrefutable. Dr. Norman Geisler writes, "The evidence for Christ's death is greater than that for almost any other event in the ancient world." One of the reasons this is true is because of the nature of crucifixion. People did not survive being nailed to a cross, especially after being beaten and whipped. Jesus bled from His hands and feet and from the thorns that pierced His brow. Crucifixion required that the person push and pull themselves up by their nailed hands and feet in order to breathe. Eventually, you were unable to do this, meaning you could no longer breathe. On top of that, Jesus was speared to prove that He had died.

The soldiers, trained executioners, pronounced Him dead. The practice was to break the legs of those crucified to expedite death, so that the person could no longer breathe. In Jesus' case, they decided it wasn't necessary.

Both Jewish and Roman historians recorded His death. There's overwhelming evidence that Jesus died.

Christianity stands or falls with the resurrection of Jesus Christ. If the resurrection is true, then only a fool would not confess Jesus as Lord. For there to be a resurrection, Jesus had to die. Yesterday, we showed that the evidence of His death is overwhelming. But what about His resurrection? It's no big deal that someone died on a cross. It's a game-changer if they rose from the dead. Let's explore some of the reasons to believe that the resurrection took place.

He appeared first to women. If someone made up the resurrection in hopes that people would believe, they never would have Jesus appearing to women. The testimony of women wasn't accepted back then. Claiming that women were the first to see Him did not give the story credibility. No one would add this to the story if it were false.

Jesus then appeared to the disciples. He appeared to 500 people at one time. He was touched, and He ate food. Eyewitness accounts demand an explanation. The effects of the resurrection are also unexplainable if they're not true. After Jesus was crucified, all of His followers lived in fear. What happened that turned them into the fearless men and women who transformed the Roman world? There is no question that His followers believed the good news of the resurrection and were willing to die for it. Nothing else accounts for that transformation.

Here are some other unexplainable things. The tomb was heavily guarded and found to be empty. The authorities who killed Jesus didn't conduct a search or produce a body but instead organized a cover-up. The conversion of skeptics, such as the Apostle Paul, is strong evidence in and of itself. Christians and skeptics alike agree that:

- Jesus died.
- His tomb was empty, and the body was never found.
- Jesus' disciples believed and were transformed following their alleged resurrection observations.

If one believes that Jesus didn't rise from the dead, they must come up with a plausible explanation for all of these facts.

There's little in the Bible about how to go to Heaven. Especially when you compare it with the amount of verses that speak of good behavior. There's so much of that, one could get the idea that we must be good enough to go to Heaven.

Much in the Sermon on the Mount is about being good. Matthew 6:1 speaks of doing good deeds… just don't do them to be seen by men. Much of Matthew 5 is about good behavior. Jesus tells us how to really keep the Ten Commandments. He teaches us how to give to please God. He tells us to love our enemies. I could go on and on. There's a lot that could give us the idea that I can be good enough to go to Heaven.

Because of the emphasis on good behavior in the Bible, and especially in the Sermon on the Mount, Matthew 5:20 is a fascinating verse. Jesus said, "For I tell you that unless your righteousness surpasses that of the Pharisees and the teachers of the law, you will certainly not enter the kingdom of heaven." These men were the professional do-gooders. They were the most righteous people of 1ˢᵗ-century Jerusalem. This must have been a shocking statement to His disciples. What hope did they have to be righteous in their behavior if the Pharisees and the teachers of the law fell short?

They sought to have a righteousness, a goodness, of their own. They thought they could be good enough for Heaven. Speaking of these men, Paul wrote, "Since they did not know the righteousness of God and sought to establish their own…" (Romans 10:3). That was the problem. They didn't understand the truth of our lifeword for today: "There is no one righteous, not even one" (Romans 3:10).

Don't be fooled into trying to be good enough. Join the crowd that says, "We're not good enough." These people are "not far from the Kingdom of God" (Mark 12:34).

We're talking about being good enough. Our world is concerned with being good. At least the religious world is. They have a desire to do good things because many of them think they can be good enough to go to Heaven. Much of the world's religions are based on being good enough.

I remember the first person I ever led to the Lord. When I asked her, "If you died tonight, would you go to Heaven?" she replied, "Yes." I then asked her why. She said she always forgives people. She was in the "good enough" crowd.

I was watching this guy on YouTube that goes to college campuses and does street preaching. He had a coed in front of him, and she said she was a practicing Catholic. He asked her, "What's the gospel?" Her response? "Do unto others as you would want them to do to you." That's a "good enough" response.

There's one biblical way to be good enough. You must have the righteous, or the goodness, of God. Theologically, it's called **imputed righteousness.** Imputed is an accounting term. Something has been credited to your account. You didn't earn it; it was credited to your account. It's what God does for you.

Our lifeword today is from 2 Corinthians 5:21. "God made him who had no sin to be sin for us so that in Him we might become the righteousness of God." Repeat the words In Him - In Him - In Him. That's imputed righteousness. That's how we get good enough. God imputes His goodness to our account.

For me to be good enough, I have to admit I'm not, and then submit to God's goodness. Remember our lifeword from yesterday. "Since they did not know the righteousness of God and sought to establish their own, they did not submit to God's righteousness" (Romans 10:3).

Yesterday, we mentioned the theology of the "good enough" crowd. They believe you make it to Heaven by doing good things and not doing bad things. To these folks, I'd like to ask a question. "How good do you have to be?" My guess is they will stumble and stammer around but won't answer the question. That's because they can't. No one knows how good you have to be. If this "good enough" theology was right, wouldn't there be a list somewhere that told us how good we had to be?

Maybe God has a set of scales that He weighs our life upon. If we are a little more good than bad, we get into Heaven. Or maybe there's a grading scale. A score of 60 is the lowest D. Since it's pass/fail, all I need is to pass. So, a 60 is good enough.

Some people say this list is the Ten Commandments. If I keep nine of the Commandments and only break one, is that good enough? That's 90%. That surely ought to be good enough. The problem with that is that nowhere in the context of the Commandments does it say these were given so you can go to Heaven. Go look at them right now. It won't say that this is the path to eternal life. If God is good, wouldn't He tell us what we have to do to be good enough? You see, "good enough" theologians have a problem.

The truth is that being good enough has nothing to do with it. God didn't expect us to be good enough. That's not a part of His plan. Our lifewords today tell us of God's plan for salvation: "...apart from the law the righteousness of God has been made known, to which the Law and the Prophets testify. This righteousness is given through faith in Jesus Christ to all who believe" (Romans 3:21-22). Those verses do away with "good enough" theology.

For the last few days, we've been speaking of the people who think they can be good enough to go to Heaven. Here's the truth that the "good enough" crowd needs to hear: No matter how good you are, it's not good enough. Now, that's bad news! You thought Christianity was about good news, didn't you? Well, it certainly is, but first, I must understand the bad news. I have no righteous of my own, and any that I try to have is "filthy rags" in God's sight (Isaiah 64:6). The "good enough" crowd has difficulty believing the bad news. They think we can do enough good things to merit Heaven. When I come to terms with the bad news, then I'm ready for the good. I need the good. I'm searching for the good. I'm desperate for good news IF I understand the bad.

The good news is the imputed righteousness we spoke of two days ago. A righteousness, a goodness that God gives me, that God credits to my account. Our lifeword today is from Romans 4:3: "What does the scripture say? Abraham believed God and it was credited to him as righteousness." Abraham didn't just believe IN God. He believed Him. He took God at His word. He believed God's promise of a son even in Abraham's old age. The Bible says that belief was credited as goodness, or righteousness. It was imputed goodness, not a goodness of his own. God pronounced him good because of Abraham's belief and trust.

Paul used to be part of the "good enough" crowd. He was focused on all the good things he could do. But after He met Christ, he called the good things "rubbish." "I consider them rubbish that I may gain Christ and be found in him not having a righteousness of my own...but that which comes through faith in Christ" (Philippians 3:8-10). Only when Paul gave up his "good enough" theology was he able to gain Christ.

I've been trying to explain the good news of imputed righteousness. While that's really good, there's more good to the good news! It's based in the fact that the New Testament calls us Christians to exhibit good behavior. You can't deny that. Because of that, God not only does something for us- imputed righteousness, He also does something IN us-imparted righteousness. I like to call it a gospel goodness.

To explain this, let's go back to my basketball coaching days. I'm having tryouts, and there's one kid who's not good enough. But I like him a lot. He's a great kid, but he's not nearly good enough. Some kids have it, and some kids don't. This kid doesn't. But I'm the coach. I can put him on the team and sit him at the end of the bench. I have the power to do that. But I don't have the power to make him a good player. He has no ability. I can put a jersey on him and <u>impute</u> basketball skills to him and pronounce him on the team. That's all I can do.

The Bible says that once you are Christian, there's a whole lot of good He wants you to do. But I'm just a sinner saved by grace, right? Imputed righteousness, remember? All that's left for me to do is try real hard and fall short of the person God calls me to be. Is that the Christian life? No, it's not, because to whom God imputes, He also imparts. He not only does something for you; He does something IN you.

What I can't do for the kid at the end of the bench, God does for us. God imparts power to us. He imparts newness. It's called a new birth. It's called a new creation. It's called being born again. You are not the person you used to be. You have new desires. You have a new nature inside of you. Our lifewords today are from 2 Corinthians 5:17: "If any man be Christ, he is a new creation." This is the good news. It's the gospel goodness.

The old song says, "I'm just a sinner, saved by grace." Of course, that's true, but it's incomplete truth. Righteousness is not only imputed; it's imparted. I'm a Holy Spirit-filled, grace-empowered sinner saved by grace. Our lifewords today are from 2 Peter 1:3-4: "His divine power has given us everything we need for a godly life through our knowledge of him who called us by his own glory and goodness. Through these he has given us his very great and precious promises, so that through them **you may participate in the divine nature...**"

First of all, the text says, God's power has given us all we need to live a godly life. Wow! If that's not good enough, the text goes on to say we somehow participate in the divine nature of God. I'm not totally sure what that means, but it's got to have something to do with impartation. I tremble as I write this, but Peter says we can participate-share-partner with the divine nature. Somehow by the grace of God, we participate in the Trinitarian nature of God. How can that NOT be some kind of impartation? It's a gift, and it's gospel goodness.

Now, you can take this way too far. You can teach that we are divine or that we can become angels. That's heresy. But He's given us something that empowers us for all the good behavior that's called for in the Old and New Testaments. To whom He imputes, He also imparts. Believe that truth. Walk in that truth. It will change your Christian life.

Referring back to yesterday's devotion, God has not only put you on the team. He's not only given you a jersey. He's also imparted you with divine ability to "play basketball". He has given you a desire to live a life that pleases and glorifies Him (Titus 2:14). It's a gift of His grace. Take it by faith. Believe it and walk in it. If you do, you'll no long be just a sinner, saved by grace.

When I went to Asbury Seminary, the president was Dr. Maxie Dunnam. He often spoke to us about a morning ritual he went through. It's based on Colossians 1:27, and these are our lifewords for today: "To them God has chosen to make known among the Gentiles the glorious riches of this mystery, which is Christ in you, the hope of glory." He quoted the end of that verse and used it as a daily discipline. "The secret is simply this: Christ in you! Yes, Christ in you... bringing with Him the hope of all glorious things to come" (Phillips translation).

Dr. Dunnam was pastoring a Methodist congregation in Mississippi in the early 60s. The level of racial hatred there was unlike in any other state. Dr. Dunnam found the emotional and physical demands of pastoral leadership during that time to be unbearable. His own words are, "I was losing confidence in my call, feeling totally inadequate and ready to throw in the towel."

It was at this time he discovered the "secret." He discovered the indwelling Christ. The fact that Christ's invitation is to "abide in Him" (John 15). Paul calls this putting on the "new self which is created to be like God in true righteousness and holiness" (Ephesians 4:24). This is nothing more than Christ imparting Himself in us so that we can live a godly life.

Some of you may think this is "preacher talk," that this is not meant for the everyday Christian but only the super–duper saints like Mother Teresa. I leave you with Ephesians 3:20: "Now to Him who is able to do immeasurably more than all we ask or imagine, according to **His power** that works within us..."

Gospel goodness, God's righteousness, is not only imputed; it's imparted. The secret is, "Christ in you, Christ in you, bringing with Him the hope of all the glorious things to come."

An important but difficult truth of God is that He wants to use the pain and hurt in our lives. When difficult times happen, so many of us ask God "Why?" when we should be asking "How?" How do You want to use this in my life?

Sometimes, the answer lies in the truth that God wants to use your painful and hurtful circumstances to teach you to trust and rely on Him more. I don't know about you, but the smooth-sailing times in my life weren't the times I learned to lean more and more on His grace.

When bad things happen in our lives, we have a choice. We can draw closer to God, or we can run away from Him. How do you draw close to God in your pain? Well, tell Him how you feel. Cry out to God. Battle it out in prayer. Draw close to Him in worship and through His Word.

Our lifeword today is from 2 Corinthians 1:8. Paul writes, "We do not want you to be uninformed about the troubles we experienced. We were under great pressure, far beyond our ability to endure. This happened that we might not rely on ourselves but on God." You see, God wants to use our pain to teach us to rely on Him.

Another way God wants to use our hurt and pain is seen in Galatians 6:2: "Carry each others burdens, and in this way you fulfill the law of Christ." What is the law of Christ? Loving God AND loving others, which is the great commandment. When we allow others to help us in our pain, and we join with others in their suffering, we draw closer to each other and come closer to fulfilling God's greatest commandment. Don't allow difficult times to isolate you from others. Drawing closer to other people is a good thing, and it's one way God wants to use the pain in our lives.

Yesterday, we spoke of how God wants to use our pain. C. S. Lewis said, "God whispers to us in our pleasures, speaks in our conscience, but shouts in our pain...it's His megaphone to rouse a deaf world." We are most keenly aware of God's power in our suffering. It is then our self-sufficiency is peeled away, and we become aware of how weak we really are. It's in that moment of weakness we experience God's power.

Our lifeword is from 2 Corinthians 12:9. God tells Paul, "My power is made perfect in weakness." In our pain, in our weakness, we can sense His power most. It's in our pain we learn that His grace is sufficient in our lives. God uses pain as a megaphone to teach us that He is sufficient to meet our deepest needs. Learning that lesson is worth a lot, even the pain we must go through to teach us that truth.

As we trust God through the difficulties of life, He builds our character. God always uses our rough spots as opportunities for growth. Christian character is seen in the Fruit of the Spirit, "love, joy, peace, patience, kindness, goodness, gentleness, faithfulness, and self-control" (Galatians 5:22-23).

How do you learn them? You learn joy when you grieve. You learn peace in chaotic times. You learn patience when you have to wait. You learn kindness when people are not kind to you. You learn faithfulness when you're tempted to not be faithful. You learn self-control when those around you are out of control. You learn these things in difficult situations.

Don't allow painful and hurtful situations to make you bitter. Make the choice to allow pain to make you better. The wise person allows the hurt to help. The Christian asks God to use these situations and learns "When I am weak then I am strong" (2 Corinthians 12:10). This is because of His power, not mine.

One truth that needs to be remembered in times of hurt is that our personal pain speaks to others. C. S. Lewis says our pain is God's "megaphone to rouse a deaf world." People listen to the cancer patient who has hope and peace.

We've had two infants die in our church in the last year. These parents witness loudly to God's grace as they go on with life with trust and faith in their good God. Friends are watching as we go through the hurt and pain in our lives.

So, our pain gives us a platform. In our hurt, what will we say to the world? Will I testify to the goodness of God even when my circumstances are not good? God does not change when suffering comes. The old song says, "He's the God of the mountain and the God of the valley. The God of the good times and the God of the bad." As I trust God through the hard times, my life speaks, and I impact those around me with the platform pain has given me.

Our lifeword today is from 2 Corinthians 1:3-4: "Blessed be the God and Father of our Lord Jesus Christ, the Father of mercies and God of all comfort, who comforts us in all our affliction, so that we may be able to comfort those who are in any affliction, with the comfort with which we ourselves are comforted by God."

Read that again. The Apostle Paul says that Christ comforts us so that we can comfort others. Our pain allows us to minister to others. Just as we're not to put our light under a bowl (Matthew 5:15), His comfort to us is meant to shine to a watching world.

May we use the platform God has given us as a "megaphone to rouse a deaf world." May our lives shout that "God is good" even through our pain and hurt.

Our lifeword today is from Matthew 6:25: "Do not worry about your life, what you will eat or drink; or about your body, what you will wear." Worry is the desire to control the uncontrollable. We can't control our children, so we worry about them. We can't control the future, so we worry about it. Much of our health we can't control, so we worry about it. Worry never solved a thing! For that reason, **worry is unreasonable.**

To worry about something you can't change doesn't make sense. It's not smart, and it's certainly not logical. Worry can cause us to deal with a problem twice. Once in our minds as we anticipation the problem, and again when (or should I say if) the difficulty happens. Why would I want to go through the problem twice? Worry doubles the trouble! How unreasonable is that? It makes no sense whatsoever.

Matthew 6 continues, "Do not worry about your life, what you will eat or drink; or about your body, what you will wear. Look at the birds of the air; they do not sow or reap or store away in barns, and yet your heavenly Father feeds them. Are you not much more valuable than they?" (Matthew 6:25-26)

Did you hear those last words of Jesus, "Are you not much more valuable than they?" Jesus says that worry is not worthy of God's children. We are created in His image. The birds weren't created in God's image, yet God cares for them. For us to worry, therefore, is beneath us, and Jesus plainly says as much. "Are you not much more valuable than they?" Jesus uses the birds to teach us. He basically says if the birds can trust, why can't humans? Worry is not worthy of the greatest of God's creation.

We get the word "worry" from both an English and German word that literally means "to strangle" or "to choke." When we worry, we are choking the very life out of us. Jesus is plain in His words. "Do not worry..." (Matthew 6:25).

Yesterday, we said that worry is not reasonable, and it's not worthy of us who are created in God's image. Our lifeword today is from Matthew 6:27: "Can any one of you by worrying add a single hour to your life?" What is Jesus saying here? It's pretty plain that He's trying to tell us that worry is not helpful. You cannot even add an hour to your life through worry.

It would be one thing if there was some kind of payoff for worry. If it could add something to my life, it might make some sense. But since worry adds nothing to my life, it's unproductive. It's a complete waste of my time. It has no ability to correct a past wrong or erase a bad choice. It cannot control the future. It only will make me miserable and unproductive today.

When I worry about a problem, it doesn't bring me one inch closer to a solution. Worry only shortens and saddens your life. It produces nothing of real and lasting benefit. Worry is unproductive, so why do we do it?

Jesus says worry tears you up. The Greek word translated here as worry actually means "to divide, rip, or tear apart." The Bible's most common word for "worry" is a compound of a verb and a noun. The verb is "divide." The noun is "mind." To worry is to divide the mind in a dozen different directions. So, when you worry, your focus and your energy is divided. The division caused by worry makes it harder for you to concentrate and accomplish what God wants you to do.

Jesus told Martha in Luke 10 that she was worried and bothered about many things, but only one thing was necessary. You get the message here, right? Some of the things we worry about take our energy and focus away from more important things. Don't allow worry to divide, rip, or tear you apart. It's completely unhelpful.

November 12th

Worry is a serious issue because Jesus says it's a spiritual problem. It stems from unbelief. Jesus has harsh words for those who worry: "O you of little faith!" (Matthew 6:30).

Worry and anxiety reveal a lack of faith in the goodness and power of God. Worrying is not trusting that God is with me and cares about me. Worry is unbelief because God plainly tells me in His Word not to worry.

Worrying is borrowing trouble from tomorrow because God has told us that tomorrow has enough worries of its own (Matthew 6:34). God, help me live one day at a time.

If I worry about tomorrow, I can't enjoy today. I'll miss today's blessings. The future can overwhelm me. God will give me the grace I need for the future when I get there. Right now, I need to trust Him... believe Him. Believe that His grace will be sufficient today.

God has promised to take care of all my needs. When I doubt that, it flows from unbelief. I'm acting as if there is no God and no promises in Scripture. Someone has said that worry is "practical atheism." Philippians 4:19 says, "And my God will meet all your needs according to His glorious riches in Christ Jesus." Is there anything not included in the word "all?" God knows about your needs. Do you believe that?

Our lifeword today is from 1 Peter 5:7: "Cast all your worries and cares on God, for He cares about you." This verse says we are to "cast" our cares on the Lord. The word "cast" doesn't simply mean to throw off. It means to throw off with vigor. The picture here is of a hiker at the end of a long hike unhooking his backpack and casting it down. As we cast our worries, we act in faith. When we carry them, we act in unbelief.

As we conclude our look at worry, let's look at the truth of Scripture that helps us battle against the temptation of worry.

When I'm tempted to worry **about what people will do to me**, I should remember Romans 8:31: "If God be for us, who can be against us?" Also, Joshua 1:9: "Have I not commanded you? Be strong and courageous. Do not be afraid; do not be discouraged, for the Lord your God will be with you wherever you go."

When I'm tempted to worry **about being too weak**, I must remember 2 Corinthians 12:9: "My grace is sufficient for you, for My power is perfected in weakness." Also, Isaiah 40:29: "He gives strength to the weary and increases the power of the weak."

When I'm tempted to worry **about future decisions**, I must remember Psalm 32:8: "I will instruct you and teach you in the way you should go; I will counsel you with My eye upon you." Also, Proverbs 3:5-6: "Trust in the Lord with all your heart and lean not on your own understanding; in all your ways acknowledge Him, and He will direct your paths."

When I'm tempted to worry **about loved ones**, I must remember Matthew 7:11: "…how much more will the Father give what is good to those who ask." Also, Proverbs 22:6: "Train up a child in the way he should go; even when he is old he will not depart from it."

When I'm tempted to worry **about getting old**, I must remember Isaiah 46:4: "Even to your old age and gray hairs, I am He, I am He who will sustain you." Also, Psalm 92:12-14: "But the godly will flourish like palm trees and grow strong like the cedars of Lebanon…Even in old age they will still produce fruit; they will remain vital and green. They will declare, 'The LORD is just! He is my rock!'"

The Book of Proverbs talks a lot about fools. I have to admit, I've done some foolish things in my life. Things that could have been avoided if I had followed the wisdom found in Proverbs.

When we know better but still do something we shouldn't, the Bible calls us a fool. A fool is someone who is in touch with the realities of life and knows the way the world works, but for some reason doesn't follow that way. The Bible speaks to a certain order that God has established for this world. When you deny that order, bad things can happen. There's a fiscal, moral, social, and spiritual order. If you don't follow that order and suffer consequences because of it, you shouldn't be shocked. If you are, you are the biblical definition of a fool.

Our lifeword today is from Proverbs 8:27-30. Wisdom is speaking and says, "I was there when he set the heavens in place. When He marked out the horizon on the face of the deep, when He established the clouds above and fixed securely the fountains of the deep, when He gave the sea its boundary so the waters would not overstep His command, and when He marked out the foundations of the earth. Then I was constantly at his side." Wisdom was there as God put the world in order.

There's a physical order to this world. I can eat all kinds of fattening foods with high cholesterol and all the things that are bad for me. The odds are great that's going to have an effect on my body and on my heart. So, I shouldn't be shocked if I die at the age of 60 of a heart attack. The Bible calls me a fool if I know all that to be true but don't follow it.

Proverbs 1:7 says, "Fools despise wisdom and instruction." Following the wisdom of the Book of Proverbs will foolproof your life. I don't know about you, but my life would have gone a lot smoother if I had submitted to God's wisdom and instruction.

Yesterday, we said a fool is one who understands God's order of things but chooses to live their life opposite of that order. They know the structure God has given this world, but for some reason, they deny it. When these people suffer consequences, they should not be surprised. Galatians 6:7 says, "Do not be deceived: God cannot be mocked. A man reaps what he sows."

The Book of Proverbs is filled with wisdom that will keep our lives on the right path. But it's important to understand that much of Proverbs are not promises. They are general rules that the world follows. Rules that are true most of the time. We live in a fallen world. The world doesn't go as it should, because of sin. That's why Proverbs aren't always promises but general rules.

So, let's say I'm a moralist and I believe that if a person does this and doesn't do that, their life will be grand. From life experience, we all know that's not true. The truth is a person could do the right thing and not do the wrong things and they can still have bad things happen to them. Why? Because we live in a fallen world.

A biblical fool is one that disregards the fact that this world is fallen. Things don't go as they would in a perfect world. That's why the good Christian man or woman, whom everybody knew to be a pillar of the church, gets killed in a car accident. We live in a fallen world. You're a biblical fool if you don't take that into account.

From Genesis 3 on, the Bible says this world isn't going as it should. That's why biblical proverbs are general rules of how life goes, but not promises. I'm a fool in biblical terms if I don't acknowledge that this world is fallen.

The next two days we'll look at a few Proverbs that speak to foolishness.

Proverbs 10:14 – "The wise store up knowledge, but the mouth of a fool invites ruin." Fools run off at the mouth. Fools love to hear themselves talk. My dad used to say, "Better to keep your mouth shut and be thought a fool than to open it and remove all doubt." That's actually a paraphrase from Proverbs 17:28. "Even fools are thought wise if they keep silent, and discerning if they hold their tongues."

Proverbs 12:15 – "The way of fools seems right to them, but the wise listen to advice." The Bible speaks of the wisdom of many counselors. Over and over again, we are told not to rely on our own wisdom. Fools don't ask anyone else's opinion. They either know it all, or they are too timid to approach others for counsel. "There is safety in a multitude of counselors" (Proverbs 11:14).

Proverbs 17:21- "To have a fool for a child brings grief; there is no joy for the parent of a godless fool." The issue is not left up to fate. Parents who neglect their parental duties may create a fool that otherwise would not have existed. Neglectful parents, especially fathers, contribute greatly to their children's foolishness. Parents who do not train their children, are creating their own misery. Children who are undisciplined bring shame to their mother (Proverbs 29:15).

Let's continue our look at a few Proverbs that speak to foolishness.

Proverbs 26:11 – "As a dog returns to its vomit, so fools repeat their folly." A heart attack will get a fool's attention. For a short while, the fool will adhere to the diet and exercise program prescribed for them. He or she wants the specific details of super nutrition and the best exercise program. Too often, after three months of no angina, the fool is a couch potato again. There are many examples of this. Remember the definition of a fool: one who knows the good they should do but does not do it.

Proverbs 29:11 – "Fools give full vent to their rage, but the wise bring calm in the end." Wise men know when and how to speak, but fools say everything without preparation or thought. A wise man speaks carefully. A fruit of God's Holy Spirit is self-control.

Anger is a natural human emotion. How that anger is dealt with is the difference between foolishness and wisdom. "In your anger, do not sin" (Ephesians 4:26). A fool's wrath is quickly known. They cannot keep in their angry words. "Fools show their annoyance at once" (Proverbs 12:16). Wise men and women keep words in and allow anger to dissipate.

Psalms 14:11 - The fool says in his heart, "There is no God." Remember the biblical understanding of a fool: Someone who knows the truth but does not practice it. That makes me think of Romans 1:20. "For since the creation of the world God's invisible qualities—his eternal power and divine nature—have been clearly seen, being understood from what has been made, so that people are without excuse." Because of the truth of creation, we all know of the existence of God. Unfortunately, some suppress that truth.

Our lifewords today are written by the Apostle Paul in Galatians 3:1: "O foolish Galatians! Who has bewitched you?" Wow! Paul calls the Galatians fools and then asks them who bewitched them. He doesn't mince words, does he? Paul never does when he speaks of eternal issues.

These Galatians had come into a relationship with Jesus by grace through faith. But Paul speaks throughout the Book of Galatians that they were allowing themselves to go back to obeying the law as a means of justification. Paul calls it "foolish."

Paul tells the people of the Galatian church that they did not receive the Holy Spirit by obeying the law, nor did they experience the daily supply of the Holy Spirit in their lives because they kept the law. "Are you so foolish? Having begun by the Spirit, are you now being perfected by the flesh?" (Galatians 3:2).

Those who attempt to be righteous through their obedience to the law of God, Paul calls fools. If by obeying traditions created by men, they try to be righteous, Paul calls them fools. He would call us the same.

The gospel says that "...no one will be declared righteous in God's sight by the works of the law...but now apart from the law the righteousness of God has been made known...this righteousness is given through faith in Jesus Christ to all who believe" (Romans 3:20-23).

It's human nature to think we can find acceptance on the basis of our behavior. Paul would say "Stop it!" He may even call us fools! It's foolishness to try to be good enough. Just how good do you have to be? How would you know if you've been good enough?

The only wise thing to do is to rest in the finished work of Christ. It's foolishness to try to satisfy God with your obedience. Believe the promise of God and rest in Christ alone by faith alone. It's the only wise thing to do.

As humans, we are prone to forget. It sure is easy to forget how good the gospel is. Our lifewords today were written by Paul, who was admonishing the forgetful Galatians: "O foolish Galatians! Who has bewitched you? ...are you so foolish? Having begun by the Spirit, are you now being perfected by the flesh?" (Galatians 3:1-3). Paul essentially says, "What were you thinking? Have you forgotten the gospel?"

There is something in us that causes us to be the very thing Jesus came to prevent: self-righteous fools. It's really hard for us to believe that God's grace could be that amazing. Even for those of us who are preachers and teachers of grace, it's easy to revert to working hard to get in God's good graces. How foolish of us!

You have that problem too, don't you? We are all attracted to our own self-righteousness. There is something in us that causes us to be proud of doing it right and trying harder than other Christians. But Jesus was a friend of sinners (Matthew 11:19). He hung out with people who knew the gravity of their sin. They knew they were lost and needed a Savior. That's the opposite of foolishness. That's wisdom.

"For the message of the cross is foolishness to those who are perishing, but to us who are being saved it is the power of God" (1 Corinthians 1:18). To the self-righteous, the ones who are proud of their behavior, its foolishness to put faith and trust in what Someone else has done for you. But for us who are saved, it is the wisdom of God. "Where is the wise person? Where is the teacher of the law? Where is the philosopher of this age? Has not God made foolish the wisdom of the world?" (1 Corinthians 1:20). The wisdom of the world says you have to earn God's approval. God calls that wisdom foolishness. It's best we don't forget that.

In 1859, Charles Blondin stretched a wire over Niagara Falls and walked from side to side. He also did it with his manager on his back! What if the manager, when they were halfway across said, "I think I'll do the rest myself." He would have died. Having been carried that far, why would he attempt to go the rest of the way by himself?

This is the very same thing that Paul addresses in Galatians 3:1-3. "You foolish Galatians! Who has bewitched you? Before your very eyes Jesus Christ was clearly portrayed as crucified. I would like to learn just one thing from you: Did you receive the Spirit by the works of the law, or by believing what you heard? Are you so foolish? After beginning by means of the Spirit, are you now trying to finish by means of the flesh?" Those are our lifewords for today.

In this passage, Paul tackles one of the greatest misconceptions about the Christian life. Many Christians seem to think we're saved by grace through faith, but then it's up to us to mature as believers. It's like getting to the middle of the tightrope and saying, "I think I'll take it from here." We all must continue in the Christian life exactly the way we started: by grace, not behavior. Paul says it would be foolish to start one way and finish another.

Paul is not saying that the choices I make as a Christian don't matter. It's through the choices we make that God changes us. But the power to make those choices doesn't come from ourselves; it comes from the Spirit. Paul writes, "But by the grace of God I am what I am, and his grace to me was not without effect. No, I worked harder than all of them--yet not I, but the grace of God that was with me" (I Corinthians 15:10). We start with grace, and we must finish with grace.

What do you think of when your mind goes to Thanksgiving? Turkey, family, football, Christmas shopping? All of those are great, but as we enter into this week, we're reminded of the goodness of God to whom we give thanks. Governor William Bradford of Massachusetts gave the first Thanksgiving proclamation: "Now I, your magistrate, do proclaim that all ye Pilgrims, with your wives and ye little ones, do gather at ye meeting house, on ye hill, between the hours of 9 and 12 in the daytime, on Thursday, November 29th, in the year of our Lord one thousand six hundred and twenty three...there to listen to ye pastor and render thanksgiving to ye Almighty God for all His blessings." These November celebrations have been around for nearly 400 years!

Although November comes and goes, our expressions of gratitude to God should continue year-round. This not only honors Him, but it's good for us. Like any wise father, God wants us to learn to be thankful for the gifts He has given us. "Every good gift and every perfect gift is from above..." (James 1:17). That's our lifeword for today. It's in our best interest not to forget that everything we have is a gift from God. We can become self-centered if we don't have a thankful heart. Thankfulness keeps our hearts in right alignment with the Giver of all good and perfect gifts.

In the Old Testament, to help keep His people thankful, God prescribed an offering called a sacrifice of thanksgiving, and it was performed twice daily (Leviticus 22:29-33). The offering was to remind the Hebrews that the Lord brought them out of Egypt and started the nation Israel. He provided for them.

As New Testament people, we're not called to give a sacrifice offering. But pausing and giving thanks to God every morning and evening would be a good spiritual discipline for all of us. "It is a good thing to give thanks unto the LORD..." (Psalm 92:1).

We finished yesterday's devotion with Psalm 92:1: "It is a good thing to give thanks unto the Lord, and to sing praises unto thy name, O Most High." That's our lifeword for today. The Psalmist says it's good for me to be thankful. Why would that be?

Thanksgiving magnifies the Lord. As we acknowledge Him as the source of all our blessings, it has an effect on us. But it can also have an effect on those who hear us. When we praise and thank God, we point others to the Source of our blessings. Thanksgiving is the most natural time to share the grace of God with our family and friends.

Jesus told a man he had healed, "Go home to your friends, and tell them how much the Lord has done for you, and how He has had mercy on you" (Mark 5:19). A thankful heart is also the heart that will open up to others and share their joy for their blessings. We can connect thankfulness to a positive witness for Christ.

We are not all pastors. Some may not know Scripture well. But one of easiest things to share about Christ is what we are thankful for. It's important for us to give voice to the good things God has done. Thanksgiving is a great time to do this.

The founder of Evangelism Explosion, Dr. James Kennedy, said, "If you're a Christian, you will be a grateful person." So, this Thanksgiving, make a point to let your family and friends know how grateful you are. In your Thanksgiving prayer, point everyone to the Source of those blessings. Allow His Holy Spirit to flow through you to fill your home with love and gratitude this Thanksgiving. It's a great opportunity to point others to Christ.

This Thanksgiving, I hope your pumpkin pie is mouthwatering. But pray about sharing your thanksgiving to God with others so they may not just taste the pie but "taste and see that the Lord is good" (Psalm 34:8).

Yesterday, we looked at Psalm 92:1, which tells us that "it's good to give thanks to the Lord." We spoke of how easy it is to give a witness of Christ at Thanksgiving.

Another reason it's good to give thanks to the Lord is that thankfulness allows us to focus on what's really important in life. So many things that cause stress in life are temporal. While many are necessary parts of our lives, most are not eternal issues. When we praise and thank the Lord, the demands of daily life feel lighter. Instead of having our minds distracted by the temporal cares of this world, God and His goodness—eternal things—come into focus. Thanksgiving helps us remember the eternal things in life.

Gratitude also lessens our anxiety. It's hard to feel grateful when we're burdened, but that's a crucial time to offer God our thanksgiving. Psalm 42:6 says, "My soul is downcast within me; therefore I will remember you." As we remember God, thank Him, and praise Him, there's a change that occurs within us. We feel the burdens lifted.

This all helps reinforce our faith. As we focus on the eternal, our anxiety will lessen. Our faith is buoyed as we sense ourselves dealing with the difficulties of life. We can add this experience to all the other times that God came through for us. This helps us recall our blessings and the many ways God has expressed His goodness toward us. This memory makes us thankful. Knowing that He has worked in the past helps us to trust Him for the future.

Adopting an attitude of gratitude is a very good practice for us. We can begin by becoming aware of the everyday blessings that God provides. The vehicle I drive, the income I earn, my family, and home are all reasons to be thankful. Too often, we take these for granted, but they are all provided by our loving heavenly Father.

Thanksgiving is about being thankful for what we have. It's about having an attitude of gratitude. It's about counting our blessings. All of that is well and good, but it falls short unless we **say it out loud.** Having an internal feeling of thanksgiving is great, but thanksgiving must be expressed. So, **say it out loud.** People aren't mind readers. They can't hear our attitudes of gratitude. We must verbalize our thankfulness.

Around the thanksgiving table this year, why don't you take turns **saying it out loud.** One by one, each family member could express thanks to another. There's something about **saying it out loud.** It makes it more real. It's a humbling experience and one that everyone around the table will remember. No one knows what tomorrow holds, and there may not be another Thanksgiving for everyone at the table. Take advantage of this one by verbalizing our thanks.

While it's important to **say it out loud** to each other, the same holds true in our relationship with God. Our lifeword today is from Hebrews 13:15 which says, "Therefore by Him let us continually offer the sacrifice of praise to God, that is, the fruit of our lips, giving thanks to His name." Notice the phrase "fruit of our lips." That obviously refers to **saying it out loud.** Over and over again the Bible urges us to worship:

"Sing praises to the Lord, for He has done gloriously: let this be made know in all the earth." Isaiah 12:5

"Oh come, let us sing to the Lord; let us make a joyful noise to the rock of our salvation!" Psalm 95:1

"Let everything that has breath praise the Lord! Psalm 150:6

During the Thanksgiving season, we are reminded to **say it out loud.** By God's grace and through the power of His Spirit, may we verbalize our thankfulness all year 'round.

As we prepare to celebrate Thanksgiving, let's take a look at a verse that's very tough to obey. It's our lifeword for today from 1 Thessalonians 5:18: "Give thanks in all circumstances for this is the will of God in Christ Jesus for you." What fuels thanksgiving when life seems to be one difficulty after another?

Before his death, Jesus "took bread, and when he had given thanks, he broke it and gave it to them, saying, 'This is my body, which is given for you. Do this in remembrance of me'" (Luke 22:19). Essentially, Jesus was saying, "Thank you, Father, for this bread, which symbolizes My body that is about to be broken and bruised. Thank you, Father, for this cup, which symbolizes my blood that will be poured out for the salvation of many."

Jesus' grateful spirit was not based on His present circumstances. It was fueled by His belief in future grace and future joy. That's what the author of Hebrews meant when he wrote, "For the joy set before him he endured the cross, scorning its shame, and sat down at the right hand of the throne of God" (Hebrews 12:2). Paul wrote, "I consider that our present sufferings are not worth comparing with the glory that will be revealed in us" (Romans 8:13). Both knew that "in all things God works for the good of those who love him, who have been called according to his purpose" (Romans 8:28). Not that everything is good, but He works all things for good.

It's possible for us to be thankful and patient in all things. The troubles we endure have a purpose. A future purpose that we wait for. Paul writes about it saying, "For our light and momentary troubles are achieving for us an eternal glory that far outweighs them all" (2 Corinthians 4:17).

So, how can you give thanks in all circumstances? There's only one way: Look to the future joy. Look to the future grace.

Thanksgiving is an oft-overlooked holiday. Between the costumes and candy of Halloween and the snowmen and elves of Christmas, Thanksgiving gets the short stick. For all the merchants, Thanksgiving is simply not a big money-maker.

As Christians, it's easy to follow the world's example and allow this time to be squeezed from our calendars. King David in Psalm 103:1-2 doesn't want us to do that. "Praise the Lord, my soul; all my inmost being, praise His holy name. Praise the Lord, my soul, and forget not all His benefits…" These are our lifewords for today.

This psalm is a prayer but without request, petitions, or pleas. It is nothing but praise to God. David was thankful for God's blessings. The old hymn, "Count Your Blessings," was not written until thousands of years later, but that's exactly what David is doing. Looking at his life, David realizes how much God had done for him and how good God has been to him. He is thankful and seems to be bursting with gratitude.

A psalm is a song. The book of Psalms is a hymn book. In fact, many of us grew up singing, "Bless the Lord, O my soul, and all that is within me bless His holy name." That's straight from Psalm 103, a psalm of David. He was certainly a praiser. Many of you will remember his wife being embarrassed by David's praise in 2 Samuel 6. David was also a musician. He sang and praised with all his heart. Maybe that was one reason why God called him a "man after my own heart" (Acts 13:22).

David had a thankful heart that just had to praise the Lord. This was not something that was kept in the temple during a worship service. The Bible records that it was part of his everyday experience. He was grateful, and he could not help but praise the Lord. If we have this kind of a heart toward God, we won't allow Thanksgiving to be crowded out between Halloween and Christmas.

Yesterday, we looked at King David's thanksgiving and praise in Psalm 103. In verse three, David continues to praise his God who forgives sin. It's interesting that David lists this as first among the blessings he's thankful for. Saint Augustine would agree. He wrote, "God's benefits will not be before our eyes unless our sins are also before our eyes."

A mature Christian is one who understands his distance from God. This distance is because of our humanity and our sin. Praise and thanksgiving flow freely from the one who understands that God has bridged the gap between a holy God and a sinful man.

But as we continue to read, David is also thankful because he has been made whole, "...who forgives all your sins and heals all your diseases" (Psalm 103:3). Those are our lifewords for today.

Please notice that in our Psalm, David is addressing his soul. He is reminding himself, as he praises the Lord, of all that God has done. This is crucial to a correct interpretation of verse three. If he is addressing his soul, what kind of healing is he speaking of here? Some take this to mean physical healing. While God certainly can touch the sick in a miraculous way, physical healing is not the kind spoken of here. Remember, he is talking to his soul, telling it that God heals all its diseases. Sin, fear, depression, lust, pride, to name a few. God can give permanent healing to the soul. Psalm 147:3 says, "He heals the brokenhearted and binds up their wounds." The healing of the soul is His first priority.

Please hear me, God does bring physical healing today. He has the power to heal any and every disease. He sometimes chooses not to though. We all know of Christians who died at a young age. They were prayed for over and over but did not receive healing on this earth. They are healed now, as all Christians will be one day. The Bible promises a day when there will be "no more death, or mourning or crying or pain..." (Revelation 21:4).

Rick Warren wrote *The Purpose Driven Life*, which is the bestselling hardback non-fiction book ever written. It also is the second-most-translated book after the Bible. That book struck a chord with many people because everyone needs purpose in life. Everyone understands their need for meaning and significance.

Our lifewords today are from Psalm 103:4. In this verse, we see David praising God that his life is now meaningful. "Who [God]redeems your life from the pit and crowns you with love and compassion..." This verse could be translated, "He keeps your life from going to waste." David seems to be saying that he thanks God and praises Him for not only forgiving his sins and healing his soul, but for saving him from the depths of a wasted life. David is grateful that God is a redeeming God who brings direction to a rudderless life.

If we live for temporal things, we'll one day realize that we've wasted years of our lives on things that, in the long run, really don't count. If our days are spent in pursuit of fleeting things, one day, we'll wake up empty, tired, and feeling like there is no purpose in life. No wonder 3,000 people worldwide commit suicide each day. For each individual who takes their life, 20 attempt to do so. I wonder how many people end up feeling betrayed because the things they worked hard to obtain did not bring them the meaning, purpose, and satisfaction for which they longed. Money, possession, power, and position, may bring happiness temporarily, but it is short-lived. We need eternal things to really sense satisfaction in life.

"For I know the plans I have for you...plans to prosper you and not to harm you, plans to give you hope and a future" (Jeremiah 29:11). God gives His people purpose in living. All lives not lived under the lordship of Christ are only a shell of what they could be. As King David thanks God for his blessings, he knows his life counts. His life is not lived in vain.

Do you remember the feeling of being the last one picked for a team on the playground? Well, I don't, because I was a pretty good athlete. But I do remember the feeling of not being accepted by my peers. More times than I can remember, I gave in to peer pressure because I wanted to be accepted and was fearful of rejection. This fear can make us seek the approval of others more than the approval of God. It can turn us into people-pleasers instead of God-pleasers.

When we are addicted to the approval of man, we will be miserable as we are controlled by other people. We may end up living the life our parents want us to live, or our boyfriend or girlfriend wants us to live. We miss the life God has for us because we can't escape from this fear of rejection as we try to please others. Our lifeword today is from Proverbs 29:25: "Fearing people is a dangerous trap, but trusting the Lord means safety."

The desire to get approval from other people is not a bad thing unless you allow it to dominate your life and determine your self-worth. But in reality, it's narcissistic to not care at all about pleasing other people. The enemy comes and does what he does—perverts good things and makes them harmful to us. Thus, we have something called approval addiction.

If I'm a people-pleaser, I will miss God's purpose for my life. Paul writes in 1 Thessalonians 2:4, "Our purpose is to please God, not people." People pleasing will keep me from maturing as a Christian. John 5:44 says, "You try to get praise from each other, but you do not try to get the praise that comes from the only God. So how can you believe?" The antidote is found in Romans 12:2. It says, "Do not conform any longer to the pattern of this world, but be transformed by the renewing of your mind." We'll spend the next few days learning how we can escape the trap of pleasing people.

How do I get free from the approval of others? How can I break the chains of approval addiction? Have you ever considered that even God can't please everyone? I'm sure that many times, God hears prayers that are directly opposite each other. To answer one would be to not answer the other. If God can't please everyone, what makes me think I can?

Happiness is not found in everyone approving of me. I don't have to please everyone, and God doesn't expect me to. No matter how I act, no matter what I do or say, someone won't like it. It's a waste of time to try to gain the approval of others because there will always be people who don't like you.

Do you have a big God? If you do, the approval of others doesn't matter as much. People have less influence on you when God is big. Isaiah 51:12 says, "I, even I, am he who comforts you. Who are you that you fear mere mortals, human beings who are but grass?" Those are our lifewords for today.

God says He is the one in whom you should find comfort. Others will let us down, but God has promised to never leave us or forsake us (Deuteronomy 31:8). Psalm 27:10 says, "Even if my father and mother abandon me, the Lord will hold me close."

Being addicted to the approval of others is short-sighted. Immature people get caught up with the here and now rather than long-term issues. My dad would tell me that "you've got to look farther than the end of your own nose." Things that seem so important now usually aren't in a few weeks.

John compares short- and long-term perspectives in 1 John 2:17: "The world and its desires pass away, but whoever does the will of God lives forever." Short-term thinking leads to people-pleasing. An eternal perspective breaks the chains of approval addiction.

December 1st

As a pastor, I know how easy it is to get addicted to the approval of others. In my early days of ministry, there were times I "feared man" as the Bible refers to it. I reflect on those occasions with regret. Nothing positive comes from a ministry devoted to pleasing people. Instead, pastors need faith to have a single-minded devotion to the Lord. Our obligation is to deliver what God's people need, not what they want.

The pastor, as well as the laity, have only one person to please. That uncomplicates my life and causes much less stress. Jesus said in John 5:30, "...I seek not to please myself but Him who sent me." Those are our lifewords for today.

Anything, including pleasing people, that is put before God becomes a god. When I fear rejection so much that I become addicted to approval, I have allowed something or someone else in my life to take first place. The Bible has a term for this; it's idolatry. If this continues in my life, I will have to give an account of this behavior. This should act as an antidote for the addiction of approval. Romans 14:12 says, "Each of us will give a personal account to God." All of us will be judged on the Christian life we've lived. If I can remember that, it helps with that long-term thinking we discussed yesterday.

If I have an eternal perspective and take seriously the judgement of God, it gives me confidence and courage. I can stand up and be the person God wants me to be when I feel the pressure to be politically correct or socially acceptable.

Jesus said, "If anyone is ashamed of me and my message, the Son of Man will be ashamed of that person when he returns in his glory and in the glory of the Father and the holy angels" (Luke 9:26).

A few days ago, Proverbs 29:25 was our lifeword, and we'll use it for this day as well. "Fearing people is a dangerous trap, but trusting the Lord means safety." Older translations will use the phrase "the fear of man." The opposite of trusting in God is fearing man. Since the fear of God is the beginning of wisdom, the fear of man is basically a worship issue.

A. W. Tozer writes about the Hebrew word *fear*: "It includes being afraid of someone, but it extends to holding someone in awe, being controlled or mastered by people, worshipping other people, putting your trust in people, or needing people."

If I'm to deal with my approval addiction, I must come to terms with what is going on inside my heart. If I live in light of what other people think of me, I ought to ask myself, "What is going on in my heart right now?" The fear of man is making me tremble, and only God should do that. I'm giving power to people that really only belongs to God. You see, people-pleasing is a worship issue.

How do I know if I'm an approval junkie? Here's a few ways to find out: Do I struggle to challenge or question the opinion of others? Do I shade the truth to avoid offending others? Do I put myself down in hope that others will disagree? Do I fish for compliments?

The opposite of the fear of man is trusting in the Lord. That's what today's lifeword says. People who fear man do not trust the Lord. Paul tells us in Galatians 1:10, "For if I still pleased men, I would not be a bondservant of Christ."

The Hebrew word translated as "trust" means to hide for refuge or to be confident in something. It means to be persuaded about something so much that you rely upon it. Those who trust in God place their confidence in Him. They hope in God and rely upon Him. That's why approval addiction is a worship issue.

Our lifeword today is from Proverbs 3:5-6: "Trust in the Lord with all your heart and lean not on your own understanding; in all your ways submit to Him, and He will make your paths straight." This is one of the foundation verses in all of God's Word. As we said yesterday, to trust God means to place confidence in Him. We hope and rely on Him, or as I like to say, "lean real hard." Whatever or whoever we lean on, we trust.

This verse says to trust God when things happen we don't understand. "Lean not on your own understanding." We as humans like to understand things. We want to figure things out. But how arrogant of us to want to figure out God. He has infinite knowledge, and we somehow think we can understand His way.

"For my thoughts are not your thoughts, neither are your ways my ways…" (Isaiah 55:8). The prophet continues, "As the heavens are higher than the earth, so are my ways higher than your ways and my thoughts than your thoughts" (Isaiah 55:9). Oswald Chambers wrote, "Trustfulness is based on confidence in God whose ways I don't understand; if I did, there would be no need for trust."

Kirk Gentrup was the best high school basketball player I ever coached. He was a shoe-in for a Division 1 basketball scholarship. As a sophomore playing left field in a high school baseball game, a lightning bolt came out of the sky and killed him.

I remember getting the news. I was a new Christian at the time, and this death really rocked my world. I sat down with my Bible and starting reading. I finally came to Romans 11:33-34: "Oh, the depth of the riches of the wisdom and knowledge of God! How unsearchable his judgments, and his paths beyond tracing out!" I closed my Bible and decided to trust God when things happen I don't understand. I encourage you to as well.

We continue today with our look at Proverbs 3:5-6. These verses encourage us to trust God when we don't know what to do. "In all your ways submit [or acknowledge)] Him and He shall direct your paths" (Proverbs 3:6). When you're faced with a decision and don't know what to do, acknowledge God. That means submit to Him. The promise is that He will direct your path.

When we acknowledge God, it's more than just a belief in His existence. We recognize not only that He is supreme but that He has a right to rule our lives. We give more than a nod in His direction; we place our lives in His hands.

To acknowledge God is to keep Him in mind with all you do. To acknowledge God means to care about what He thinks and submit our plans to Him. To acknowledge Him means to submit to His desires and His ways.

When you have a tough decision, acknowledge Him. Pray about it and read Scripture asking God for direction. Seek out godly friends whom you respect and get their counsel. After all, there is "safety in a multitude of counselors" (Proverbs 11:14). That's how to acknowledge God in all your decisions.

As I was graduating from Asbury Seminary, I had to decide on where I was going to plant a church. I had three options: Rockford, IL; Orlando, FL; or Henry County, Ga. I prayed, I read Scripture, I asked for counsel. Still, I had no leading.

I went to Dr. John Oswalt, one of my Seminary professors, and told him I didn't know what to do. He gave me sound advice. He said, "God doesn't care as much about where you go as the person you're going to be once you get there."

He was telling me to make my decision. I had acknowledged God; now I had to trust that He would guide me. After all, God is more concerned with my character than where I live.

There's a promise at the end for our lifeword today: "Trust in the Lord with all your heart and lean not on your own understanding; in all your ways submit [or acknowledge] Him, and He will make your paths straight." As we trust, lean not, and submit, He will direct our path, or as this translation says, "make your paths straight." Trust God when your future seems uncertain. When you don't know what the future holds, His promise is to direct your path.

This Christian journey is a faith walk. "For we live by faith, not by sight" (2 Corinthians 5:7). If we lived by sight, we wouldn't need faith. There will always be an element of uncertainty when we are dealing with faith issues. That's why God asks us to trust Him. We are to live based on a confidence that God is true to His character and keeps His promises. He WILL direct our path.

Proverbs 4:18 is instructive here: "The path of the righteous is like the morning sun, shining ever brighter till the full light of day." Walk in the light God gives you! The light may not be bright, kind of like the morning sun. But stay in step with Him, and He will direct your path.

Your car headlights only illuminate a short distance in front of you. When you're driving home at night, you cannot see very far, certainly not all the way to home. But as you begin driving in the light provided, you will have enough light to get home. Your lights guided you all the way there, as you trusted them each mile. That's a good illustration of walking by faith when the future seems uncertain.

"Even though I walk through the darkest valley, I will fear no evil, for you are with me" (Psalm 23:4). Psalm 36:9 says, "For with you is the fountain of life; in your light we see light." Trust God that His light is enough to guide you in uncertain times.

Let's deal the next few days with a very sensitive topic. I would even call it a heated topic. No matter what side of this issue you're on, it's difficult to understand those who think differently. This is a deeply personal topic that adds to its sensitive nature. It's a topic about real people. People we love. People we work and live next to. Our topic is about people who are gay.

The Church has not always handled this issue well. We're called to deal with this and all issues with grace and truth. Too often, it's all grace or all truth. It needs to be both-both biblical and loving. If we neglect either of those, we lose. If we're not biblical, we lose. God's Word is authoritative, and we must go where the text leads, even if I don't like that direction. If we're not loving, we lose. I'm committed to be a person of grace as much as I am a person of truth.

We can't ignore that marriage is defined throughout Scripture, and confirmed by Jesus, to be the union between a male and a female. We only have to go 39 verses into the Bible to read, "Then the LORD God said, 'It is not good that the man should be alone; I will make him a helper fit for him'" (Genesis 2:18). Those are our lifewords for today.

A few verses later, we read, "Therefore a man shall leave his father and his mother and hold fast to his wife, and they shall become one flesh" (Genesis 2:24). What's fascinating is that when Jesus was asked about marriage, He quoted this verse. Jesus also quotes Genesis 1:27, which speaks of maleness and femaleness. This doesn't settle the issue, but it's significant. According to Scripture and the teaching of Jesus, marriage is defined as a union between a male and a female. Nowhere in God's Word do we see marriage between any two humans. No matter where you are in this debate, this is an undisputed fact.

Same-sex relationship are to be understood at the intersection of grace and truth. We bring to this issue not only grace, but truth as well. Today, we continue to look at what the truth of Scripture says concerning this sensitive topic.

No one can deny that when the Bible mentions sexual relationships and practice between the same sex, it always refers to them in a negative way. There are only five passages that talk about homosexual practice. Let's look at just one of these passages: Romans 1:26-27. "For this reason, God gave them up to dishonorable passions. For their women exchanged natural relations for those that are contrary to nature; and the men likewise gave up natural relations with women and were consumed with passion for one another, men committing shameless acts with men and receiving in themselves the due penalty for their error." These are our lifewords for today.

Paul indicates in this passage that homosexual behavior, whether male or female, is not God's intent. There is no diversity in His Word about whether same-sex sexual behavior is properly aligned with the intent of God in creation. With issues like divorce, women teaching in the local church, and baptism, there is some diversity and tension in Scripture, but none when it comes to homosexual practice. God's Word always prohibits them.

In today's world, almost every television show and movie disagrees with our lifeword today. Our government, our schools, and even some churches, define truth based on their own opinion rather than on the truth of Scripture. Truth for the modern world is a moving target.

Jesus says we are the light of the world (Matthew 5:14). Being light doesn't just mean love and grace. It means grace and truth. Jesus couldn't be one without the other (John 1:14). Neither can we. If we love someone, we tell them the truth in a gracious way.

Concerning same-sex sexual relationships, God's Word is plain in its admonitions against it. The Church of Jesus Christ has upheld this biblical teaching since its inception 2,000 years ago. There always has been a strong consensus among Bible-believing Christians, in all places in the world, that human sexuality was to be expressed between a man and a woman. Christians' views on this have been universal no matter the Christian tradition: Catholic, Protestant, or Orthodox. Only in the last 50 years has this issue been called into question. We depart the historic positions of the Church with extreme caution. The wisdom of our Church fathers should not be ignored, and we should not forget what we have always believed.

In the history of the Church, there are times when she was wrong. Invariably, it was when we drifted from the authority of God's Word. Tradition alone is not enough. We always make sure tradition is subservient to Scripture. Only the Bible can prove that same-sex sexual relationships are sinful. But the argument from tradition does show that we aren't reading into the text what we want it to say.

Protestant reformer Martin Luther, says this: Homosexuality "...departs from the natural passion and desire, planted into nature by God...the devil puts such great pressure upon his nature that he extinguishes the fire of natural desire and stirs up another, which is contrary to nature."

John Chrysostom, an early Roman Catholic Church theologian said, men "...have done an insult to nature itself. And a yet more disgraceful thing than these is it, when even the women seek after these intercourses, who ought to have more shame than men."

The tradition of the Church is an important added voice in this debate. As we stand on Scripture and tradition, we come to the unmistakable position that homosexual behavior is incompatible with Christian teaching.

With all issues in the Christian life, we need to approach them as Jesus would: with grace and truth (John 1:14). So, as we seek to walk in His footsteps, what does this mean for us as we decide our stance on the homosexual issue? How do we approach this area with grace and truth?

First of all, remember that we're not dealing with the homosexual issue; we're dealing with homosexuals— people made in the image of God. We are to love the gay people in our lives. What in the world does that mean? Love is such a tough word to get your mind around, unless you are a person of truth. For the Christian, love is easy to define because the Bible does it for us: "Love is patient, love is kind. It does not envy, it does not boast, it is not proud. It does not dishonor others, it is not self-seeking, it is not easily angered, it keeps no record of wrongs. Love does not delight in evil but rejoices with the truth. It always protects, always trusts, always hopes, always perseveres. Love never fails." Those are our lifewords for today from 1 Corinthians 13:4-8.

If you are gay, I want to tell you that I love you, and I'm glad you're in my life or in my church. If you've been hurt by Christians or by the Church, I'm sorry. Because I love you, you can disagree with me, and I won't be mad at you.

As a person who wants to speak the truth in love (Ephesians 4:15), I hope you hear this in the way it's intended: Jesus welcomes sexual sinners. Actually, Jesus welcomes all kinds of sinners. You are the type of person He came to minister to. He won't turn you away. You matter to Him. Because you matter to Jesus, you matter to me. I love you enough to want to spend time with you and hear your heart and allow you to hear mine. We may never come to agreement, but that's okay. A lot of people I love disagree with me!

As the body of Christ, what can we do to make LGBTQ+ people fell welcome among us? First of all, we do not have to change our beliefs or water them down. According to research done by Andrew Marin:

- 3% say they left primarily because of the Church's belief that homosexual practice was wrong.
- 18% did not feel safe.
- 14% felt a relational disconnect with the leaders.
- 13% left because they saw an incongruence between the teaching of the Church and the actions of its' members.
- 12% left because of an unwillingness to dialog.
- 9% said they were kicked out.

Wow, as the church, we have a lot of work to do. Every church member should repent as we read those statistics. Only 3% said the church would have to change its beliefs for them to return. Here's what gay people say needs to change:

- 12% say they want to feel loved.
- 9% said they want to be given time.
- 6% said they don't want us to try to change their sexual orientation.
- 5% said they want us to be authentic.
- 4% said they want the support of family and friends.

Based on this research, LGBTQ+ people are asking that we be what the Bible says Christians should be: loving, patient, realistic, authentic, and supportive. People don't have to be right for us to love them. Nor do they have to have all the eggs in the right sexual basket for us to show them grace and love.

Jesus came full of grace and truth (John 1:14). Those are our lifewords for today. All of us who follow in His footsteps and desire to live a Christ-like life should come to this issue, and all others, like Jesus would: full of grace and truth.

The great majority of unbelieving people would say Christianity is "anti-homosexual." This is defined as having contempt and unloving attitudes toward those in the gay and lesbian community. Many Christians view homosexual behavior as a "bigger sin" than adultery or two heterosexual people having sexual relations outside of marriage. It's not, by the way. As followers of Jesus, we must do better as we talk with and about people who identify as gay.

Jesus demonstrated what God desires for His people. As disciples of Jesus, we should seek after the perfect balance of grace and truth that Jesus lived out (John 1:14). We don't do this by avoiding people with whom we're uncomfortable. As we read the Gospels, Jesus was intentional about going to places where the good religious people would not go. He spent time with people that other religious people would not. John 4:4 says, "Now he had to go through Samaria." Those are our lifewords for today. The text says Jesus *had* to go through Samaria. There, He met not only with a female but one with a sinful past.

Later in the same text, John tells us that "Jews do not associate with Samaritans" (John 4:9). Samaritans were despised by the Jews. Jewish people traveling to Jerusalem would not go through Samaria. They would add a day or more to their trip by avoiding Samaria. Jesus, however, "had to go to Samaria."

The message is clear: Jesus *had* to go to a rejected group of people. He *had* to speak to a rejected gender (a woman). He *had* to minister to a rejected person (because of her adulterous lifestyle). Jesus valued and respected this rejected person.

As we reflect on Jesus' actions, what walls of prejudice does God want us to climb in order to show respect and value to a rejected person? As we climb that wall, others will take note and may follow. Also, like the Samaritan woman (John 4:28-29), the recipient of our efforts may go and tell others in their community of the Jesus we represent.

As we minister to our gay and lesbian friends and family, we must do it as Jesus did: "full of grace and truth" (John 1:14). As we do this, we must place relationships before directives. That's another way of saying we put grace before truth. Here's what I mean by that: Jesus didn't always start the conversation with the preaching of forgiveness of sins. He didn't always say, "Go and sin no more" before He developed a relationship with the person.

Luke 19 tells us the story of a rejected man named Zacchaeus. He was a tax collector, which meant society had stigmatized him and viewed him as one to be ignored. Instead of telling him to clean up his life, Jesus invited Himself to Zacchaeus' home. Luke tells us that "...the Son of Man came to seek and to save the lost" (Luke 19:10). Those are our lifewords for today.

Don't try to win an argument; make a friend. No one, once they lose the argument, falls on their knees and accepts Christ. Remember, it's not your job to change their minds. We simply point people to Jesus and allow God to change their heart.

Don't try to prove a point; listen to their point of view. As you listen, you know better how to tailor the conversation to their wants and needs. Ask lots of questions. Don't do all the talking. God will open the door and nudge you when it's time for you to share the truth. More times than not, that will come after we've listened.

These truths are crucial. To people far from God, Jesus led with grace. To religious people who thought they knew it all, Jesus emphasized truth. We would be wise to follow that strategy.

It's important for all of us evangelical Christians, who are conservative in our political beliefs, to be acquainted with the teachings of Jesus in Mark 12:13-17. It's here where the Savior gives us a template for how we as Christians should engage in politics.

Should we be above it and stay clear from the muck and mire of political debate? Should we be heavily involved? After all, as Christians we are called to make this world a better place. As I wade into this subject, I know that I will turn many off. There's no way I can please everyone because we are so divided on this issue. Allow me to do the best I can to see what Scripture teaches.

Here we see a confrontation between Jesus and His religious opponents, the Pharisees and Herodians. They approached Jesus and tried to trap Him in His words. They asked, "Is it lawful to pay taxes to Caesar, or not? Should we pay them, or should we not?" (Mark 12:14). No matter how Jesus answered, He was going to look bad to either His followers or the Roman government.

It's important to know that Jesus regarded the pagan government as legitimate when He said, "Render to Caesar the things that are Caesar's" (Mark 12:17). Those are our lifewords today. Human government is rooted in Scripture. Governmental authority is simply a reflection of God's authority. "For there is no authority except from God, and those that exist have been instituted by God" (Romans 13:1). We all would agree that order, even order that is non-Christian, is better than everyone doing what is right in their own eyes (Judges 17:6).

We Americans are an independent bunch, and we often rebel against authority. But as Christians, we are called to submit. "Pay to all what is owed to them: taxes to whom taxes are owed, revenue to whom revenue is owed, respect to whom respect is owed, honor to whom honor is owed" (Romans 13:7). Government is not inherently bad. It's mandated by God. Christ-followers should be respectful even of pagan political leaders. We can be respectful even as we voice our different values.

We continue to look at the implications from Jesus' words in Mark 12:13-17 and, in particular, verse 17: "Render to Caesar the things that are Caesar's." Those are our lifewords for today. If Jesus told His 1ˢᵗ-century followers to support a corrupt Roman government, surely there is no authority today that we as Christians can't support. This means that Christians can survive and even thrive no matter the political climate.

Peter echoes Paul's words when he says, "Be subject for the Lord's sake to every human institution, whether it be to the emperor as supreme, or to governors as sent by Him to punish those who do evil and to praise those who do good" (1 Peter 2:14).

Living in exile has always been familiar to God's people, Old Testament and New. The old song says "This world is not my home, I'm just a passin' through." As we are involved in political discussion and take part in the arena of politics, we would do well to remember that we are "citizens of Heaven" (Philippians 3:20).

Being citizens of Heaven means not expecting our homeland to reflect the values of our real home. An American living in Berlin does not expect Germany to be the United States. The foreigner may take part in German culture, but it is still foreign and unfamiliar. There is no reason to try to force American values while in Germany. There is also no reason to avoid German society because it's not American.

"Since you call on a Father who judges each person's work impartially, live out your time as foreigners here in reverent fear" (1 Peter 1:17). We shouldn't get bent out of shape when we feel as if we don't belong here. We should embrace our status as foreigners, strangers, and people in exile. Christians should not totally fit into any political system. We're not meant to.

Jesus said, "Render to Caesar the things that are Caesar's," but that's not the whole verse. It concludes with render "to God the things that are God's." Those are our lifewords today from Mark 12:17. While Jesus commanded obedience to the political system, He undermined its supreme authority with this phrase. Jesus called for submission to earthly authorities, but it's a limited authority. When our allegiance to God clashes with our allegiance to earthly political structures, the Christian's choice is clear.

Examples of this are throughout God's Word. Peter and John were jailed because they would not stop speaking and teaching in the name of Jesus. This was in stark disobedience to a human authority, the Sanhedrin (Acts 4:18). Peter's words are direct: "We must obey God rather than men" (Acts 5:29). This opens the door for some level of civil disobedience when the dictates of the government clash with the commands of God.

An Old Testament example is found in Exodus 1:17. The Egyptian Pharaoh commands Hebrew midwives to kill all male Jewish babies. A patriot would have carried out the order, yet the midwives "feared God, and did not do as the king of Egypt had commanded them, but let the boys live" (Exodus 1:17). The Bible goes on to say the midwives lied to Pharaoh about the incident. God seemed to be pleased because the text continues by saying, "God was good to the midwives, and the people multiplied, and became very mighty. Because the midwives feared God, He established households for them" (Exodus 1:20-21).

There are moral outrages that no Christian of conscience can overlook. It's left up to the individual to determine when civil disobedience is required of us because of our faith. We must do that prayerfully as we seek the counsel of godly friends. May God give us grace to know when we must not flinch from speaking the truth in love, even under the penalty of law. Remember, "Render to Caesar the things that are Caesar's and to God the things that are God's" (Mark 12:17).

May I express some concern about Christians in the political arena? One area that grieves me is the tone of political debate. I know of people, many of them Christians, who will unfriend you on Facebook if you don't agree with them politically. This breaks the heart of Christ. Paul wrote in Romans 12:18, "If it is possible, as much as it depends on you, live at peace with all men." Those are our lifewords for today. As much as it depends on me, I should live at peace. I can't control you, but I am in control of myself. And I should live in peace and harmony with those I disagree with and who disagree with me.

One political hot button today is secure borders. How do we deal with the illegal immigration issue? No matter where you fall in this tough debate, we know that God speaks often about justice for the poor and the alien. Whatever side we are on, let us remember this is more than an argument about illegal immigration; it's about people. Many times, they are young people, even children, who are caught in the crosshairs of adult action. As one who believes our borders should be secured, I also believe we should care for those, especially the children, who are pawns in the debate.

Bible-believing Christians will disagree on politics, but *how* we disagree is more important than agreeing. Because it's difficult to be gracious in our disagreements, many people of faith avoid expressing an opinion for fear of someone taking offense. This is a mistake.

Our political differences can be a very good thing. None of us have all the truth. As we converse and have civil debates with each other, we can all benefit from each other's wisdom. Our lifeword today is from Proverbs 27:17: "As iron sharpens iron, so one person sharpens another."

Please know this: The Bible doesn't instruct on who to vote for or what policies to support. While there does seem to be foundational principles to follow, the application of those is debatable. In those debates, let's honor Christ and speak "our" truth in love.

"Give back to Caesar what is Caesar's, and to God what is God's" (Matthew 22:21). Those are some of the most God-focused words Jesus ever said. It would be a good prayer of all of us who enjoy politics. I hope we're not first focused on the Republican or Democratic party. Those who claim the name of Christ should be God-focused. That focus must dictate the way we think about political matters.

Our political allegiance should not define our identity. If we allow Caesar (government) to determine our identity, we give to Caesar that which doesn't belong to him. As I listen to politicians, I hear all kinds of ways that Caesar tries to define me: American, Democrat, or Republican. I live in a red or blue state. None of those are bad. They're simply not our first identity as followers of Jesus. I can be boxed into being a liberal, conservative, or moderate. All of these labels divide the Body of Christ.

As Christians, our identity in Christ should be where we get our value and self-worth. The most important thing about us is that we are "foreigners and strangers on earth." That's our lifeword today from Hebrews 11:13. We align with the people who are "looking for a country of their own" (Hebrews 11:14).

What is your identity as a disciple of Jesus?

- I am God's child ~ John 1:12
- I am forgiven ~ Colossians 1:13-14
- I am free from condemnation ~ Romans 8:1-2
- I am a citizen of Heaven ~ Philippians 3:20
- I am a new creation in Christ ~ 2 Corinthians 5:17
- I am an ambassador of Christ ~ 2 Corinthians 5:20
- I can do all things through Christ ~ Philippians 4:13

As Christians, our identity is not determined by how we define ourselves. It's defined by what God has done for us and what He says about us. This is so much greater than husband or wife, father or mother, and certainly, Republican or Democrat. It's crucial to our Christian walk that we understand this truth.

Political campaigns, especially at the national level, are becoming nastier and nastier. Because of that, many followers of Christ are asking questions concerning the legitimacy of our involvement in this less-than-desirable activity. That's a valid concern. But even though we must be careful, I want to make the case that political involvement is part of what it means to live fully in God's world.

Engagement in the political process is a matter of Christian stewardship. Paul says in Romans 13:1-2, "Let everyone be subject to the governing authorities, for there is no authority except that which God has established. Consequently, whoever rebels against the authority is rebelling against what God has instituted..." Those are our lifewords for today.

It could be argued that taking a "hands off" policy when it comes to politics is rebelling against the government that God has put into place. In the United States, we are the government. We put into office those who lead us. We the people function in certain ways as Caesar. We can't be passive about what God has given us. The privilege of voting and expressing our opinions is a stewardship from God that we must not shirk.

Jesus said that loving our neighbors is as important as loving God (Matthew 22:40). For that reason, we should engage in politics as an expression of our love for one another. We should engage in politics because we love our neighbors.

How can we love our neighbor if we ignore the social structures that affect him or her? How can we love our neighbor if we neglect the government that will rule over him or her? If we aren't engaged politically, we aren't engaged with the people we're called to love. Jesus needs us to be people aware of and involved in the political process. Then, we can love those we are called to love.

As long as this earth endures, we have stewardship over the government that God has put in place because we are that government. We are Caesar. Think about that.

For the last few days, we've been looking at an important verse of Scripture dealing with our involvement in the political arena. "Give back to Caesar what is Caesar's, and to God what is God's" (Matthew 22:21). Those words give us a God-centered vision of politics. Each of us must come to grips with how that works out in the voting booth. There is no biblical voting guide.

So, give to Caesar what belongs to him. Go ahead, get engaged in the political process, study the voter's guide, give money to the candidate of your choice, and by all means, vote. If you feel so persuaded, hit the pavement and knock on doors. All of this is appropriate for a disciple of Jesus.

As we engage in the political process, have your antenna up because the enemy of our souls is crafty. He may convince you to get so involved in politics that your allegiance may shift. You may be tempted to give to Caesar what is God's. Remember from two days ago, your identity is in Christ. He deserves your ultimate allegiance. He is your basis of hope.

Scripture is clear: "Give to Caesar what is Caesar's, but to God what is God's." This is your focus. This is your mindset. Don't allow your life to become man-centered, Caesar-centered. Your life should be lock, stock, and barrel centered in the person of Jesus Christ. Our lifewords today speak of that: "And whatever you do, whether in word or deed, do it all in the name of the Lord Jesus, giving thanks to God the Father through him" (Colossians 3:17).

Each of us must come to terms with the answers to the following questions. Am I keeping the main thing the main thing? Am I giving to Caesar what rightfully belongs to God? Where do I get my self-worth, my identity? Where is my true allegiance found? In what, or Whom, am I placing my trust and hope?

Let me finish by paraphrasing King David. This was a song the people of God sang thousands of years ago, but the words are just as true today as they were when they were written. "Some will place their trust in chariots and others in horses, some put hope in political candidates and the ballot box, but we—as God-focused followers of Jesus Christ—find our hope and place our trust in the name of the Lord our God." That's my translation of Psalm 20:7.

The Christmas story is filled with many serendipities, things you find when you're looking for something else. We go to the Christmas story looking for the baby Jesus, Joseph, and Mary, but we find some unexpected things.

We find the birth place of the Savior of the world. That stable would have been dirty, smelly, and dark. I can't imagine too many places that would have been worse to birth a child. But because of Jesus, soon after He was born, that stable changed into a church! (Well, since it was the 1st century, maybe I should say it turned into a synagogue.) A few hours after the birth, it became a place of worship for shepherds! When Jesus shows up, He completely changes a situation.

He changes our situations as well. When we experience the new birth, our lives change. Jesus brings grace that is greater than all our sins. That same grace gives us a hope for a new future on the earth and in the next world. This change is the serendipity of the Christmas story.

We find another serendipity in the story of the wise men. They were warned in a dream not to return to Herod, so they returned a different way. The biblical text says, "And having been warned in a dream not to go back to Herod, they returned to their country by another route." That's our lifeword today from Matthew 2:12. After these wise men met Jesus, they returned to their home a different way.

That's a great illustration of conversion. When we truly meet Christ, when we are born again, all of us leave different than when we came. We go back home different men and women. New Testament persons from Matthew to Peter, and from Paul to Lydia, could all testify to the difference Christ made in their life. Tens of millions of followers after them would have the same testimony. He made a change in my life, and He can make a change in yours as well.

Thomas Adams, an inventor in the 19th century, was experimenting with the sap from a South American tree. He was trying to find a substitute for rubber. Failure after failure, Adams was about to give up. Then, he popped a piece of sap into his mouth, and chewing gum was born!

In 1943, James Wright was an engineer for General Electric. In an effort to help the World War II effort, he was looking for a cheap alternative to rubber for tank treads and boots. He failed to find what he was looking for but found something else instead. The engineers found that the material could bounce, stretch and transfer comics onto paper. Silly Putty was born! Those are two examples of serendipities, things you find when you are looking for something else.

We go to the Christmas story looking for the baby Jesus, angels, shepherds, but we find unexpected things.

In the person of Joseph, we find a great example of godly living. Joseph is described as a righteous man who didn't want to embarrass Mary by leaving her. He knew he needed to because she had been unfaithful to him. Virgin birth! Who in the world would believe that story? So, he decided to leave her but with as few people knowing as possible. The text says this: "Because Joseph her husband was faithful to the law, and yet did not want to expose her to public disgrace, he had in mind to divorce her quietly" (Matthew 1:19).

He was going to obey the Old Testament and put her away, but he was going to do it privately - doing the right thing in the right way. Remember, right in deed but wrong in spirit is wrong. He was going to do the godly thing but with a gracious and kind spirit. That's a prescription for godliness, and it's a serendipity of the Christmas story.

At the risk of receiving threatening phone calls, angry emails, or you throwing this book in the trash, let me share a few thoughts with you.

You've seen the signs this year. You know the ones. They come out every year at this time and sound so spiritual. Some people have this on the bumper sticker of their car. Churches will put this on their sign out front. You see it posted all over Facebook. You see it on lapel pins. Some hang it proudly as an ornament on a tree. You will see it on Christmas cards. The message is clear and points to Jesus. But it's wrong, I tell you. It's well-meaning but theologically wrong. In fact, it robs Christmas of all of its meaning. Are you ready for it? Here goes… "Jesus is the reason for the season."

He's not, you know. I know that some of you will misunderstand, but I must tell you the truth. *You* are the reason for the season. He came for you. He didn't have any reason to come to earth if it weren't for a lost sinner like you and me. We are the reason for the season.

Jesus is NOT the reason for the season. I know that sounds harsh, and I know the reason people say this, and they are very well-meaning… but it's just not true. You are the reason for the season. Christmas celebrates Jesus coming to earth. What was the reason He came? It was for you and for me. We are the reason for the season.

Our lifeword today is from Luke 19:10; "Jesus came to seek and to save that which was lost." We live in a consumer society that focuses on ourselves, so I hate to say this. Even with all our selfies posted for everyone to see, I must tell you the truth. He came for us. We are the reason for the season.

As Christians, we must be people of the truth. After all, "the truth will set you free" (John 8:32). So, I must share the truth with you. Jesus is NOT the reason for the season. Now, I understand the "Jesus is the reason for the season" crowd. It's a reaction to all the modern-day political correctness that surrounds Christmas. Some even want to leave the name of Jesus out of what is supposed to be the celebration of His birth. While it's right to keep Jesus front and center of your Christmas celebration, and while it's right to fight the commercialization of Christmas, it's even more right to live by the truth.

In the mystery of the Trinity, Jesus existed before the season ever did. Colossians 1:15-16 says, "He is the image of the invisible God, the firstborn of all creation. For by him all things were created, in heaven and on earth, visible and invisible, whether thrones or dominions or rulers or authorities— all things were created through him and for him." Jesus is God—God the Son, and He's always existed. So, He's not the reason the season exists. YOU ARE.

Jesus didn't come into this world for Himself. The Father didn't send His only Son to earth—or to the cross—for Himself. Isaiah 9:6 states, "For unto us a Child is born, unto us a Son is given; And the government will be upon His shoulder. And His name will be called Wonderful, Counselor, Mighty God, Everlasting Father, Prince of Peace." We are the reason for the season!

We sing it in our Christmas carols: "Born that man no more may die...born to raise the sons of earth...born to give them second birth." You see these lyrics, and many verses of Scripture scream to us the truth: We are the reason for the season.

Our lifeword today is from Luke 2:11: "For there is born to you today in the city of David, a Savior who is Christ the Lord."

There's a lot of bad things about Christmas. It's way too commercial. It starts way too early. There's way too much pressure on parents to max out the credit card. I feel the need to apologize because Christmas is my fault... and it's yours too. In fact, if it wasn't for me and you, there wouldn't be a need for Christmas.

We are the reason His hands and feet were nailed to the cross. Christmas had to happen so that He could live the life we couldn't. Christmas had to happen so that He could die a death we deserved. It might as well have been us that betrayed Him for a few pieces of silver. It might as well have been us who denied Him three times.

Christmas is my fault, but I really needed it to happen... or at least something like it. The Scriptures say there are none that are righteous (Romans 3:10). We are like sheep who have gone astray and turned to our own way (Isaiah 53:6). I really need something like Christmas, and you do too. God knew that, and in His love and grace, He came up with an idea: "For God so loved the world that He gave..." (John 3:16).

Our lifeword today is from 2 Corinthians 8:9: "For you know the grace of our Lord Jesus Christ, that though He was rich, yet for your sake He became poor, so that you through His poverty might become rich." That verse says Christmas is for us. We are the reason for the season.

If the gifts that we exchange at Christmas are examples of the greatest gift ever given, Jesus Christ, then is Jesus the reason, or are you? The spiritual purpose of Christmas is the giving of a gift. There would be no need for the gift if there weren't lost sinners like you and me. We are the reason for the season. Christmas is our fault.

This is the time of the year many people say, "Merry Christmas." I'm one of those people who prefer that to "Happy Holidays," although I don't get bent out of shape about it. I try to remember that Christmas, while a happy and festive time for many, is a tough time for those who are grieving.

Some may have lost a loved one, and this time only reminds them of how lonely they are. Things that once made people happy at this time of year now make them sad. Others have lost their job. Because of that, this is not the most joyful time of the year, with so much emphasis placed on materialism at Christmas. Their lack of financial security keeps them from buying a lot of gifts.

There are many who need encouragement at Christmas. It's not a Christmas present they need; they need His presence. They need to be reminded of what Christmas is all about. It is not about things. It is not about presents. It's not about trees, tinsel, or any of those other good things. The essential message of Christmas is this: Jesus' name is Immanuel, which means, God is with us. Those are our lifewords today from Matthew 1:23.

For the one who is hurting, lonely, or grieving, this is the perfect time to bring the gift of encouragement to them and say, "The message of Christmas is: God is with you. He will help you and strengthen you." Christmas is always a reminder that God keeps His promise and hasn't forgotten His people. His presence came in the person of Jesus Christ and is still here today through the ministry of God's Holy Spirit.

Psalm 139:7 says, "Where can I go from your Spirit? Where can I flee from your presence?" The Psalmist was clear. God is everywhere. There is nowhere I can go that God is not already there.

This is the message of Christmas and the essence of our faith — God is with us. Encourage someone today with this truth.

We are flooded with reminders of Jesus' birth this time of year — in Christmas sermons, in devotionals like this one, in Christmas cards, Christmas carols, church nativities, TV specials, and family traditions.

But how many of us are confident that God is with us? I mean, really with us. How many of us believe the promise the Old Testament prophet Isaiah spoke of as a sign from the Lord? "A son will be born to a virgin and his name will be Immanuel, which means 'God with us.'" That's from Isaiah 7:14, and it's our lifeword for today. Matthew opens his Gospel by leaving no doubt that this sign was fulfilled in Jesus (Matthew 1:23).

Jesus is God with us. Through Jesus, God came to earth in the form of a little baby. He walked among His creation and lived and died to make a way to restore our relationship with Him. He also gave us His Spirit so that we're never without Him. Our actions and attitudes change when we really believe God is with us. A belief that's not in our heads only, but is in our hearts as well.

Because God is with us, we know that we can never be separated from His love (Romans 8:38-39). Because God is with us, we are assured that we can accomplish His will for us (Philippians 2:13).

Jesus promises His presence as an encouraging and motivating factor as we make disciples. "...Therefore go and make disciples of all nations, baptizing them in the name of the Father and of the Son and of the Holy Spirit, and teaching them to obey everything I have commanded you. And surely I am with you always, to the very end of the age" (Matthew 28:19-20).

Do you struggle sometimes to believe God is with you? It's okay to know He is in theory, but real change happens when we carry this truth into our everyday lives. Really believe it, lean on it, and depend on it. This Christmas, may the knowledge that God is with us allow us to live a more abundant, generous, and confident life.

At Christmas, we have a wonderful thing called "the Christmas spirit." People are friendlier. There is peace and good tidings in the air. People's attitudes change. Generosity abounds. Families who usually don't like each other get together for meals and good times.

Have you noticed the problem with "the spirit of Christmas"? It doesn't hang around too long. It slips away, and that old January-through-November feeling creeps back in.

There's a story I've heard many preachers tell that goes like this. In World War 1, there was something called trench warfare. German and British soldiers were huddled down in trenches not far from each other. Sometimes, they were so close, they could hear each other talking. On one Christmas Eve, a British voice began to sing, "The Lord Is My Shepherd." Then, from the German trenches, came a German voice. For a few minutes, there was beautiful music and worship.

Early on Christmas morning, some of the British soldiers climbed out of their trenches carrying a soccer ball. Some of the German soldiers climbed out as well, and England played Germany right there on Christmas Day. The next morning, the fighting resumed.

The Christmas spirit may bring a truce, but it doesn't bring lasting peace. Maintaining this truce is too hard, and old ways creep back in. We need something more than the spirit of Christmas. We need the Spirit of Christ.

You may say that this could never happen year-round. Luke 1:37 is our lifeword for today. It says, "...nothing is impossible with God." As we rely on God's Holy Spirit, we can have lasting peace in our spirit because the Spirit of Christ is eternal.

December 28th

As we said yesterday, we have a problem with Christmas... it passes. Those Christmas feelings that we call the spirit of Christmas don't hang around long. But the good news of the gospel is this: The Christ that was born in Bethlehem wants to be born in people's lives by the Holy Spirit. Our lifeword today is from Romans 8:11: "If the Spirit of Him who raised Jesus from the dead is living in you, He who raised Christ from the dead will also give life to your mortal bodies through his Spirit, who lives in you" (Romans 8:11).

God, who can accomplish the impossible (Luke 1:37), makes it possible that the Spirit of Him who raised up Christ from the dead comes into people's lives. Paul says that Christ is formed in us (Galatians 4:19).

The Christmas spirit is a feeling; the Spirit of Christ is a fact. The Christmas spirit happens once per year; the Spirit of Christ is 24/7. The Christmas spirit is sentimental; the Spirit of Christ is supernatural.

The angel told Mary that "The Holy Spirit will come upon you" (Luke 1:35). That same Holy Spirit wants to live in us so we can experience "love, joy, peace, patience, kindness, goodness, faithfulness, gentleness and self-control" (Galatians 5:22-23). That's not the Christmas spirit, it's the Spirit of Christ.

No one can maintain a human spirit of love, joy, and peace all year-round. Our spirit may be willing, but our flesh is weak. Remember, nothing is impossible with God. The Spirit of God can produce in us what we can't produce ourselves. But we have to be willing to surrender to God's Spirit. If we do that, His promise is that you will "walk by the Spirit, and you will not gratify the desires of the flesh" (Galatians 5:16).

During this Christmas season, we're used to seeing the Salvation Army bell ringers. It's part of the Christmas season and helps bring in the spirit of Christmas. Whenever I see one of these bell ringers, I think of a story I heard many years ago.

There was a simple, illiterate man who was saved through the work of the Salvation Army. He went regularly to the Salvation Army to receive help and reading tutoring from them. One day, he came home upset. His wife said, "What's the matter?"

He said, "All the officers at the Salvation Army wear red sweaters, and I don't have one." She said, "I'll knit you one." So, she knitted him a red sweater, and the next Sunday, he wore it proudly to the church service at the Salvation Army.

After the service was over, he was still upset. He told his wife, "I noticed all their red sweaters have yellow writing." Now, remember, they were both illiterate. The wife said, "I'll embroider some writing on it for you."

The yellow writing on the red sweater was the motto of the Salvation Army: blood and fire. The man's wife, being illiterate, had no idea what the letters said. So, she copied some letters on a sign from a store window close to their home and embroidered the letters onto his red sweater.

The next Sunday after church, his wife asked him if they liked his sweater. He replied, "They loved my sweater. They even liked my sweater better than their own!" Obviously, neither of them knew the letters on the store window spelled, "This business under new management." That's what it means to have the Spirit of Christ come and take residence in you.

Our lifeword today is from Galatians 5:25. "Live by the Spirit…" If we do that, we will see something like the Christmas spirit on a routine basis, only it's much better. It's the Spirit of Christ.

For the last three days, we've been speaking of the difference between the Christmas spirit and the Spirit of Christ. Spiritually, this is illustrated by the battle between our flesh and God's Spirit. Paul speaks of this in Romans 7 and Galatians 5. The flesh fights against the Spirit, and the Spirit fights against the flesh. There's a battle within us. The story of the cuckoo bird may help explain this.

The cuckoo mother bird lays her egg in another bird's nest. Believe it or not, that's all the cuckoo does when it comes to parenting. When the bird whose nest has been invaded comes back, she doesn't notice the additional egg. Evidently, birds can't count.

After the eggs have hatched, you will have three to four little mouths and one big cuckoo mouth. When mother bird comes back with the worm, who do you think gets it? Of course, the cuckoo dominates. The cuckoo gets fed, and the little birds do not. The cuckoo lives, and the tiny baby birds do not.

What in the world does this have to do with the battle between our flesh and God's Spirit? Well, there are two natures in one nest, or in our case, one body. The nature you feed will grow, and the nature you starve will die. Read that last line again. Don't miss that truth.

"...I say, walk by the Spirit, and you will not gratify the desires of the flesh" (Galatians 5:16). Those are our lifewords for today. Also, in Galatians 6:8, Paul writes, "Whoever sows to please their flesh, from the flesh will reap destruction; whoever sows to please the Spirit, from the Spirit will reap eternal life."

This sowing to the Spirit must happen if we are to have the type of life God envisions for us. That life is not an annual attempt to have the Christmas spirit, but a 24/7 recognition of the Spirit of Christ. Remember, the nature you feed will grow, and the nature you starve will die.

On that first Christmas, there were many different reactions to the birth of Jesus. Many were threatened by the newborn King. King Herod certainly was.

Herod was worried he was going to lose his power to this baby. When Herod heard the wise men were searching for a baby, he was struck with paranoia. He told the wisemen to "...'Go and make a careful search for the child. As soon as you find him, report to me, so that I too may go and worship him'"(Matthew 2:8).

Of course, Herod didn't want to worship Jesus at all. All of this leads to one of the worst atrocities in the Bible. You can read about it in Matthew 2:16. King Herod killed all young boys two years of age and under because he was threatened by Jesus.

It's not only King Herod who's threatened by the birth of the newborn King. In our lives, we know there's not room for two kings, and we enjoy sitting on the throne of our life. We don't want another telling us what to do and how to live. When we come to the end of our life, we want to sing with Frank Sinatra, "I did it my way." That's the theme song for all the modern-day Herods of the world.

The first reaction in the Bible to someone else sitting on the throne of our life wasn't worship, praise, or adoration. It was murder. Herod was threatened by the birth of this newborn King. Don't make the same mistake; to be a Christian means we must be willing to give up our kingdom for His. After all, "...if you confess with your mouth Jesus as Lord, and believe in your heart that God raised Him from the dead, you will be saved" (Romans 10:9). That's our lifeword for today.

As you are on the brink of a New Year, resolve to get off the throne of your life. Allow Jesus to be who He is; your Savior and your Lord.

About the Author

Mark Atherton has been an adopted son of God since August 29, 1993. He married Sue on November 18, 1995. They have two children, Christopher, and Levi. They reside in Xenia, Ohio.

Mark graduated from the University of Kentucky and Asbury Theological Seminary. He has been a pastor since June of 1996. He currently pastors the Xenia Church of the Nazarene and is constantly amazed that they have put up with him since August of 2010.

Made in the USA
Columbia, SC
01 December 2021